acadiana profile's

CAJUN COOKING

Edited by

TRENT ANGERS and SUE McDONOUGH

ON THE COVER: *Mrs. Amelie Naquin, peeling shrimp for cooking at her home in New Iberia, La., is one of thousands of south Louisianians who have mastered the art of Cajun cooking. She owns and operates Naquin's Seafood in New Iberia, preparing and selling a wide variety of frozen seafood.*

– Photography by Lee Millet

For information, contact Acadian House Publishing, P.O. Box 52247, Lafayette, Louisiana 70505, or via e-mail: info@acadianhouse.com.

Published by:
ACADIAN HOUSE PUBLISHING
Lafayette, Louisiana

Library of Congress Catalog Card Number: 00-111691

ISBN: 0-925417-38-6
(Previously ISBN: 0-939524-02-3 and 0-925417-03-3)

Fifth Edition

Printed in the United States of America

A short story about...

Acadiana

Homeland of the best cooks in the world

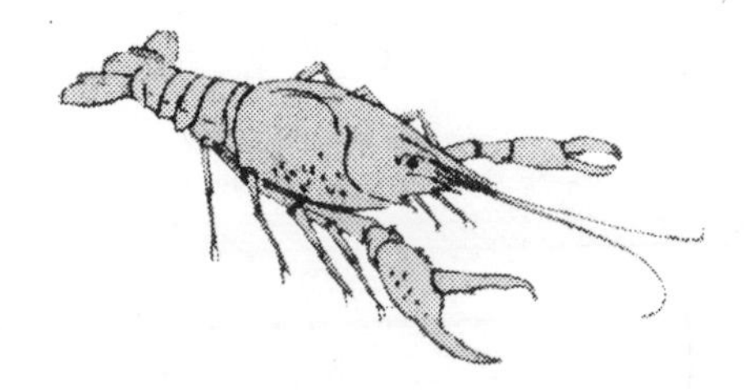

Illustrations by TOM SOMMERS

By TRENT ANGERS

The Cajun Country of south Louisiana has a reputation for being one of the most intriguing parts of the United States. Cajun cooking is recognized nationally as a leading regional cuisine. The local people's ability to truly enjoy life (*joie de vivre*), even when their lot in life is modest, has filled many a visitor with wonder. And the fact that this region has festivals to celebrate everything under the sun—from crawfish and shrimp to sugarcane and yams—continues to fascinate people from other parts of the country.

Indeed, this 22-parish region of south Louisiana known as "Cajun Country," or "Acadiana," is unique in several ways, including the fact that it is the homeland of most of the true masters of Cajun cooking.

The Cajuns, along with their tradition of excellence in cooking, have been in south Louisiana now for more than two centuries. Cajun traditions of various kinds form one of the dominant cultural influences in the region. In recognition of this fact, the State Legislature in 1970 approved an act officially designating the area as "Acadiana," a word formed by combining Acadia and Louisiana. The

---

*This article is adapted from the book, *The Truth About The Cajuns*, and from an article in *Acadiana Profile* magazine titled "The Other Side of Cajun Country," both by Trent Angers. (Copies of the book and the magazine may be ordered using forms provided in the back of this cookbook.)

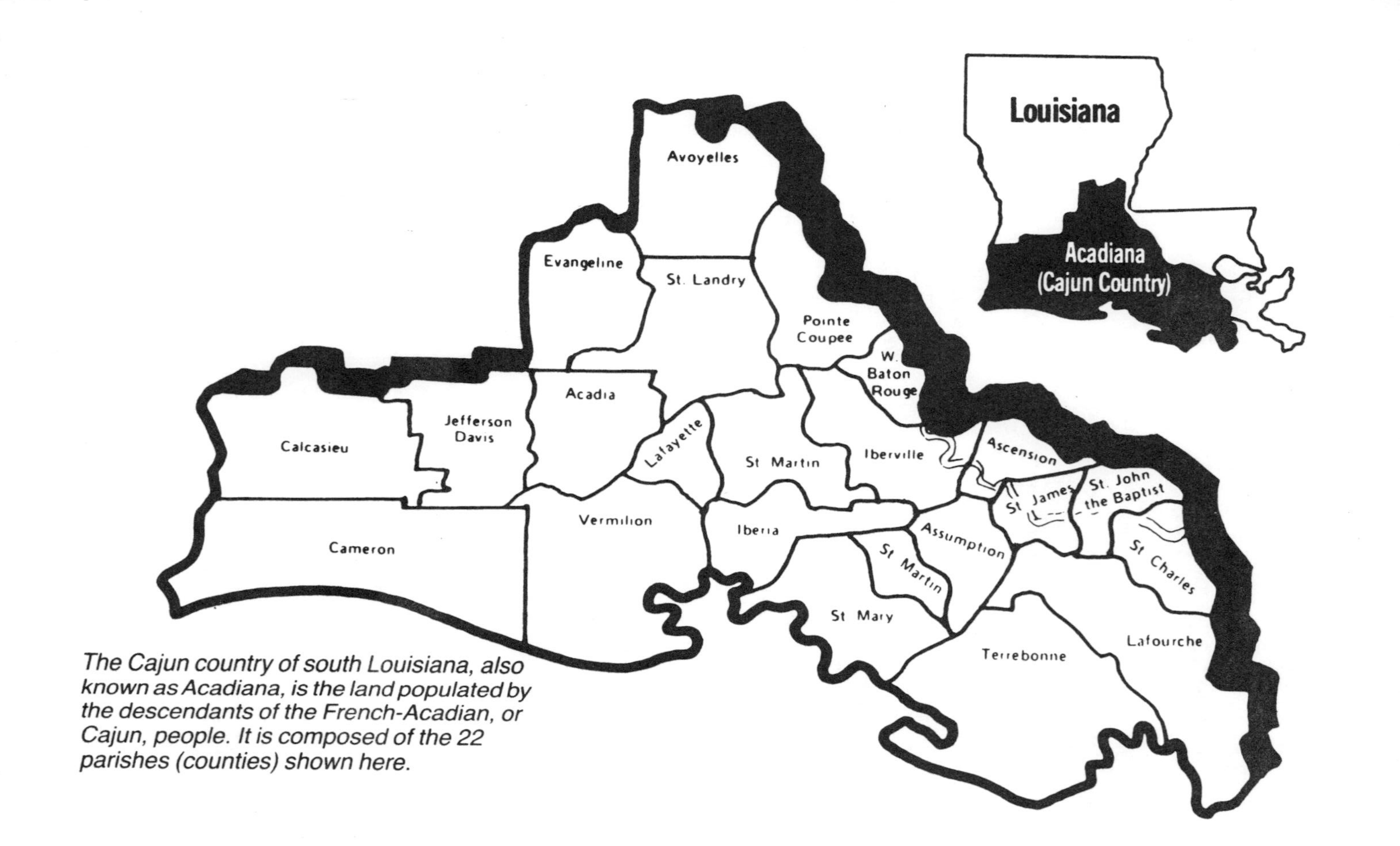

The Cajun country of south Louisiana, also known as Acadiana, is the land populated by the descendants of the French-Acadian, or Cajun, people. It is composed of the 22 parishes (counties) shown here.

region forms a triangle, which is situated at the base of the state (see map).

Not everyone living in Acadiana is a Cajun, of course, but many are. Of the 1.25 million people in the region, about 250,000 are Cajuns. Others include English, French, blacks, Irish, Italians, Germans, Spaniards, Orientals and Native Americans.

A Cajun is a person of French-Acadian descent; that is, a person whose ancestors can be traced to the land of Acadia, particularly Nova Scotia, on one or both sides of the family.

Many of the Cajun cooking traditions used today began in Nova Scotia in the 1600s and 1700s. Others are newer customs that were not begun until after the Acadians reached Louisiana following their tragic exile from their homeland in the mid-1700s. (Some 10,000 Acadians were expelled by the British from what is now Nova Scotia because the British perceived them to be a military threat. To the dismay of the British authorities, the Acadians continued their allegiance to the French crown and continued to embrace Roman Catholicism even after the country was placed under British rule. Thus, the Acadian exile.)

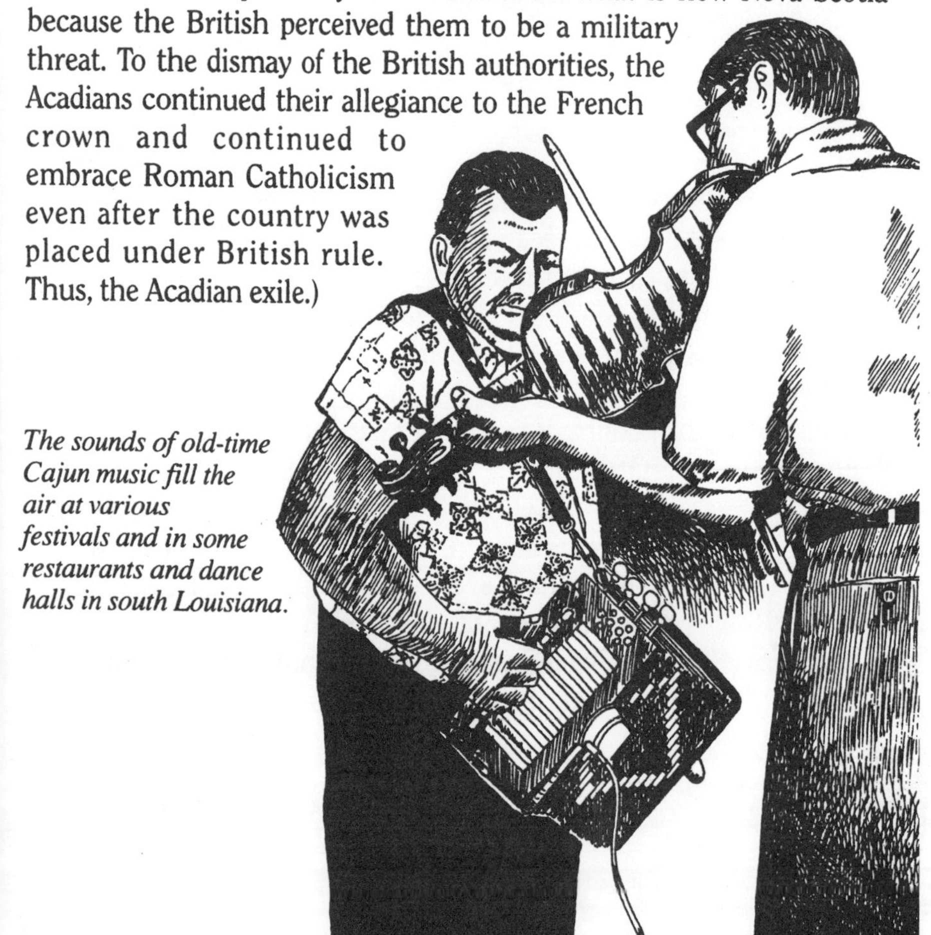

The sounds of old-time Cajun music fill the air at various festivals and in some restaurants and dance halls in south Louisiana.

Geographic features of Acadiana

The land of the Cajuns today is green and fertile, and the weather is generally mild or warm for most of the year. Live oak trees, many of them draped with grey moss, are plentiful in south Louisiana, and in the spring the whole area is alive with the beauty of azaleas and dogwoods.

This part of the country is pretty well flat, but it has a number of uncommon geographical features. For one thing, it has one of the most extensive, most complex systems of waterways in the world; these bayous, rivers and canals are used for drainage, navigation, flood- control and recreation.

The largest of the much-publicized swamps of Louisiana is the great Atchafalaya River Basin

Duck hunting and bass fishing are two of the recreational opportunities available to sportsmen throughout the region. The great hunting and fishing in Acadiana is one reason why Louisiana is known as "Sportsman's Paradise."

swampland, which is about 17 miles wide on the average and about 100 miles long. It is teeming with fish and wildlife of many species. Some of the early Acadian settlers drew life from the basin, harvesting timber and moss, catching fish and crawfish, hunting deer, ducks, rabbit and squirrel. Many hunters and hordes of fishermen enjoy the basin's bounties today. And, yes, there are alligators and snakes in the swamps.

Another interesting geographical feature of this region is the vast coastal marsh that separates the land from the sea. An incredible variety of wildlife lives here year-round, and their ranks are increased greatly each year as tens of thousands of ducks and geese arrive for the winter. Like the swamp, the marsh was a source of life for many Acadians of the eighteenth and nineteenth centuries, and it still is today, though for fewer Acadians.

Louisiana has been called "Sportman's Paradise" for some years now because of the great hunting and fishing that are the envy of the nation. The bass fishing in the Atchafalaya Basin is one good reason; another is the duck and goose hunting in the coastal marshes. Other reasons include dove and quail hunting in several places in this area, and the highly productive salt-water fishing around the offshore oil

***Above:** Old Southern mansions dot the landscape of Acadiana, serving as reminders of a bygone era. **Right:** The backyard crawfish boil is a unique south Louisiana social event and gourmet dining experience.*

rigs. Also, horse racing is attended by many at Evangeline Downs near Lafayette and Delta Downs near Lake Charles and at various less formal "bush tracks" out in the country.

The 'Bayou State'

Louisiana is also officially called the "Bayou State," and for good reason. The presence of so many bayous in the Acadiana area is one of its distinguishing characteristics. There are bayous in the country, bayous running through farmland, bayous running through most of the main towns and cities. Many Acadian communities were built on the bayous' banks, since water transportation was the way to go in the old days. Bayou Teche and Bayou Vermilion snake their ways through

the Cajun country, and dozens of towns can be found on their banks.

Perhaps the most interesting bayou of all is Bayou Lafourche, which dissects Lafourche Parish, in the southeast corner of the Acadiana region. Dubbed by local tourism promoters as "The Longest Main Street in the World," this waterway runs the entire length of the parish, some 90 miles, and spills into the Gulf of Mexico. More than a dozen Acadian communities were founded on the banks of this bayou, and the bayou was far and away the primary source of transportation in that era. It was, indeed, Main Street. Early Acadians traveled by *pirogue* or other boats up and down the bayou. Some lived in houseboats. Today, there are highways on both sides of Bayou Lafourche, running parallel to the bayou.

The economic fabric of the region

Another distinguishing characteristic of the Cajun country is the sprawling sugarcane fields that cover about a quarter of a million acres in the southeast and south-central parts of the region. The presence of

the cane, sometimes 10 feet tall and taller, gives this area a bit of the flavor of the tropics, where cane was grown and harvested by hand for centuries. While the harvesting of cane in Acadiana has been highly mechanized for many years now, in some cases, such as when a hurricane has twisted the cane, there is no way to get it out of the fields except to send in people with cane knives to cut it by hand.

Slow-moving tractors hauling cane to the mill for grinding is a common sight here in the fall. And so are the fires in the cane fields at dusk as farmers burn off the excess leaves which are no longer of any use once the cane has been cut.

While sugarcane has been a major crop in Acadiana for well over a century, a crop that has surpassed it in terms of acreage planted and total cash value is soybeans. Farmers in the western reaches of the area specialize in rice, and the Port of Lake Charles is the nation's leading exporter of rice. Other crops grown in Acadiana include wheat, sorghum and corn and a variety of fruits and vegetables such as strawberries, tomatoes, cucumbers, eggplants and peppers.

Agriculture is a major part of the economic fabric of Acadiana. This fabric also includes the oil and gas industry, the petrochemical industry, boat-building, commercial fishing, food processing, shipping,

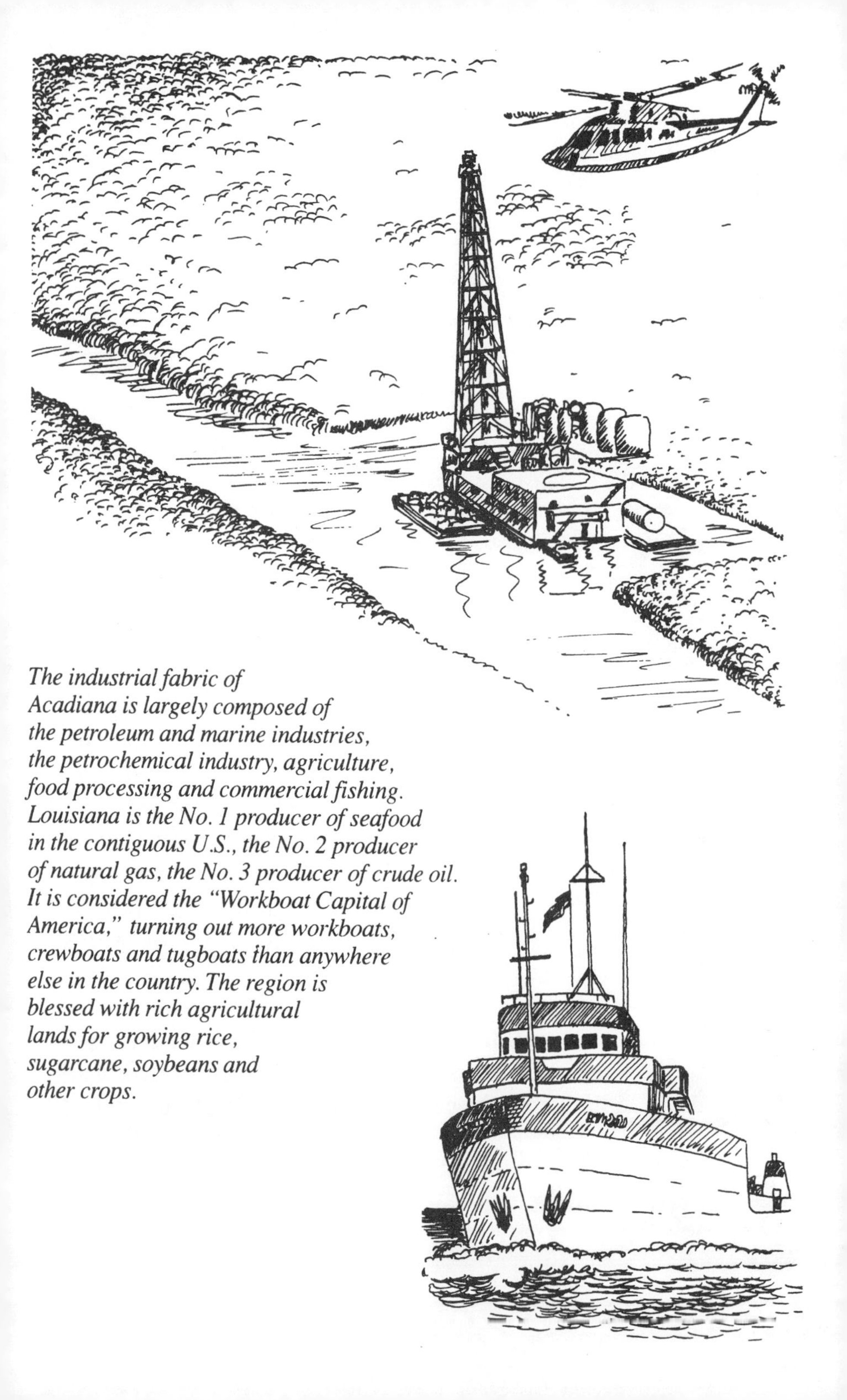

The industrial fabric of Acadiana is largely composed of the petroleum and marine industries, the petrochemical industry, agriculture, food processing and commercial fishing. Louisiana is the No. 1 producer of seafood in the contiguous U.S., the No. 2 producer of natural gas, the No. 3 producer of crude oil. It is considered the "Workboat Capital of America," turning out more workboats, crewboats and tugboats than anywhere else in the country. The region is blessed with rich agricultural lands for growing rice, sugarcane, soybeans and other crops.

Below: *Fresh Louisiana seafood is the key ingredient in many Cajun dishes.* ***Right:*** *Mardi Gras is a day of fun and frolic for the masses in several Acadiana towns annually.* ***Right, bottom:*** *Horse racing provides entertainment for many at Evangeline Downs at Lafayette and at Delta Downs in Vinton, near Lake Charles.*

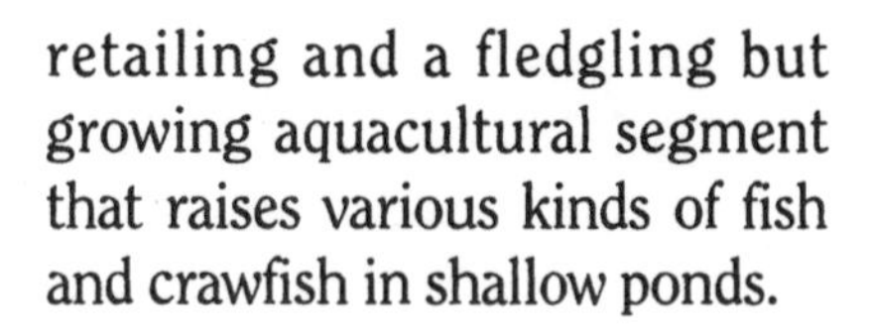
retailing and a fledgling but growing aquacultural segment that raises various kinds of fish and crawfish in shallow ponds.

Festivals and other tourist attractions abound

Tourism is also a very big business in the Cajun country. Next to the health care industry, it is the leading non-agricultural revenue-producer. The well-publicized Cajun restaurants are a top drawing card, but in addition to that there are some 400 other points of interest for the visitor to see in the 22-parish region.

These include countless Southern mansions and Civil War battle sites, picturesque beaches and fishermen's docks, tours of the swamps and marshes, beautiful old churches and an array of museums, numerous lakes and bayous and bird sanctuaries, quaint Acadian villages and rice and sugar mills.

Additionally, tourists are attracted by the hundreds of festivals and public celebrations that take place 12 months out of the year. There's always something going on. Incidentally, the tremendous number of festivals is one of the reasons the people of the Cajun country have the reputation of being a partying lot!

There are festivals to celebrate the harvests of sugarcane, rice, cotton, shrimp, crawfish, soybeans and much more—you name it. The blessing of the fleet or the crop is always part of the ceremonies, reflective of the region's religious heritage.

In addition to carnival rides, games, cake sales, live entertainment and the like, the festivals also offer a wide array of Louisiana cooking. Some offer boiled crawfish or shrimp, alligator *sauce piquante* and catfish courtbouillon;

others may offer red beans and rice, jambalaya, crawfish pie and filé gumbo. Cajun bands and local people dancing the old-fashioned two-step always seem to find their way into the festival programs. Some of the festivals feature special events that are not found anywhere else in the country: crawfish races, *pirogue* races, alligator-cooking, muskrat-skinning and Cajun story-telling.

The many festivals serve as occasions for the people of this region to showcase some of the things that make Cajun country unique and interesting—the delicious food, the Cajun music and dancing, the often-present spirit of celebration.

Cajun cooking isn't for women only. In Acadiana, there is a large number of male cooks who take a great deal of pride in their cooking – and some of these guys are downright possessive about their kitchens!

Preface

The Cajun country of south Louisiana has a reputation for having some of the best food in the world, and this cookbook contains the cream of the crop of the dishes that have made it so.

Five years in the making, this is the first truly Acadiana-wide cookbook ever published, incorporating recipes from all 22 parishes (counties) of Acadiana, the Cajun country.

The recipes were gathered from every corner of Acadiana, from the pecan orchards of Pointe Coupee and Avoyelles parishes to the shrimp docks of Vermilion and Cameron, from the oyster boats off Terrebonne and Lafourche to the crawfish boats out in the Atchafálaya Basin swampland, from the sugarcane fields of Iberia and St. Mary to the rice fields of Acadia and Jeff Davis.

These recipes were first published by *Acadiana Profile* magazine (Lafayette, La.) in a series of four special cooking sections that were issued as part of the magazine in 1976 through 1979. They were obtained primarily from the readers of the magazine and from the Louisiana State University Cooperative Extension Service offices throughout Acadiana.

In editing the recipes, we have attempted to present them in such a way that anyone can use them even if they are not experienced cooks. The ingredients are listed in the order in which they are used and the directions are presented in simplified, easy-to-follow steps.

While many of the recipes are for classic Cajun cuisine, others that may seem to be ordinary American fare are considered Cajun because of the herbs and spices used in them, because of the method and/or amount of time required to prepare them, or because they are made with foods indigenous to the Cajun country.

Though the main feature of this cookbook is Cajun recipes, we have included additional elements in an attempt to make it perhaps the most unique of all Louisiana cookbooks. One is the brief essay and illustrations depicting Acadiana, the homeland of the best Cajun cooks in the world. Another is the cover picture of a real master Cajun cook. The other special aspect of this book, though not necessarily related to Cajun cooking, is the homemade babyfoods section, presented in an attempt to promote and emphasize the tremendous importance of proper nutrition in feeding your little ones.

—Trent Angers

Lafayette, Louisiana
October 1980

Introduction

When we went out into the field to begin gathering recipes for this cookbook in 1976, our idea was to get ahold of authentic Cajun recipes. But the first woman we encountered—who was typical of many others we talked with—seemed a bit surprised that anyone could be so naive as to think that a *real* Cajun cook would have recipes in written form.

"I don't have any written recipes," said the lady, who was bound to have mastered a thousand recipes if she had mastered one.

Seeing that gathering these recipes wasn't going to be a simple matter of transcribing from the recipe card to the notebook, our next approach was to attempt an interview, asking the lady if she would tell us how she made shrimp and okra gumbo, for instance.

"I can't tell you how I do it; I just do it. You're welcome to come back later this afternoon and watch, though," she said.

It was almost as though there were some kind of instinct at work here.

Though the real Cajun cooks of decades past may have cooked without written recipes, this is more the exception than the rule today. What does remain true today, though, is that good Cajun cooks take a great deal of personal pride in their cooking. As they have for generations, they put a lot of tender loving care into preparing meals for their families, and it shows.

Cajuns, or French-Acadians, have a tradition of excellence in the culinary arts dating back two centuries and more. The tradition was brought with them to south Louisiana after being exiled from their homeland of Nova Scotia in French Canada by the British for religious and political reasons in the mid-1700s. Once they were re-settled in Louisiana, their storehouse of knowledge and experience in the culinary arts was greatly expanded because of the abundance of wild game, the diversity of seafood and the productivity of the rich alluvial agricultural lands in this semi-tropical part of the country. The cuisine was further enriched by the absorption of African, German, Spanish and Italian influences.

But the element that may give Cajun cooking its richness more than any other is patience—the willingness to put in the time to do it well no matter how long it takes. The Acadians of two and three centuries ago were rural people, tied strongly to their homes and lands; they had plenty of time and an abundance of patience to try many kinds of recipes and to work with them until they were perfected. They prepared dishes requiring eight and ten ingredients and took the time to allow those ingredients to blend one into the other, gradually and completely, until real gourmet fare was created.

This tradition of patience has found its way down through the decades and, together with knowledge and skill, remains today the hallmark of *real* Cajun cooking.

—Trent Angers

TWO BASIC RECIPES IMPORTANT IN CAJUN COOKING

ROUX

–4 tablespoons of oil
–6 tablespoons of flour

1. Heat oil in pot; add flour, stirring constantly over medium-high heat until brown.
2. Lower heat and continue cooking and stirring until dark brown.

Some other recipes in this cookbook vary, but these are the basic proportions of oil to flour. Specific quantities differ with different recipes, of course.

RICE

–1 cup of rice
–2 cups of water
–1 tablespoon of oil or butter
–1 teaspoon of salt

1. Put all ingredients in a two-quart saucepan and bring to a boil.
2. Lower heat to medium and cook until rice and water are at the same level.
3. Cover, lower heat to low and cook 20 minutes.
4. Remove from heat and let stand five to ten minutes before serving.

Another way to measure the proportions of rice to water is to add enough water to the pan to cover the rice by the depth of one finger joint (index finger). This rule applies no matter how much rice you're cooking.

ACKNOWLEDGEMENTS

We are appreciative of the contribution of recipes made by the readers of Acadiana Profile magazine and by the Louisiana State University Cooperative Extension Service offices in all 22 parishes of Acadiana. We are also very grateful to the people who helped produce this book, namely Steve Angers and Al Esteve, commercial artists who worked long and hard to prepare the book for printing; Cheryl Loughlin and Christie Molinet for patient assistance to the publisher; Debbie Romero, who typeset the majority of the book; Theo Harvey, Phil Hubbell and Bill Hakes of Harvey Press, who took great pride in the printing of the book and great pains in all the details leading up to it. —T.A.

TABLE OF CONTENTS

Appetizers

CONTENTS

PICKLED EGGS

–15 to 18 hard-boiled eggs
–3 cups of white vinegar
–1 cup of water
–1 teaspoon of salt
–Pickling spices or hot pepper, if desired

1. Carefully shell eggs.
2. Bring vinegar, water, salt and spices or pepper to boiling point.
3. Place eggs in hot sterilized jars and cover with boiling liquid.
4. Store in refrigerator.

Makes about 12 quarts.

—Mrs. Mildredge Broussard
Grand Chenier (Cameron Parish)

DEVILED EGGS

–6 boiled eggs, cut in half lengthwise, with yolk removed
–1 teaspoon of sweet pickles, finely chopped
–½ teaspoon of green hot peppers, finely chopped
–1 tablespoon of tuna fish (optional)
–¼ teaspoon of salt
–1 teaspoon of bellpepper, finely chopped
–1 teaspoon of celery, finely chopped
–2 tablespoons of mayonnaise
–1½ teaspoons of evaporated milk

1. Mash egg yolks well and add other ingredients; mix well.
2. Stuff egg whites with mixture.

—Isabelle Thibodeaux
Lafayette Parish

OYSTERS BIENVILLE

–1 bunch of green onions, chopped
–3 tablespoons of butter
–3 tablespoons of flour
–¾ cup of milk
–¼ cup of white wine
–1 pound of shrimp, chopped
–1 2-ounce can of mushrooms
–2 dozen oysters on half-shell
–2 tablespoons of breadcrumbs
–2 tablespoons of cheese, grated

1. Cook green onions in butter; add flour, milk and white wine.
2. Cook until thick, about 15 minutes; add chopped shrimp and mushrooms and cook for a few minutes.
3. Cook oysters in shells for about 10 minutes in 400-degree oven, until oysters begin to shrivel.
4. Remove from oven and drain liquid; place shrimp sauce over oysters.
5. Sprinkle with breadcrumbs mixed with cheese; bake until brown at 400 degrees for about 10 minutes.

—Rita S. Roussel
Lutcher (St. James Parish)

BOUDIN

- –2 pounds of pork meat
- –1½ pounds of pork liver
- –Salt and pepper, to taste
- –1 large onion, cut up
- –2 bunches of green onions, chopped
- –1 bunch of parsley, chopped
- –6 cups of cooked rice
- –Sausage casings, soaked in cold water

1. Cook pork meat, liver and seasonings in water to cover until meat falls apart; remove meat and reserve some broth.
2. Grind meat, onion, green onions and parsley (reserving about one-half cup each of green onion tops and parsley).
3. Mix ground meat mixture with the one-half cups of green onion and parsley, rice and enough broth to make a moist dressing.
4. Stuff dressing into casing, using a sausage-stuffer.

—Sue C. McDonough
New Iberia (Iberia Parish)

WHITE BOUDIN

- –2 pork hearts
- –4 pork kidneys
- –1 pound of liver
- –4½ pounds of shoulder roast
- –1 bellpepper
- –3 onions
- –4 cups of cooked rice
- –Salt and pepper
- –2 bunches of green onions, chopped
- –1 cup of chopped parsley

1. Boil first six ingredients until tender; grind or mash.
2. Add rice, salt, pepper, green onions and parsley.
3. Stuff in pork casings.

—Mrs. Helen Leger
Rayne (Acadia Parish)

SHRIMP REMOULADE

- –4 tablespoons of horseradish mustard
- –½ cup of tarragon vinegar
- –3 to 4 tablespoons of catsup
- –1 tablespoon of paprika
- –1 teaspoon of salt
- –½ teaspoon of red pepper
- –1 garlic clove, sliced
- –1 cup of oil
- –½ cup of chopped green onion
- –½ cup of chopped celery
- –Boiled and peeled shrimp

1. Combine all ingredients (except shrimp) in blender; blend until thoroughly mixed.
2. Pour mixture over shrimp; marinate at least four hours.

—Sue C. McDonough
New Iberia (Iberia Parish)

CHOPPED CHICKEN LIVER PATÉ

–1 pound of chicken livers
–2 medium onions, chopped
–1/3 cup of rendered chicken fat
–2 hard-boiled eggs
–1 teaspoon of salt
–½ teaspoon of pepper

1. Saute livers and onions in fat until livers are no longer pink inside and onions are soft and transparent.
2. Chop livers and eggs and mix; add salt and pepper.
3. Pat mixture into oiled mold and chill for several hours.
4. Unmold and garnish with hard-boiled egg and parsley and serve with crackers or french bread.

—Keith E. Courrege
New Iberia (Iberia Parish)

PIQUANT PECANS

–¼ cup of butter or oleo
–2 teaspoons of garlic salt
–¼ to ½ teaspoon of liquid pepper seasoning
–4 tablespoons of worcestershire sauce
–4 cups of pecan halves

1. Melt butter in pan; add next three ingredients, stirring well.
2. Spread pecans in single layers in shallow bake pan; pour butter-seasoning mixture over pecans, coating all pecans.
3. Bake at 375 degrees, stirring occasionally, for 30 minutes or until deep brown and crisp. Drain on absorbent paper.

—Lou Goodman
Convent (St. James Parish)

PATÉ DE FOIS GRAS
(Liver Paté)

–4 pounds of pork livers
–3 pounds of pork meat
–2 pounds of pork fat
–7 small garlic cloves, minced
–3 tablespoons of salt
–4 teaspoons of black pepper
–1 tablespoon of red pepper

1. Grind liver, meat and fat together twice; mix well and place in a large pot.
2. Add garlic, seasonings and water to cover (about four and three-fourths cups).
3. Cook until fat rises to the top (about three hours), stirring often.
4. Pour in jars; refrigerate. (The fat will rise to the top of the jar; this acts as a seal.)
5. Before serving, bring to room temperature; with a fork, work the fat back into the paté. (This makes it easier to spread).
6. Serve with crackers or french bread.

—Mrs. Sam Broussard
New Iberia (Iberia Parish)

HOG'S HEAD CHEESE

–Head, ears and feet of a hog
–1 tablespoon of salt
–1 tablespoon of black pepper
–1 tablespoon of red pepper
–3 cups of finely chopped green onions
–2 cups of finely chopped parsley

1. Remove eyes and brains from head and split head in half.
2. Wash and scrape head thoroughly, removing excess fat.
3. Singe pig feet; wash and scrape.
4. Singe, wash and clean ears thoroughly with hot water.
5. Place all pieces of hog in large pot; cover with hot water. Boil until meat drops from bones. Reserve two cups of broth.
6. Put meat through meat grinder.
7. Add seasonings, broth and vegetables to five pounds of meat.
8. Put in pans; press with weight and refrigerate overnight.
9. Slice; store in jars covered with vinegar.

—Mrs. Mildredge Broussard
Grand Chenier (Cameron Parish)

DAUBE GLACÉ

–3 pounds of cooked pot roast, shredded
–1½ quarts of liquid from pot roast
–3 envelopes of unflavored gelatin
–1 cup of cold water
–Red pepper, salt and black pepper, to taste
–1 tablespoon of worcestershire sauce
–2 tablespoons of minced parsley
–1 garlic clove, pressed
–½ cup of chopped green onion tops

1. Combine all ingredients (dissolving gelatin in cold water before adding); mix well.
2. Pour in molds; cover and refrigerate at least 12 hours.
3. Serve, sliced, with crackers or french bread.

Will keep for five days in refrigerator.

—Sue C. McDonough
New Iberia (Iberia Parish)

OYSTER MOLD

–2 to 3 tablespoons of mayonnaise
–2 8-ounce packages of creamcheese
–2 teaspoons of worcestershire sauce
–2 garlic cloves, mashed
–½ of small onion, chopped fine
–1/8 teaspoon of salt
–1 bunch of fresh parsley, chopped fine
–2 cans of smoked oysters

1. Cream mayonnaise with creamcheese until soft. Add worcestershire sauce, garlic, onion and salt; mix well.
2. Line a mold with plastic wrap; sprinkle parsley in bottom of mold.
3. Alternate layers of creamcheese mixture and oysters, using all ingredients. Chill.
4. Unmold and serve with melba toast or garlic rounds.

—Mrs. Ann Hall
Lafayette (Lafayette Parish)

CRAB MOLD

- –1 can of mushroom soup
- –2 envelopes of unflavored gelatin
- –3 tablespoons of cold water
- –1 cup of mayonnaise
- –1 8-ounce package of cream-cheese
- –1 cup of chopped green onions
- –1 pound of crab meat
- –Salt and pepper, to taste

1. Heat mushroom soup until melted; add gelatin which has been mixed with water.
2. Add remaining ingredients and mix well; pour into two or three molds and refrigerate overnight.

Serve with crackers.

—Marguerite M. Kramer
Franklin (St. Mary Parish)

PICKLED SHRIMP I

- –1½ pounds of raw shrimp, peeled and cleaned
- –½ cup of chopped celery leaves
- –¼ cup of whole mixed pickling spice
- –2 quarts of boiling water
- –2 cups of sliced onions
- –5 bay leaves
- –1½ cups of salad oil
- –1½ cups of white vinegar
- –¼ cup of chopped pimento
- –2 tablespoons of capers and liquid
- –1½ teaspoons of celery seed
- –1½ teaspoons of salt
- –¼ teaspoon of liquid hot pepper sauce
- –Salad greens

1. Rinse shrimp with cold water.
2. Tie celery and pickling spice loosely in a piece of cheesecloth; place in boiling water and simmer for about 20 minutes.
3. Add shrimp and simmer for five minutes; drain.
4. Arrange sliced onions and shrimp in alternate layers in a bowl; add bay leaves.
5. Combine remaining ingredients except salad greens; mix thoroughly and pour over onions and shrimp.
6. Cover and chill for about six hours, stirring occasionally.
7. Drain and serve on salad greens.

Makes six servings.

—Marilyn Langston
Franklin (St. Mary Parish)

MIRLITON PICKLES

- –6 mirlitons, peeled, cored and cut into strips
- –3 medium onions, sliced ¼-inch thick
- –½ rib of celery, cut into ¼-inch sticks
- –1 quart of white vinegar
- –1 cup of sugar
- –¼ cup of salt
- –½ fresh green hot pepper per pint

1. Soak mirliton, onions and celery in ice water at least three hours or preferably in refrigerator over night.
2. Boil vinegar, sugar and salt.
3. Drain vegetables.
4. Put one-half green hot pepper in each pint jar. Pack vegetables into jars tightly while still cold. Pour hot vinegar mixture over vegetables and seal.

Makes four to six pints.

—Mrs. J. O. Smith
New Roads (Pointe Coupee Parish)

PICKLED SHRIMP OR CRAWFISH II

–1 cup of oil
–½ cup of lemon juice
–½ cup of vinegar
–1 tablespoon of worcestershire sauce
–Dash of hot pepper sauce
–2 teaspoons of sugar
–1 tablespoon of salt
–2 pounds of boiled shrimp (or crawfish), peeled
–¾ cup of mixed sweet pickle relish
–2 medium-size onions, sliced thin
–3 tablespoons of pickling spices

1. In a quart jar, combine oil, lemon juice, vinegar, worcestershire sauce, hot pepper sauce, sugar and salt. Shake well.
2. In a large mixing bowl toss together shrimp, pickle and onions. Pour sauce over shrimp.
3. Tie spices in bag and drop in mix. Let set for 24 hours.

—Mrs. Adolph Castille
Breaux Bridge (St. Martin Parish)

FIG PICKLES

–1 tablespoon of baking soda
–1 gallon of water
–7 pounds of fresh figs, unpeeled
–3 pounds of sugar
–1 pint of vinegar
–1 tablespoon of cinnamon
–½ teaspoon of cloves
–3 lemons, sliced thin

1. Dissolve soda in water; heat to boiling and pour over figs.
2. Let stand a few minutes, drain and rinse thoroughly in cold water.
3. Dissolve sugar in vinegar; add cinnamon, cloves and lemons and heat to boiling.
4. Add figs that are well-drained and cook until syrup is clear; lift out figs and pack in sterile jars.
5. Boil down vinegar syrup until thick and pour over figs; seal jars at once.

Makes seven pints.

—Mrs. Charles F. Hebert
Cameron (Cameron Parish)

PICKLED VEGETABLES (Carrots, Cauliflower, Okra, Etc.)

–Vegetable
–White vinegar
–Salt
–Cayenne pepper

1. Wash and clean vegetable of your choice.
2. Stuff into quart jars and completely cover with vinegar; and two teaspoons of salt and at least one-fourth teaspoon of cayenne pepper per jar.
3. Shake jar until vinegar is cloudy.
4. Refrigerate for at least a week before serving.

—Kathryn Leonard
Lafayette (Lafayette Parish)

CRAB PICKUPS

- 1 tablespoon of butter
- ¼ cup of finely chopped onion
- 1 tablespoon of flour
- ¼ cup of grated Parmesan cheese
- 6- to 8-ounce package or 7½-ounce can of Alaskan king crab meat
- Finger Pastry (Recipe follows)
- 1 cup of lightly packed grated Swiss cheese
- 3 large eggs
- 1 cup of milk
- ½ teaspoon of salt
- ¼ teaspoon of pepper

1. In a medium skillet, melt butter and gently cook onions until wilted.
2. Stir-in the flour, the Parmesan cheese and the crab meat; spread over finger pastry.
3. Sprinkle with Swiss chesse.
4. In a medium bowl, beat together until blended the eggs, milk, salt and pepper. Carefully pour over the crab and cheese.
5. Bake in a preheated oven at 350 degrees on the rack below center for 35 to 40 minutes; cool slightly.
6. Cut into squares, each about two inches by two inches.
7. Remove with a spatula and serve at once or keep warm in a low-heat oven for a short time.

FINGER PASTRY

- 1 1/3 cups of flour
- ½ teaspoon of salt
- ½ cup of butter
- 3 tablespoons of water

1. Stir together flour and salt.
2. With a pastry blender, cut in butter; sprinkle with cold water.
3. Stir with a fork until dough holds together.
4. Pat into the bottom and one-half inch up the sides of a 9x13-inch pan.

Makes 24 pieces.

—Nancye Duhon
Gueydan (Vermilion Parish)

OYSTER PIE OR PATTIES I

- 3 tablespoons of butter
- 3 tablespoons of flour
- ¼ cup of chopped green onions
- 1 rib of chopped celery
- 1 bunch of parsley, chopped
- 3 dozen oysters, shucked (reserve juice)
- 1½ cups of milk
- 1 teaspoon of salt
- ¼ teaspoon of pepper
- 1 9-inch pie shell, unbaked (or 1 dozen large patty shells)

1. Melt butter in heavy skillet; add flour and cook over medium heat until light cream-colored.
2. Add green onions, celery, parsley and oysters; stir until edges of oysters curl.
3. Add the oyster juice, milk and seasonings. Cook 20 to 25 minutes, until thick.
4. Pour mixture into pie shell or patty shells and bake at 400 degrees until crust is done, in 30 to 40 minutes.

—Mrs. Adrian R. Beatty
Port Allen (West Baton Rouge Parish)

CRAWFISH PATTIES

–1 bellpepper, ground
–1 rib of celery, ground
–2 pounds of crawfish, ground
–Salt
–Red pepper and black pepper
–½ cup of breadcrumbs
–1 tablespoon of crawfish fat
–Biscuit dough

1. Mix bellpepper, celery and crawfish. Cook uncovered on low heat for 15 minutes.
2. Season with salt and pepper, to taste; add breadcrumbs and crawfish fat and stir.
3. Make pie shells out of biscuit dough. Fill with cooked crawfish and bake in oven about six minutes at 350 degrees.
Makes 30 patties.

—Mrs. Lelia Breaux
Breaux Bridge (St. Martin Parish)

OYSTER PATTIES II
(Makes 200)

–1 pound of butter
–4 bunches of green onions, chopped
–1 quart of oysters, drained (reserve liquid)
–2 cans of cream of mushroom soup
–Kitchen Bouquet
–Salt and pepper, to taste
–200 baked miniature patties (available at bakery)

1. Melt butter in saucepan; add green onions, and saute lightly.
2. Add oysters (chop in half or quarter if large) and cook until edges curl; add mushroom soup.
3. If mixture is too thick, oyster liquid or wine may be added.
4. Add Kitchen Bouquet for a little color, and season, to taste; put into patties. (May be frozen at this point; thaw before baking.)
5. Place in preheated oven at 350 degrees for about ten minutes.

—Mrs. Ward Fontenot
Cameron (Cameron Parish)

CRAB PARTY PIES

–4 tablespoons of oleo
–¾ cup of chopped onions
–¾ cup of chopped bellpepper
–3 garlic cloves, minced
–1 6½-ounce can of crab meat
–1 2-ounce can of chopped pimentoes
–1 tablespoon of dry sherry
–1 teaspoon of salt
–1 teaspoons of black pepper
–2 teaspoons of red pepper (or to taste)
–Cheese Sauce (Recipe follows)
–2 dozen bite-size pie shells, baked

1. Melt oleo and saute onion, bellpepper and garlic until wilted.
2. Add crab meat, pimentoes, sherry, seasonings and cheese sauce. Cook over low heat for 10 minutes. Pour into baked pie shells.

CHEESE SAUCE

–2 tablespoons of butter
–2 tablespoons of flour
–1 cup of milk
–5 slices of American cheese, cut into small pieces
–¼ teaspoon of salt

1. Melt butter; add flour and milk and cook over low heat until thick, stirring.
2. Add cheese and salt; stir until melted.

—Mrs. Joyce Breaux
Scott (Lafayette Parish)

MARINATED MUSHROOMS

–1 pound of fresh mushrooms
–6 tablespoons of olive oil
–¾ cup of dry white wine
–1½ teaspoons of salt
–1/8 teaspoon of red pepper
–¼ cup of parsley, chopped
–¼ teaspoon of dried leaf oregano
–2 tablespoons of chopped onion
–3 tablespoons of lemon juice

1. Slice mushrooms and place in glass or earthenware bowl.
2. Combine remaining ingredients in saucepan and simmer 15 minutes; remove from heat and pour over mushrooms.
3. Cover and refrigerate several hours.

—Newty Jeansonne
Ville Platte (Evangeline Parish)

MARINATED OYSTERS

–1 gallon of oysters, drained
–3 medium onions, sliced and separated in rings
–Dash of worcestershire sauce
–1 teaspoon of lemon juice
–6 ribs of celery, cut in slices
–1 large bottle of Italian style salad dressing
–Hot pepper sauce, to taste
–Salt and pepper, to taste

1. Combine all ingredients in large bowl.
2. Refrigerate for one full day.

—Mrs. Raymond Blanchard
Lockport (Lafourche Parish)

MARINATED SHRIMP

–2 to 3 quarts of fresh, unpeeled shrimp with heads on (preferably the jumbo)
–Salt, pepper and red pepper, to taste
–¼ pound of oleo, melted
–½ cup of olive oil
–3 medium garlic cloves, crushed
–½ cup of lemon juice
–¼ cup of worcestershire sauce
–Fine herbs (optional)
–Thin lemon slices

1. Using scissors, first snip whiskers, then snip shell of shrimp starting just behind the head. Engage scissors deep enough to remove vein while snipping shell. (This allows marinade to penetrate. The fat of the head enhances the flavor.)
2. Season shrimp (with shells still on) with salt, pepper and red pepper. Set aside.
3. Mix oleo, olive oil, garlic, lemon juice and worcestershire sauce; pour over prepared shrimp and marinate one to three hours.
4. Place shrimp in single layer in pan; sprinkle with fine herbs and garnish with lemon slices.
5. Bake at 350 degrees for 10 to 15 minutes or broil for 10 to 15 minutes. Do not overcook. Baste occasionally as they cook.
6. Serve with hot french bread, as the sauce is as good as the shrimp.

—Mercedes Lampo
Jeanerette (Iberia Parish)

MARINATED BOILED CRABS

–2 dozen crabs, boiled
–1 cup of olive oil
–1 cup of Italian dressing
–1/3 cup of wine vinegar
–2/3 cup of green onions, chopped
–½ cup of chopped celery
–5 garlic cloves, minced
–½ cup of chopped green olives
–¼ cup of dill or sweet pickles
–Salt, to taste
–1 teaspoon of hot pepper sauce
–1 cup of small shrimp, cooked and peeled

1. Clean crabs and cut in half, setting aside the claws; place in a large covered bowl.
2. Mix remaining ingredients and pour over crabs and claws; stir to coat with seasoning.
3. Marinate in refrigerator about 12 hours.
Serves six.

—Alzina Toups
Galliano (Lafourche Parish)

SHRIMP APPETIZER

–2 pounds of large shrimp
–1 pound of bacon
–Salt and pepper, to taste
–1½ cups of Italian breadcrumbs

1. Wash and devein shrimp.
2. Wrap each shrimp with one-third slice of uncooked bacon, using toothpick to secure bacon to shrimp.
3. Add salt and pepper to breadcrumbs; roll each shrimp in crumbs.
4. Place on wire rack (over pan to catch drippings).
5. Broil 10 to 12 minutes, turning once. Serve hot.

—Robert L. Freeman
Iberville Parish

CRAB DIP I
(Serves 100)

–¾ cup of oleo
–2 onions, chopped
–2 stalks of celery, chopped
–3 tablespoons of chopped parsley
–3 pounds of crab meat or 7 6½-ounce cans
–1 large can of evaporated milk
–1½ to 2 pounds of Velveeta cheese, cut in small pieces
–½ teaspoon of garlic powder
–1 can of cream of mushroom soup
–½ teaspoon of thyme
–1 teaspoon of Kitchen Bouquet (optional)
–Salt and red pepper
–Breadcrumbs

1. Melt oleo in large black iron pot; add onions and celery.
2. Cook with lid on pot on low heat for 20 to 30 minutes, stirring occasionally to prevent burning or sticking.
3. Add parsley, crab meat, evaporated milk, cheese, garlic powder, cream of mushroom soup and thyme. Add Kitchen Bouquet if a tan dip is desired rather than a white dip.
4. Cook about one hour on low heat with lid on pot, stirring occasionally to prevent sticking.
5. Add salt and pepper, to taste; check dip for thickness and add breadcrumbs to dip to thicken if desired.
6. Cook about another 15 minutes. Makes more than a gallon. Serves about 100.

—Mrs. John Daigre
Lafayette (Lafayette Parish)

CRAB DIP II

- –1 small onion, finely chopped
- –2 tablespoons of bellpepper, chopped
- –2 tablespoons of onion tops, chopped
- –¼ pound of butter
- –1 8-ounce package of cream-cheese
- –1 pound of white crab meat
- –Hot pepper sauce, to taste
- –Red pepper
- –Black pepper

1. Saute onion, bellpepper and onion tops in two tablespoons of butter; set aside.
2. In a double boiler, melt cream-cheese and remaining butter; blend well.
3. Add crab meat, seasonings and sauted vegetables.
4. Serve in chafing dish with melba toast.

—Cheryl Bordelon
St. Martin Parish

CRAWFISH OR SHRIMP DIP I

- –1 cup of chopped onions
- –½ cup of chopped bellpepper
- –½ cup of chopped celery
- –2/3 cup of chopped onion tops and parsley
- –1 small jar of pimentos
- –2 teaspoons of oleo
- –2 to 3 pounds of crawfish or shrimp
- –2 to 4 cans of cream of mushroom soup
- –Garlic powder, salt and red pepper, to taste

1. Saute onions, bellpepper, celery, onion tops, parsley and pimentos in oleo; add crawfish or shrimp that have been cut in halves (or thirds, if large) and cook for one minute.
2. Add mushroom soup and cook until crawfish are fully cooked, about 15 to 20 minutes; season, to taste.

The key ingredient in this recipe is the garlic powder, and the more used the better it tastes.

—Paula Faulk
Ebenezer (Acadia Parish)

CRAWFISH DIP II

- –3 large onions, chopped
- –¾ cup of butter
- –2 pounds of crawfish tails and fat, ground
- –2 cans of cream of mushroom soup
- –1 can of cream of celery soup
- –Salt and pepper, to taste

1. Saute onions in butter until cooked; add crawfish and cook about 15 minutes over medium heat.
2. Add fat and soups and cook another five to ten minutes.
3. Season, to taste; serve hot.

Note: This can be frozen and reheated.

—Clara Habetz
Rayne (Acadia Parish)

SHRIMP SPREAD I

- –1 8-ounce package of cream-cheese, softened
- –½ cup of mayonnaise
- –Lemon juice, to taste
- –Hot pepper sauce, to taste
- –3 tablespoons of grated onion
- –¼ cup of French dressing
- –Worcestershire sauce, to taste
- –1 cup of chopped shrimp, cooked

Cream together all ingredients except shrimp. Then add shrimp.

(Optional: Add crab meat to this mixture. Mound high on a serving platter and serve with crackers. Much better if made eight hours prior to serving time. Add more seasonings if necessary.)

Serves 15 generously as hors d'oeuvres.

—Mrs. William Mouton
Lafayette (Lafayette Parish)

SHRIMP DIP II

- –1 8-ounce package of cream-cheese, softened
- –Juice of one lemon
- –2 pounds of shrimp, boiled, peeled and coarsely ground
- –10 green onions, minced
- –Mayonnaise
- –Salt and pepper, to taste
- –Worcestershire sauce and hot pepper sauce, to taste

1. Add lemon juice to softened creamcheese; add shrimp and green onions, mixing well.
2. Add enough mayonnaise to give a consistency for dipping.
3. Season with salt, pepper, worcestershire sauce and hot pepper sauce.

Good for dipping with crackers, chips or raw vegetables.

—Mae Clement
Garyville (St. John the Baptist Parish)

SHRIMP SPREAD OR SHRIMP SALAD II

- –1 pound of fresh shrimp, boiled and peeled (or 2 cans)
- –1 boiled egg, chopped fine
- –2 tablespoons of mayonnaise
- –1 tablespoon of sweet pickle relish
- –2 tablespoons of grated onion
- –1 tablespoon of bellpepper, grated or chopped fine
- –Dash of hot pepper sauce
- –Salt and pepper, to taste

1. In a bowl combine shrimp with next five ingredients, mashing shrimp slightly as you mix together.
2. Add hot pepper sauce, salt and pepper, mixing well.
3. Serve on lettuce leaf with crackers or as a spread on toast triangles.

Serves four, as a salad.

—Norma M. Hicks
St. Landry Parish

SHRIMP DIP III

–1 quart of shrimp, boiled, peeled and deveined
–1 onion
–½ cup of mayonnaise
–1 tablespoon of mustard
–Juice of ½ lemon
–Few drops of worcestershire sauce
–2 tablespoons of French dressing
–Light cream

1. Grind boiled shrimp and onions.
2. Add other ingredients and mix with light cream until soft enough to dip.
3. Serve with crackers or chips.

—Mrs. Frank Daviet
Lockport (Lafourche Parish)

TANGY EGGPLANT RELISH

–2 medium eggplants, cubed
–3 tablespoons of salt
–1/3 cup of vegetable oil or olive oil
–½ cup of chopped white onions
–½ cup of chopped green onions
–3 garlic cloves, diced or crushed
–¼ cup of chopped parsley
–1 small can of tomato sauce
–2 small or 1 medium chopped tomato
–¼ cup of vinegar
–1 tablespoon of sugar, brown or white
–1/8 teaspoon of black pepper
–1/8 teaspoon of red pepper

1. Put eggplant in bowl; sprinkle with salt and let set for a couple of hours.
2. Drain; saute eggplant in oil and remove from skillet.
3. Saute onions, garlic and parsley; add eggplant and remaining ingredients.
4. Cover; simmer slowly about 10 minutes, stirring occasionally.
5. Pack into hot jars; seal and process in hot water bath at 10 pounds for 20 minutes.

Make five to six half pints.

—Mrs. Marian Zachary
Erwinville (West Baton Rouge Parish)

STUFFED BANANA PEPPERS

–1 small tomato, finely chopped
–½ cup of finely chopped onions
–¼ cup of finely chopped sweet pickle
–¼ cup of finely chopped bell-pepper
–2 finely chopped hot peppers
–½ pound of grated sharp cheese
–1/8 teaspoon of salt
–1/8 teaspoon of black pepper
–6 to 8 large banana peppers
–6 to 8 slices of bacon

1. In a large bowl mix together tomato, onion, pickle, bellpepper, hot pepper, grated cheese, salt and black pepper.
2. Cut banana peppers open and remove seeds; stuff with cheese mixture.
3. Starting at one end wrap bacon around the stuffed pepper until cheese mixture is covered; fasten with toothpick at each end.
4. Place in large pan lined with foil; bake at 400 degrees, 30 to 40 minutes.

—Mrs. Ray Dimas
Creole (Cameron Parish)

COCKTAIL BURGER BALLS

–½ cup of prepared onion dip
–3 tablespoons of fine dry bread-crumbs
–¼ teaspoon of salt
–Dash of pepper
–1 pound of ground beef
–1/3 cup of catsup
–2 tablespoons of prepared mustard
–1 teaspoon of worcestershire sauce

1. Combine onion dip, bread-crumbs, salt and pepper.
2. Add ground beef; mix well. Shape into 24 walnut-shaped meat-balls.
3. Grill over medium coals for seven to ten minutes or to desired doneness, turning frequently to brown all sides.
4. Combine catsup, mustard and worcestershire sauce. Spear meat-balls on wooden picks; dip in sauce.
Makes 24 appetizers.

—Leona Roberson
Ascension Parish

CHEESE COOKIES

–1 pound of sharp cheese, grated
–1 pound of oleo
–4 cups of sifted flour
–2 cups of chopped pecans
–½ to 1 teaspoon of red pepper
–½ teaspoon of salt

1. Mix all ingredients.
2. Drop on baking sheet by the teaspoonful.
3. Bake at 350 degrees for 15 to 20 minutes.
Freezes well.

—LSU Cooperative Extension Service,
St. Charles Parish

TARTAR SAUCE

–3 tablespoons of mayonnaise
–1 medium onion, chopped fine
–2 tablespoons of dill pickle relish
–1 tablespoon of horseradish

Combine all ingredients and let stand about 30 minutes before serving. (Great with fried fish, shrimp or oysters.)

—Brenda Conner
Cameron (Cameron Parish)

SEAFOOD SAUCE

–½ cup of chili sauce
–½ cup of catsup
–3 tablespoons of freshly squeezed lemon juice
–1 tablespoon of mayonnaise or salad dressing
–1 teaspoon of worcestershire sauce
–½ teaspoon of grated onion
–¼ teaspoon of salt
–3 drops of hot pepper sauce
–Dash of pepper

Combine all ingredients and chill thoroughly.
Yields one and a half cups.
Serve with boiled seafood.

—Gerald Richard
Grand Chenier (Cameron Parish)

Vegetables, Salads & Salad Dressings

CONTENTS

ARTICHOKE CASSEROLE

–1 medium onion
–1 large rib of celery
–1 small bellpepper
–4 tablespoons of oleo
– 3 14-ounce cans of artichoke hearts
–½ cup of grated Parmesan and Romano cheese
–2 tablespoons of real bacon bits
–1 tablespoon of olive oil
–½ cup of seasoned breadcrumbs

1. Chop onion, celery and bellpeppers fine; saute in melted oleo.
2. Drain and cut artichoke hearts and combine with softened vegetables.
3. Add cheese, bacon bits, oil and breadcrumbs; mix well.
4. Place in a one and one-half quart casserole dish and top with additional breadcrumbs if desired.
5. Bake uncovered at 325 degrees for 20 to 30 minutes.

—Thelma Landry
Iberville Parish

GREEN BEANS AMANDINE

–1 large can of French-style green beans
–1 can of cream of celery soup
–½ cup of slivered almonds

Combine the above in a baking dish. Bake uncovered at 375 degrees 15 to 20 minutes, or until bubbly.

For variety top with onion rings.

—Verna Mae Ruiz
Reserve (St. John the Baptist Parish)

CROWNED ASPARAGUS

–3 cans of green asparagus
–1 4-ounce package of blue cheese
–1 8-ounce carton of sour cream
–5 tablespoons of butter
–2 cups of cheese-flavored crackers, crumbled

1. Drain asparagus; layer in a baking dish.
2. Crumble blue cheese over asparagus.
3. Spread sour cream over blue cheese and asparagus.
4. Melt butter; toss cracker crumbs in butter and sprinkle cracker crumbs over asparagus.
5. Bake uncovered in a preheated oven at 450 degrees until hot and bubbly, about 20 minutes.

—Mrs. Maybelle C. Prather
Houma (Terrebonne Parish)

BUTTERBEANS WITH ROUX

–1 tablespoon of flour
–2 tablespoons of oil
–1 small onion, chopped
–1 pound of fresh butterbeans
–1 quart of water
–Salt and pepper, to taste
–1 tablespoon of sugar (optional)

1. Brown flour in oil to make the roux; add onion and butterbeans and cook lightly.
2. Add water and cook until beans are tender and gravy is thick. Salt and pepper, to taste. Add sugar if desired.

Note: If canned butterbeans are used, use less water.

—Mrs. Louis Courtade Sr.
Brusly (West Baton Rouge Parish)

BROCCOLI CASSEROLE

–2 boxes of frozen broccoli, cooked according to directions on package
–1 6-ounce roll of nippy cheese
–¼ pound of oleo
–1 can of cream of mushroom soup
–½ cup of chopped mushrooms
–½ teaspoon of garlic puree
–½ cup of breadcrumbs

1. Place cooked broccoli in buttered casserole.
2. Melt cheese and oleo; add soup, mushrooms and garlic puree. Pour over broccoli, mixing together. Top with breadcrumbs.
3. Bake uncovered at 425 degrees for 40 minutes, until brown and bubbly.

—Mrs. Coonie Richard
Labadieville (Assumption Parish)

STEWED BELLPEPPER

–Oil
–6 large bellpeppers, sliced
–1 large onion, chopped
–1 can of tomatoes
–Italian cheese (Use as much or as little as you like)
–4 eggs, beaten
–Salt and pepper, to taste

1. Use enough oil to coat the bottom of a skillet; saute bellpeppers and onion until tender on low heat.
2. Add tomatoes and chunks of Italian cheese; cook covered about 20 to 30 minutes on low heat.
3. Add eggs and cook until they are done; season, to taste.

—Donna Sadden
Plaquemine (Iberville Parish)

BAKED BEANS
(Serves 30 to 35)

–4 large white onions, chopped
–1½ pounds of ground meat, pork and beef
–1 gallon of pork and beans
–1 cup of ketchup
–½ cup of brown sugar
–¼ cup of maple syrup
–2 or 3 tablespoons of mustard
–Red pepper and black pepper, to taste

1. Cook onions and meat until meat is brown and onions are wilted.
2. Stir-in other ingredients and bake for one hour at 375 degrees.

—U. J. Daigle
Jennings (Jefferson Davis Parish)

GLORIFIED CABBAGE

–1 bellpepper, chopped
–1 onion, chopped
–1 cup of chopped celery
–¼ pound of oleo
–2 medium heads of cabbage cut in wedges, cooked and drained
–Salt and pepper, to taste
–1 cup of breadcrumbs
–1 cup of grated cheese
–1 cup of milk

1. Wilt vegetables in oleo; mix with cabbage, seasoning, breadcrumbs and one half of the cheese.
2. Pour milk over the mixture, which has been placed in a large pyrex baking dish.
3. Top with remaining cheese and bake uncovered 15 minutes at 350 degrees.

—Mrs. Lowell Rue
Crowley (Acadia Parish)

BABY LIMA BEANS
(Serves 20)

—2 pounds of dried baby lima beans
—1 pound of bacon, chopped
—1 large onion, chopped
—¼ cup of black peppercorns, crushed
—1 tablespoon of sugar
—Salt, to taste

1. Wash beans and cover with water, about twice the depth over beans; add remaining ingredients.
2. Bring to a boil, lower heat and cook for four to five hours, until beans have turned to a thick consistency.
Serves about 20.

—Jim deCordova
Jennings (Jefferson Davis Parish)

FRESH WHITE CORN

—18 to 24 ears of fresh white corn on the cob (Don't use yellow corn)
—¼ to 1/3 pound of butter
—¼ cup of milk
—Salt and black pepper, to taste

1. Cut kernels off each ear of corn; scrape all remaining pulp off each cob, using a large tablespoon, cup side down.
2. In a large pot with a cover or roasting pot with a cover, melt the butter; add corn and corn pulp, milk and salt and pepper, to taste.
3. Cover and bring to the point of juice bubbling; reduce heat. Cover pot and stir often; if sticking occurs, lower heat further.
4. Steam for 20 minutes; remove cover and continue cooking to dry out excess juice.
5. Reduce heat still further and stir frequently to prevent sticking. (It should take about 20 minutes to dry out corn, or a little more if corn is very young and moist.)
6. Freeze in serving portions for future use.

—Arthur Randol Jr.
Lafayette (Lafayette Parish)

CORN CASSEROLE

—4 eggs
—2 cans of cream-style corn
—¼ cup of chopped bellpepper
—1 tablespoon of chopped pimento
—1 cup of chopped green onions
—1 teaspoon of flour
—Scant teaspoon of sugar
—Salt and pepper, to taste

1. Beat eggs and add to other ingredients; season, to taste.
2. Bake uncovered in greased baking dish at 350 degrees for one hour.

—Mrs. Earl Boulet
Crowley (Acadia Parish)

CORN "OYSTERS"

—1 small can of creamed corn
—1 egg
—¼ cup of fine cracker crumbs
—¼ cup of flour
—¼ teaspoon of baking powder
—½ teaspoon of salt
—1/8 teaspoon of black pepper (very important to taste)

1. Mix all ingredients and drop by the teaspoonful into hot oil until golden brown.
2. Drain on brown paper or paper towling.

—Gertilee Williams
Franklin (St. Mary Parish)

STUFFED EGGPLANT

- –4 eggplants
- –Salt
- –¾ cup of vegetable oil
- –¼ cup of olive oil
- –1 cup of breadcrumbs
- –1 cup of finely chopped onions, sauteed
- –2 large garlic cloves, chopped fine
- –2 tablespoons of finely chopped parsley
- –2 tablespoons of finely chopped green onions
- –¼ pound of oleo, melted
- –6 tomatoes (less if desired), seeded and chopped fine
- –Grated Parmesan cheese

1. Cut eggplant in half lengthwise; make a few incisions with sharp knife, sprinkle well with salt and let stand for one-half hour.
2. Wash and dry well.
3. Fry in hot oils on one side until half-cooked (about 10 minutes); turn over on other side and finish cooking.
4. Scrape out pulp, leaving skin whole.
5. Chop pulp fine; mix with breadcrumbs, onions, garlic, parsley, green onions and melted oleo.
6. Mix-in tomatoes.
7. Refill eggplant skins carefully; sprinkle the top with breadcrumbs, Parmesan cheese and a little melted oleo.
8. Brown under the broiler.

—Maude Milano
Ascension Parish

FRIED EGGPLANT OR OKRA

- –Eggplant or okra
- –Salt and red pepper
- –Flour
- –White cornmeal
- –1 egg, beaten

1. Wash vegetable and slice into one-half-inch slices; season with salt and pepper.
2. Blend flour and cornmeal and season with salt and pepper.
3. Dip vegetable in egg then in flour-cornmeal mixture; fry in hot oil until golden and crisp.

—Kathryn Leonard
Lafayette (Lafayette Parish)

EGGPLANT FRITTERS

- –1 medium-size eggplant, chopped
- –Salt and pepper, to taste
- –½ small onion, minced finely
- –1 egg, beaten
- –1 teaspoon of baking powder
- –Flour
- –Oil for frying

1. Boil eggplant until very tender. Drain in colander and remove as much water as possible. Mash until mushy.
2. Add rest of ingredients; stir-in as much flour as needed to hold together.
3. Drop by the spoonful in hot oil and fry on each side (about one-half minute for each side).

Serve while still warm.

—Mrs. Georgia Landry
Norco (St. Charles Parish)

EGGPLANT ROUNDS

- –2 large eggplants (2½ inches round), sliced ½-inch thick and peeled
- –Vegetable oil
- –Italian-style breadcrumbs

1. Pour oil into shallow bowl and coat eggplant slices on both sides.
2. Dip oil-coated slices into breadcrumbs (should be rather thickly coated with breadcrumbs).
3. Place foil on cookie sheet or in shallow baking pan. Put eggplant slices in pan, not touching each other.
4. Bake in 350-degree oven about 40 minutes (20 minutes each side) or until lightly browned on both sides, turning only once.

Goes well with broiled pork chops or beef.

—Frances W. Breaux
Opelousas (St. Landry Parish)

SMOTHERED OKRA

- –10 pounds of okra
- –Cooking oil
- –2 large bellpeppers, chopped
- –2 large onions, chopped
- –2 large cans of tomatoes (or 4 fresh tomatoes, peeled)
- –Salt and red pepper, to taste

1. Wash okra and slice into one-half inch slices.
2. Pour oil to cover bottom of large heavy roasting pan; add okra, bellpepper and onion, and blend. Cover tightly and cook in 300-degree oven for one hour.
3. Add tomatoes and stir until well-blended; re-cover and continue to cook for at least two more hours. Stir occasionally to prevent sticking.
4. When cooked, add seasonings to taste and serve hot as a side dish, or freeze for later use in gumbo.

—Kathryn Leonard
Lafayette (Lafayette Parish)

ONION PIE

- –1 cup of cracker crumbs (about 25 crackers)
- –¼ cup of butter
- –2 cups of thinly sliced onions
- –¾ cup of milk
- –2 eggs
- –¾ teaspoon of salt and pepper together
- –¼ cup of grated cheese (any kind)

1. Mix cracker crumbs with two tablespoons of butter and press in eight-inch pie plate to form shell.
2. Cook onions in two tablespoons of butter until tender (not brown), then place in shell.
3. Combine milk, eggs, salt and pepper; pour over onions and sprinkle with cheese.
4. Bake at 350 degrees until set, 20 to 30 minutes.

Great with fish!

—Iva Lee Decuir
Avoyelles Parish

SHRIMP-STUFFED POTATOES

- –4 large potatoes
- –2 pounds of shrimp, boiled and peeled (or enough to measure 1 quart of peeled shrimp)
- –1 small onion
- –1 8-ounce package of creamcheese
- –3 tablespoons of mayonnaise
- –2 to 4 tablespoons of evaporated milk
- –1 teaspoon of salt
- –½ teaspoon of garlic powder
- –½ teaspoon of Season-All salt
- –1 tablespoon of chopped parsley

1. Bake potatoes at 375 degrees for 55 to 60 minutes or until fully cooked; remove from oven and wrap potatoes separately in foil.
2. Grind one-half of the shrimp finely with onion.
3. Cream together creamcheese, mayonnaise, milk, salt, garlic powder and Season-All; mix-in the ground shrimp and onion.
4. Cut potatoes in foil in half; place a layer of the remaining whole shrimp inside of baked potato that has been partially scooped-out, then a layer of one and one-half tablespoons of creamy shrimp mixture, then another layer of six shrimp. Top with parsley.

Serves four.

Great served with grilled steak!

—N. Pitre
Bourg (Terrebonne Parish)

BAKED ONIONS

- –3 large Bermuda onions, thickly sliced
- –Salt, black pepper and red pepper, to taste
- –¾ cup of grated cheddar cheese
- –¼ cup of Italian breadcrumbs
- –3 tablespoons of oleo

1. Butter casserole; place onions in dish in a single layer.
2. Season lightly with salt, black pepper and red pepper.
3. Sprinkle grated cheese over onion slices; top with breadcrumbs and dot with oleo.
4. Bake uncovered at 375 degrees about 30 minutes.

Serves three.

Great with steak!

—Matt and Sarah Vernon
Eunice (St. Landry Parish)

SCALLOPED POTATOES

- –4 cups of potatoes, sliced thin or grated
- –Dash of salt and pepper
- –¼ cup of flour
- –1 teaspoon of minced onion
- –¼ cup of butter
- –1¼ cup of hot milk

1. Heat oven to 350 degrees.
2. Layer raw potatoes in a one-and-one-half-quart baking dish with salt, pepper, flour and minced onion.
3. Dot with butter; add hot milk.
4. Bake uncovered about one hour and 15 minutes or until golden brown.

—Mrs. Mildredge Broussard
Grand Chenier (Cameron Parish)

GREEN RICE I

- –2 cups of raw rice
- –2/3 cup of chopped bellpepper
- –1 cup of chopped green onions and tops
- –1/3 cup of minced parsley
- –¼ cup of cooking oil
- –1½ tablespoons of worcestershire sauce
- –1 teaspoon of salt
- –½ teaspoon of red pepper
- –4 cups of beef or chicken bouillon, using 6 cubes and 4 cups of hot water

1. Combine all ingredients in rice cooker and cook, or bake without stirring in a two-quart casserole with a tight-fitting cover, for 45 minutes at 350 degrees.
2. Remove cover and toss. Serve hot.

Serves eight to ten.

—Pat Mouret
Opelousas (St. Landry Parish)

RIZ AU BREME
(Rice with Eggplant)

- –3 large eggplants, peeled and cut in medium pieces
- –1 onion, chopped
- –2 tablespoons of oil
- –Salt and pepper, to taste
- –3 cups of cooked rice

1. Boil eggplant in water to cover until tender; drain.
2. Saute onion in oil; add eggplant and seasonings. Smother until moisture has evaporated.
3. Add rice and cook about 12 minutes.

—Miss Viola LeBlanc
Lockport (Lafourche Parish)

RICE DELICIOUS

- –1 4-ounce can of sliced mushrooms
- –1 4-ounce can of water chestnuts, sliced
- –¼ pound of butter or oleo
- –1 cup of raw rice
- –1 can of onion soup

1. Reserve liquid from mushrooms and water chestnuts.
2. Melt butter in saucepan; saute mushrooms and chestnuts one or two minutes.
3. Combine with rice, onion soup, and reserved liquids plus enough water to fill soup can.
4. Bake in 300-degree oven in covered dish for about one hour, or until rice is done.

—Patsy Granger
Jennings (Jefferson Davis Parish)

GREEN RICE II

- –2 cups of raw rice
- –1½ cups of milk
- –½ cup of oleo
- –1 cup of fresh chopped parsley
- –1 cup of chopped bellpepper
- –1 cup of chopped green onions
- –2 garlic cloves
- –1 pound of grated cheese
- –Salt and pepper, to taste

1. Cook rice; mix while hot with all other ingredients.
2. Place in oiled casserole; bake uncovered at 350 degrees for 35 to 40 minutes.

Note: One cup of crab meat may be added to make a main dish.

—Norma Meyers
Sulphur (Calcasieu Parish)

SPINACH-MUSHROOM CASSEROLE

- 2 packages of frozen chopped spinach
- 2 tablespoons of butter
- 2 tablespoons of chopped onions
- 1 tablespoon of chopped bellpepper
- 1 teaspoon of chopped parsley
- ½ roll of jalapeno cheese
- Celery salt
- Garlic salt
- 1 teaspoon of worcestershire sauce
- Red pepper (optional)
- 1 can of cream of mushroom soup
- Breadcrumbs

1. Cook spinach as directed; drain.
2. Mix other ingredients (except breadcrumbs) and heat to melt cheese.
3. Fold-in spinach and put in casserole dish; dot with more butter and sprinkle with breadcrumbs.
4. Bake at 375 degrees till brown and bubbly. (Can be frozen for later use.)

—Manila Marchand
Ascension Parish

SQUASH CASSEROLE

- 6 pounds of white squash, peeled, cored and diced
- 3 medium white onions, chopped
- ¼ cup of butter
- ½ cup of cream
- Salt, to taste
- Buttered breadcrumbs

1. Combine squash and onions. Cook in heavy pot over very low heat, stirring often to prevent sticking. As squash and onion get tender, mash while cooking. Add a little water if necessary.
2. When mixture is tender and mashed, add butter and cream. Continue cooking for a short time, stirring until butter and cream have blended well into the vegetables. Salt, to taste.
3. Pour into nine-inch pyrex dish and sprinkle with buttered breadcrumbs. Place in 300-degree oven for 15 to 20 minutes.

—Mrs. J. O. Smith
New Roads (Pointe Coupee Parish)

YAMS WITH CRANBERRY SAUCE

- 1½ cup of whole cranberry sauce
- ¼ cup of water
- ¼ teaspoon of nutmeg
- ¼ cup of raisins
- 3 tablespoons of dry sherry
- ¼ cup of brown sugar
- 2 tablespoons of butter
- ½ cup of chopped pecans
- 1 large can of yams, drained

1. Combine cranberry sauce, water, nutmeg, raisins, sherry and brown sugar in saucepan. Bring to boil. Cook over low heat about five minutes.
2. Stir-in butter until melted. Add pecans.
3. Arrange yams in casserole; pour sauce over them. Bake uncovered in 350-degree oven for 25 to 30 minutes.

Serves six to eight.

—Patricia Wright
Lafayette (Lafayette Parish)

SUPER YAMS

- –8 medium pre-cooked yams, cut in 1- to 1½-inch slices
- –5 tablespoons of brown sugar
- –2 ounces of dark creme de cacao
- –1½ cups of honey

1. Place yams in baking dish. Sprinkle brown sugar over them; then pour creme de cacao and honey over them.
2. Bake at 425 dgrees for 15 to 20 minutes.

—Keith Courrege
New Iberia (Iberia Parish)

RUM-BAKED YAMS

- –6 yams, peeled
- –½ cup of butter or oleo
- –1 cup of apple cider
- –1/3 cup of dark rum
- –¼ cup of packed brown sugar
- –¼ teaspoon of salt
- –¼ teaspoon of allspice
- –¼ teaspoon of mace
- –1 teaspoon of ground ginger
- –1/3 cup of raisins

1. Cut yams into one-inch cubes and place in a two-quart buttered casserole.
2. Put the butter, apple cider, rum, brown sugar, salt and spices into a saucepan and heat, stirring until the butter and sugar have melted; pour about half of it over the yams, sprinkle with raisins and pour the remaining syrup over the raisins and yams.
3. Cover tightly and bake for one hour at 325 degrees; turn the oven to 425 degrees, uncover and bake about 30 minutes longer or until the juices are thick and bubbling.

—William "Bill" O'Dea
Abbeville (Vermilion Parish)

YAM CUPS

- –½ cup of oleo or butter
- –2 3-ounce packages of creamcheese
- –2 cups of flour
- –½ teaspoon of salt
- –¼ cup of ground pecans
- –1 large can of yams, drained
- –1 small can of crushed pineapple, drained
- –¼ cup of brown sugar
- –½ cup of pecans, chopped
- –¼ teaspoon of nutmeg
- –½ teaspoon of cinnamon
- –¼ teaspoon of ground cloves
- –2 tablespoons of melted butter
- –1½ cups of miniature marshmallows

1. Soften butter and creamcheese in large mixing bowl. Gradually blend-in flour, salt and ground pecans. Blend well.
2. Form into balls, about as large as a silver dollar. With fingertips, press each ball into an ungreased muffin tin, forming a shell. Repeat until all dough is used.
3. Mash yams with fork in a large mixing bowl. Add pineapple, brown sugar, chopped pecans, spices and butter; mix well.
4. Divide yam mixture by the spoonful into unbaked shells. Sprinkle with a few miniature marshmallows.
5. Bake at 350 degrees 15 to 20 minutes. Remove from oven and allow to cool slightly before removing from pans.

These may be made ahead and placed uncooked in the freezer and then baked when needed.

—Mrs. Carl Johnson
Lafayette (Lafayette Parish)

OLD-FASHIONED CANDIED YAMS

–6 medium yams, cooked and peeled
–1½ cups of sugar, white or dark brown
–3 tablespoons of water
–3 tablespoons of butter
–½ cup of chopped pecans

1. Place yams in a heavy pan.
2. Mix sugar and water, bring to a boil and add butter; pour syrup over yams.
3. Set in moderate 350-degree oven and bake; baste occasionally until syrup is as desired.
4. Remove and sprinkle with pecans.
Serves six to eight.

—Frank Daigle
Opelousas (St. Landry Parish)

YAM BAKE

–5 medium-size yams, cooked (or a 29-ounce can of yams)
–1 cup of orange juice
–¼ cup of oleo, melted
–¼ teaspoon of salt
–½ cup of firmly packed brown sugar
–¼ cup of seedless raisins
–2 tablespoons of chopped nuts

1. Halve yams and arrange in shallow dish.
2. Combine all other ingredients; mix well. Pour over yams.
3. Bake uncovered at 350 degrees for 20 to 25 minutes.
Yields six servings.

—Mrs. Charles Arceneaux
Lafayette (Lafayette Parish)

SUCCOTASH

–¼ pound of salt pork, cut up
–1 tablespoon of shortening
–1 large onion, chopped
–1 small bellpepper, chopped
–1 cup of sliced okra, fresh or frozen
–1 8-ounce can of tomato sauce
–1 16-ounce can of corn, cream or whole
–1 16-ounce can of lima beans
–1 tablespoon of sugar

1. Bring salt pork to a boil in water and scald; drain and fry well in shortening.
2. Add onion and fry lightly; add bellpepper, okra and tomato sauce; cook at medium heat for about 15 minutes.
3. Add corn, lima beans and sugar; cook one-half hour on low heat. If mixture becomes too thick, add water as needed.

—Mrs. Joseph Moore, Sr.
Napoleonville (Assumption Parish)

SOUTHERN-STYLE VEGETABLES

–1/3 pound of bacon
–2 cups of shelled peas
–2 cups of butter beans
–1 pound of whole baby okra

1. Brown bacon in dutch oven.
2. Add peas and beans and enough water to cover mixture; simmer one hour.
3. Add okra and continue to cook 20 minutes longer. Salt, to taste.

—Sylvia Aplin
Grand Chenier (Cameron Parish)

CHICKEN SALAD RING

–1 large fryer
–1 teaspoon of salt
–½ teaspoon of pepper
–½ teaspoon of Accent
–3 cups of water
–1 envelope of unflavored gelatin
–2 ribs of celery
–¼ medium bellpepper
–3 boiled eggs
–1 whole green onion
–½ cup of sweet salad pickles
–½ cup of stuffed olives, sliced
–1 cup of mayonnaise
–1 tablespoon of lemon juice

1. Cut chicken in half; place in large saucepan; sprinkle with salt, pepper and Accent; add water and bring to boil.
2. Cut temperature to medium and boil 45 minutes to one hour or until chicken is tender.
3. Remove chicken from broth to cool; reserve one-half cup of broth and while still warm dissolve gelatin in it and set aside.
4. Pull skin from chicken while warm and take meat from bones.
5. Grind chicken, celery, bellpepper, eggs and green onions.
6. Mix well; then add pickles, sliced olives, mayonnaise, lemon juice and more salt and pepper, to taste.
7. Fold-in to gelatin mixture and pour into mold; let stand in refrigerator for one to two hours.
8. Serve on platter layered with lettuce, and garnish with olives, bellpepper and pickled quail eggs. Serves eight.

—Mrs. C. E. Saunier
Houma (Terrebonne Parish)

CRAB AND SHRIMP SALAD

–1 cup of cooked crab meat
–1 cup of cooked shrimp, peeled and cut in half if large
–½ cup of mayonnaise
–2 tablespoons of ketchup
–½ teaspoon of mustard
–Dash of worcestershire sauce
–Juice of ½ lemon
–Salt and pepper, to taste
–½ small onion, chopped very fine
–Chopped lettuce

Mix all ingredients together right before serving.

—Hubby and Loraine Foret
Luling (St. Charles Parish)

GERMAN POTATO SALAD

–1 pint of sour cream
–1/3 cup of mayonnaise
–3 medium onions
–½ teaspoon of horseradish
–¼ teaspoon of celery seeds
–1 cup of parsley, chopped
–7 red potatoes, boiled and sliced

1. Mix first six ingredients for dressing.
2. Alternate potato slices and dressing.

—Gertilee Williams
Franklin (St. Mary Parish)

HEARTY HOT CAJUN POTATO SALAD

–5 medium potatoes
–5 slices of bacon
–½ cup of chopped onion
–2 tablespoons of sugar
–1 tablespoon of flour
–1½ teaspoons of salt
–2 teaspoons of hot pepper sauce
–½ cup of water
–¼ cup of vinegar
–½ cup of sliced red radishes

1. Cook unpeeled potatoes in boiling water until tender, about 40 minutes; peel and slice.
2. Fry bacon until crisp; remove, drain, crumble and reserve.
3. Cook onion in bacon drippings until partially tender, about five minutes.
4. Blend together sugar, flour, salt, pepper sauce, water and vinegar; add to onion and cook, stirring constantly, until mixture thickens and bubbles, about five minutes. Remove from heat.
5. Add potatoes to onion mixture and heat for about five minutes; add radishes and toss.
6. Serve hot, topped with bacon.

—Jay Norris
New Iberia (Iberia Parish)

POTATO SALAD

–8 to 10 small whole red new potatoes
–1 hard-cooked egg
–½ cup of mayonnaise
–1 tablespoon of lemon juice
–¼ cup of half-and-half cream
–½ cup of minced green onions
–½ cup of minced sweet cucumber pickle slices
–¼ cup of minced bellpepper
–1 tablespoon of minced parsley
–1 teaspoon of salt
–½ teaspoon of dill weed
–¼ teaspoon of marjoram
–½ teaspoon of summer savory
–¼ teaspoon of pepper

1. In large saucepan, boil unpeeled potatoes until fork-tender, for about 20 minutes.
2. In medium bowl, mash the egg thoroughly; stir-in remaining ingredients until well-mixed.
3. Taste for flavor; the dressing may taste salty, but do not be concerned, as the potatoes will absorb the salt.
4. After potatoes are cooked, drain; plunge into cold water and drain immediately.
5. Peel and slice into medium bowl; pour dressing over warm potatoes and toss until well-coated.
6. Cool; then cover and refrigerate until chilled.

Makes four to six servings.

—Mrs. Charles A. Rogers
Cameron (Cameron Parish)

STRING BEAN SALAD

–¾ cup of peeled and diced potatoes
–2 cans of string beans, drained
–1/3 cup of sliced onions
–2 tablespoons of vinegar
–2 tablespoons of oil
–Salt and pepper, to taste

1. Boil potatoes until almost done; add string beans and boil ten minutes longer; drain.
2. Add onions, vinegar, oil, salt and pepper.
3. Serve hot or cold.

—Rosa Rodosta
Iberville Parish

SHRIMP-RICE SUPPER SALAD

–2 4½-ounce cans of shrimp
–2 cups of chilled, cooked and blanched rice
–1 8-ounce can of water chestnuts, drained and thinly sliced
–1 cup of diagonally sliced celery
–½ cup of sliced, pitted, ripe olives
–¼ cup of sliced green onions
–1¼ cups of mayonnaise or salad dressing
–1 tablespoon of lemon juice
–1 teaspoon of soy sauce
–¼ teaspoon of ginger
–¼ teaspoon of curry powder
–Crisp salad greens
–Tomato wedges or slices and black olives for garnish (optional)

1. Drain shrimp; rinse in cold water and chill.
2. Combine rice, water chestnuts, celery, olives and green onions in large bowl.
3. Combine mayonnaise or salad dressing, lemon juice, soy sauce, ginger and curry powder and mix well; pour over rice mixture and mix well.
4. Chill at least one hour; fold-in shrimp.
5. Serve on salad greens. Garnish, if desired, with tomato wedges or slices and black olives.
Makes five cups of salad mixture, four to six servings.

—Mrs. Laura Gilmore
Berwick (St. Mary Parish)

FRENCH DRESSING

–¼ cup of vinegar
–1 teaspoon of paprika
–½ teaspoon of dry mustard
–¾ cup of salad oil
–½ teaspoon of salt
–Dash of white pepper

1. Combine all ingredients in tight-fitted covered jar.
2. Shake until blended.
3. Chill; shake well each time before using.

—Gwen Seale
Ascension Parish

BLUE CHEESE SALAD DRESSING

–2½ ounces of mild blue cheese
–½ cup of mayonnaise
–1 cup of sour cream
–1 tablespoon of sugar
–¼ teaspoon of worcestershire sauce
–1 teaspoon of monosodium glutamate
–Salt and pepper, to taste

Mix all ingredients well. Keeps in refrigerator.

—Marguerite M. Kramer
Franklin (St. Mary Parish)

Soups & Gumbos

CONTENTS

CORN AND SHRIMP SOUP

—¼ cup of cooking oil
—2 tablespoons of flour
—1 large onion, chopped
—12 ears of fresh corn, cut from cob (or 2 cans of cream-style corn)
—½ can of tomato sauce
—1 large bellpepper, chopped
—1½ pounds of shrimp
—Water

1. Heat oil and add flour; brown to make a roux.
2. Add onion and saute; then add remaining ingredients.
3. Add water to soup for desired consistency and simmer about one hour.

—Mrs. Bea Laurent
New Roads (Pointe Coupee Parish)

OYSTER SOUP

—1 cup of finely chopped celery
—1 cup of finely chopped green onions
—¼ pound of butter
—1 tablespoon of flour
—1 teaspoon of chopped garlic
—1 teaspoon of chopped parsley
—2 dozen large oysters
—Oyster water plus water to make six cups

1. Saute celery and green onions in butter until tender.
2. Blend-in flour and cook five minutes, stirring over low heat; add remaining ingredients and simmer 20 minutes.
Makes one and one-half quarts.

—Georgiana Bourg
Ascension Parish

OYSTER-ARTICHOKE SOUP

—1 bunch of green onions, chopped
—3 bay leaves, crumbled
—Pinch of thyme
—Red pepper, to taste
—4 tablespoons of butter
—2 tablespoons of flour
—1 14-ounce can of chicken broth
—2 jars of oysters, drained (saving the juice)
—1 14-ounce can of artichoke hearts, chopped
—3 sprigs of parsley, chopped
—½ cup of heavy cream
—Salt, to taste
—Dash of nutmeg

1. Saute green onions, bay leaves, thyme and red pepper in butter; add flour and stir well.
2. Add chicken broth and juice from the oysters; simmer 15 minutes.
3. Add artichoke hearts, oysters and parsley; simmer 10 minutes.
4. Remove from heat; stir-in heavy cream. Add salt if necessary and nutmeg.

Note: It isn't really necessary to add the oysters; the oyster flavor comes from the oyster juice. Fry the oysters to serve with the soup.
Serves four.

—Sue C. McDonough
New Iberia (Iberia Parish)

GARLIC SOUP

- –8 garlic cloves, minced
- –2 tablespoons of olive oil
- –2 tomatoes, peeled, seeded and chopped fine
- –8 cups of beef or chicken stock or bouillon
- –Bouquet garni (bay leaf, celery leaves, thyme and parsley), tied in cheesecloth
- –3 egg yolks, beaten lightly
- –¼ cup of olive oil
- –French bread
- –Grated Parmesan cheese

1. Gently saute garlic in olive oil for just a few minutes; add tomatoes and saute a few minutes more.
2. Add stock or bouillon and bouquet garni and simmer gently for 20 minutes; remove bouquet garni.
3. While stock is cooking, with a wire whisk beat the one-fourth cup of olive oil, a few drops at a time, into egg yolks, like making mayonnaise, until mixture is thick.
4. Slowly pour about one cup of hot soup into egg mixture while beating vigorously with whisk, then pour mixture into soup while stirring well with whisk.
5. Serve accompanied by french bread and Parmesan cheese.

It may also be served by putting slices of french bread, plain or toasted, in individual bowls and pouring soup over them, then sprinkling with Parmesan.

—Keith E. Courrege
New Iberia (Iberia Parish)

CHICKEN GUMBO

- –3- to 4-pound fryer, cut up
- –Salt and pepper
- –Flour
- –Shortening
- –10 tablespoons of flour
- –1 onion, chopped
- –3 quarts of water
- –4 stalks of celery, chopped

1. Season fryer with salt and pepper; sprinkle with flour.
2. Saute in enough shortening to cover bottom of pot until dark golden brown; place in six-quart soup pot.
3. Drain all shortening from skillet, leaving residue at bottom; reserve drippings.
4. Add six tablespoons of the drippings and ten tablespoons of flour to skillet and brown until dark golden brown, 10 to 15 minutes, being careful not to burn.
5. When browned, add onion and cook until limp; add this to cooked chicken and add water and celery.
6. Bring to a boil, reduce heat to simmering and cook about two hours, stirring occasionally; season with salt and pepper.
7. Remove chicken, debone, skin and put meat back into gumbo.
8. Serve over hot rice.

—Mrs. Paul Sewall, Jr.
Lafayette (Lafayette Parish)

CHICKEN-ANDOUILLE GUMBO

–½ cup of flour
–½ cup of shortening
–1 cup each of onion, celery and bellpeppers, chopped
–1 garlic clove, minced
–1 hen, cut into serving pieces
–Salt, pepper and cayenne, to taste
–1 pound of andouille sausage, cut in pieces
–Filé, to taste

1. Make a roux by slowly browning the flour in the shortening; when golden brown, add the onion, celery, bellpepper and garlic.
2. Cook at low heat until the vegetables separate from the shortening.
3. In another pan, brown the cut-up hen in some extra shortening, using enough to sear chicken well.
4. Add the hen to the brown roux mixture and cook together for a few minutes, stirring occasionally.
5. Meanwhile, carefully pour out the extra shortening in which hen was browned, leaving only the brown drippings at the bottom; to this, add water and bring to boil.
6. Pour this over the hen, adding enough extra boiling water to cover; add salt, pepper and cayenne, to taste.
7. For best results, it will require several hours of slow cooking; add the andouille during the last hour of cooking.
8. When ready to serve, add some filé, a small sprinkle at a time, until the desired flavor has been obtained.

Serve with rice.

—Mrs. A. J. Nobile
Gramercy (St. James Parish)

CHICKEN AND SAUSAGE GUMBO

–6 tablespoons of oil
–6 tablespoons of flour
–1 pound of smoked sausage or andouille
–1 large hen
–2 gallons of water
–2 large onions
–¼ stalk of celery
–½ bellpepper
–5 onion tops, chopped
–Salt
–Cayenne
–Black pepper
–5 sprigs of parsley (or 2 tablespoons of flakes)
–2 teaspoons of filé

1. Make fudge-looking roux with oil and flour.
2. Boil sausage in separate pot.
3. Combine hen, one and one-half gallons of water, sausage, roux and chopped seasonings (except parsley).
4. Cook for two hours, adding extra one-half gallon of water if needed.
5. During last half hour of cooking, add salt, cayenne and black pepper.
6. As hen becomes tender enough, add parsley and filé. Cook ten minutes, remove from heat, skim excess fat and serve over rice. One pint of oysters may also be added if desired.

—Mrs. Pearl Credeur
Schriever (Terrebonne Parish)

CHICKEN AND OKRA GUMBO

–1 quart of smothered okra
–2 large onions, chopped
–2 to 3 ribs of celery, chopped
–3 quarts of water
–1 large chicken, cut up
–Oil
–Salt, black pepper and red pepper, to taste
–Chopped green onions
–Chopped parsley

1. To smother okra, saute sliced okra in a small amount of oil until golden brown.
2. Add onions and celery; saute until wilted.
3. Add water; simmer until vegetables are well done.
4. Brown chicken in oil to cover bottom of frypan; when brown, add to boiling okra mixture. Add salt, black pepper and red pepper; cook until chicken is tender, about 45 to 60 minutes.
5. Add green onions and parsley just before serving. Serve over rice.

—Mrs. Perfice Armentor
New Iberia (Iberia Parish)

SHRIMP AND OKRA GUMBO

–1 quart of okra, cut up
–1 medium onion, chopped
–1 small bellpepper, chopped
–3 ripe tomatoes, peeled and chopped
–1 tablespoon of oil
–1 teaspoon of salt
–Pinch of black pepper
–1 cup of shrimp, peeled
–1 quart of water

1. Smother okra with onion, bellpepper, tomatoes and cooking oil.
2. Add salt, pepper, shrimp and water. Cook on low heat for 45 minutes.

Note: Don't use iron pot for cooking okra; it will cause okra to turn black.

—Mrs. Malcolm Guillot
Avoyelles Parish

BEEF RIBS AND OKRA GUMBO

–3 pounds of short beef ribs
–2 pieces of beef brisket
–1/3 cup of oil
–2 cups of chopped onions
–1 medium-size bellpepper, chopped
–Water as needed
–2 cups of cooked okra
–½ cup of green onion tops, chopped
–Filé to taste

1. Put beef ribs and brisket in iron pot in one-third cup of oil; let brown slightly. Add onions and bellpepper. Add some water and simmer two hours. Keep adding water as needed.
2. When meat is tender, add okra and green onion tops. Let simmer 30 minutes longer. Add gumbo filé, to taste.

A can of tomatoes may be added to cut the slime of the okra.

Serve with rice or crackers.

—Mrs. Jessie Hoffpauir
Indian Bayou (Vermilion Parish)

SHRIMP AND CRAB GUMBO

–2 pounds of shrimp, peeled and deveined
–½ dozen crabs, boiled and peeled
–¼ cup of shortening
–2 quarts of water
–1 large onion, chopped
–1 garlic clove, minced
–1 bellpepper, chopped
–1 rib of celery, chopped
–2 pounds of okra, fresh or frozen (if fresh, slice and fry)
–1 can of tomato sauce
–1 bay leaf
–1 tablespoon of worcestershire sauce
–Salt and pepper, to taste
–Parsley, chopped
–Cooked rice

1. Saute shrimp and crab meat with two tablespoons of the shortening in a large pot; add water and set aside.
2. In remaining two tablespoons of the shortening, saute onion, garlic, bellpepper and celery slightly; add okra and continue sauteing until brown.
3. Add sauted vegetables to seafood, along with the tomato sauce and seasonings; stir well to remove all browned particles from the bottom of the pot.
4. Cook slowly for about two hours.
5. Add parsley and serve over cooked rice.
Serves six to eight.

—Mrs. Mary Pryolo
Lafourche Parish

SEAFOOD GUMBO

–2/3 cup of oil
–1 cup of flour
–1 big onion, chopped
–½ bellpepper, chopped
–1 small rib of celery, chopped
–2 quarts of cold water
–1½ cups of oyster juice
–2½ pounds of shrimp, peeled
–5 dozen oysters
–Crab meat or lobster (optional)
–Onion tops, chopped
–Parsley, chopped
–Filé

1. Make roux with oil and flour until golden brown, but not too dark. Let finish browning without heat. Add onions, bellpepper and celery. Stir well and put back on low, low heat. Cover pot and cook until onions wilt.
2. Add cold water and oyster juice; stir. Bring to a boil, lower heat and simmer about 45 minutes.
3. Add shrimp; bring to a boil, lower heat and simmer about 30 minutes.
4. Add oysters during the last ten minutes (also cooked crab meat or lobster).
5. Add chopped onion tops and parsley when everything is done. Serve in soup bowls with rice and a sprinkling of filē.

—Mrs. Virginia Yongue
Breaux Bridge (St. Martin Parish)

CRAWFISH BISQUE

–20 pounds of live crawfish
–6 tablespoons of butter or oleo
–½ cup of oil
–1 cup of flour
–2 large onions, ground
–1 large bellpepper, ground
–4½ cups of water
–1 tablespoon of salt
–2 teaspoons of red pepper
–½ cup of chopped green onion tops
–½ cup of chopped parsley
–Stuffed Crawfish Heads (Recipe follows)

1. Drop live crawfish in boiling water for 10 minutes or until crawfish are red.
2. Separate heads from tails; peel tails and set aside. Place crawfish "fat" in separate container and set aside. Clean 60 heads to fill with stuffing; set aside. Divide tails and "fat" equally for bisque and for stuffing.
3. Make a roux with butter, oil and flour; add onions and bellpepper. Cool until soft, stirring frequently.
4. Add one-half of the crawfish tails and one-half of the crawfish "fat;" cook over low heat for about 20 minutes.
5. Gradually add four and one-half cups of boiling water, salt and pepper; cook for about 20 minutes more.
6. Add onion tops and parsley. Just before serving, add baked Stuffed Crawfish Heads.
Serve with rice.
Serves 10.

STUFFED CRAWFISH HEADS
–¼ cup of oil
–½ cup of flour
–2 medium onions, ground
–1 large bellpepper, ground
–¾ cup of water
–2 teaspoons of salt
–1½ teaspoons of red pepper
–1½ cups of breadcrumbs
–¼ cup of chopped parsley
–¼ cup of chopped green onion tops
–4 tablespoons of butter or oleo
–60 cleaned crawfish heads
–Flour

1. Make a roux with oil and flour; add onions and bellpepper. Cook until soft.
2. Grind remaining crawfish tails and add to onion mixture; add remaining crawfish "fat" and simmer for 15 minutes.
3. Add water, salt, pepper, breadcrumbs, parsley, green onion tops and butter; mix well.
4. Fill each head with stuffing, roll in flour and bake at 350 degrees for 15 minutes.

—Mrs. August Girard
Breaux Bridge (St. Martin Parish)

REDFISH COURTBOUILLON

–1 cup of flour
–¾ cup of oil
–1 cup of chopped onion
–1 medium bellpepper, chopped fine
–2 cans of tomato paste
–1 can of stewed tomatoes
–3 garlic cloves, minced
–1 cup of chopped celery
–1 lemon, sliced thin
–2 bay leaves
–Salt and pepper, to taste
–Water
–4 to 6 pounds of de-boned fish (leave skin on for better taste)
–12 sprigs of parsley, chopped fine
–1 tablespoon of worcestershire sauce
–1 to 2 cups of sauterne wine
–2 cans of chopped mushrooms
–½ cup of chopped olives

1. Make a dark brown roux with flour and oil. Add onion and bellpepper; stir and cook until vegetables are well-smothered.
2. Add tomato paste and stewed tomatoes; cook thoroughly.
3. Add garlic, celery, lemon slices and bay leaves; season with salt and pepper. Add hot water, a little at a time, up to about four cups; simmer about 15 minutes.
4. Add fish; cook 30 minutes after boiling begins.
5. Add parsley, worcestershire sauce, wine, mushrooms and olives; bring to a boil and cook for five minutes. Turn off heat and let stand with cover on for a few minutes. Serve with rice.

Serves ten.

—Mrs. S. E. Curole
Larose (Lafourche Parish)

SEAFOOD COURTBOUILLON

–1 cup of oil
–1 cup of flour
–1¼ cups of finely minced onion
–2 to 3 ribs of celery, finely chopped
–½ cup of finely chopped bellpepper
–2 garlic cloves, finely minced
–1 8-ounce can of tomato paste
–3½ to 4 quarts of water
–2½ teaspoons of salt
–2½ teaspoons of red pepper
–2 teaspoons of seasoning salt
–4½ to 5 pounds of fish (redfish, snapper, catfish, etc.), cut into pieces
–1 12-ounce can of crab meat
–1½ pounds of shrimp, peeled and de-veined
–¼ cup of chopped green onion tops
–¼ cup of chopped parsley
–Cooked rice

1. Brown oil and flour until golden.
2. Add onion, celery, bellpepper and garlic; cook until wilted.
3. Add tomato paste and cook until oil appears on top of mixture (about 25 minutes).
4. Add water, salt, red pepper and seasoning salt; boil 15 minutes.
5. Add fish, crab meat, shrimp, green onion tops and parsley; cook 25 minutes.

Serve over cooked rice.

Serves 10 to 12.

—Jeanette M. Guidry
Breaux Bridge (St. Martin Parish)

CHICKEN SAUCE PIQUANTE

- –1 stewing hen, cut up
- –3 onions, chopped
- –4 ribs of celery, chopped
- –2 garlic cloves, minced
- –2 lemon slices
- –Salt and pepper
- –1 cup of oil
- –1 cup of flour
- –½ cup of chopped green onions
- –1 bellpepper, chopped
- –2 cans of tomato paste
- –2 cans of tomato sauce
- –½ cup of chopped parsley
- –1 pound of smoked sausage, sliced
- –Crushed red pepper, to taste
- –1 tablespoon of sugar
- –1 teaspoon of garlic powder
- –1 tablespoon of worcestershire sauce
- –1 can of mushroom pieces

1. Boil hen with one onion, two ribs of celery, garlic, lemon, salt and pepper in water to cover until tender. Remove hen and reserve broth.
2. Make a roux with flour and oil; add remaining onions and celery, green onions and bellpepper. Cook until tender.
3. Add tomato sauce and tomato paste and cook for another 10 minutes.
4. Add hen, broth, parsley, sausage and seasonings and continue cooking for one hour.
5. Add mushrooms and cook another 30 minutes.

Serve over cooked rice.

—Mrs. Donald Olinde
Ventress (Pointe Coupee Parish)

CATFISH OR GASPERGOU SAUCE PIQUANTE

- –4 to 5 pounds of fish
- –2 cups of chopped onions
- –½ cup of oil
- –1 cup of chopped celery
- –2 garlic cloves, minced
- –1 bellpepper, chopped
- –1 can of tomato paste
- –1 can of tomato sauce
- –Juice and rind of 1 lemon
- –1 teaspoon of salt
- –Cayenne pepper, to taste
- –¼ cup of green onions, chopped
- –¼ cup of parsley, chopped

1. Boil fish long enough to debone easily; save fish stock for later use.
2. Saute onions in oil until transparent; add celery, garlic, bellpepper, tomato paste, tomato sauce, lemon rind, salt and cayenne pepper.
3. Cook 45 minutes on low heat.
4. Add one cup of fish stock or more if it is too thick.
5. Add lemon juice, green onions and parsley.
6. Add fish to sauce and simmer for 15 to 20 minutes.
7. Serve over rice.

Serves six to eight.

—Tess Cavell
Ventress (Pointe Coupee Parish)

Main Dishes

CONTENTS

CHICKEN-SAUSAGE JAMBALAYA

–1 six-pound hen, cut for frying
–1 tablespoon of salt
–½ tablespoon of black pepper
–½ tablespoon of red pepper
–1 cup of oil
–1 large onion, minced
–3 garlic cloves, minced
–2 pounds of smoked sausage, cut into 1-inch lengths
–3 quarts of water
–1 bunch of green onions, chopped
–Parsley, chopped
–6 cups of short grain rice

1. Season chicken with salt and pepper.
2. In a large black iron pot, brown chicken in oil.
3. Add onions and garlic; cook until onions are clear.
4. Remove chicken, onions and garlic from pot.
5. Add sausage to oil and brown quickly.
6. Remove sausage and excess oil from pot.
7. Add chicken, onions, garlic, sausage and water to pot; cover pot and cook until chicken is tender, skimming excess fat from water. (Be sure there are at least 12 cups of stock in the pot.)
8. Add onion tops, parsley and rice; bring to rapid boil, stir and taste for seasoning.
9. Lower heat, cover and cook for 30 to 45 minutes or until rice is cooked and stock absorbed.

—Mrs. Sandy Hebert
Lafayette (Lafayette Parish)

JUBILEE JAMBALAYA

–1 pound of ground round
–1 tablespoon of oil
–1 cup of chopped onions
–1 medium bellpepper, chopped
–½ cup of chopped celery
–1 garlic clove, mashed
–1 teaspoon of worcestershire sauce
–Few drops of hot pepper sauce
–1 can of cream of mushroom soup
–1 package of onion soup mix
–1 soup can of water
–2 cups of cooked rice
–1 can of mixed vegetables

1. Lightly brown ground round in oil; remove from skillet.
2. Saute onion, bellpepper, celery and garlic in remaining drippings; return meat to skillet and add worcestershire and hot pepper sauce, stirring lightly.
3. Add cream of mushroom soup, onion soup mix, water and liquid from mixed vegetables; cover and simmer for 30 minutes.
4. Add cooked rice and mixed vegetables, mixing lightly without mashing grains of rice or vegetables; return lid to skillet and keep warm until ready to serve.

Serves six to eight.

—Dezere M. Richard
Sweetlake (Calcasieu Parish)

CHICKEN JAMBALAYA

–1 large fryer, quartered
–½ cup of olive oil
–2 onions, minced
–1 bellpepper, chopped
–2 garlic cloves, mashed
–6 green onions, chopped
–¼ teaspoon of pepper
–2 tablespoons of salt
–1 bay leaf
–1 small can of tomatoes
–Hot pepper sauce
–1 cup of raw rice
–2 cups of water
–½ cup of sherry wine
–1 medium can of mushrooms
–1 medium can of green peas

1. Brown chicken in olive oil over medium heat; remove chicken and saute onions, bellpepper, garlic and green onions in same oil, adding more oil if necessary.
2. Cook until slightly brown, about five minutes; add pepper, salt, bay leaf, tomatoes and a few dashes of hot pepper sauce and cook slowly for six or seven minutes.
3. Aad browned chicken, rice, water and wine and turn to high; bring mixture to boiling point.
4. Add mushrooms and peas; remove from heat.
5. Cover saucepan and place in oven preheated to 400 degrees and cook for about 45 minutes.
Serves four generously.

—Gene Knobloch
Thibodaux (Lafourche Parish)

RED BEANS AND RICE

–1 pound of red beans, sorted and washed
–¾ pound of pickled pork, sliced
–1 medium onion, chopped
–1/3 bellpepper, chopped
–Salt and pepper, to taste
–Cooked rice

1. Soak beans overnight in water to cover.
2. In same soaking water, bring beans to a boil; lower heat and simmer for one and one-half to two hours.
3. Add pickled pork, onion, bellpepper and salt and pepper; simmer another hour and a half or until beans and pork are tender.
4. Serve over cooked rice.

—Myrtle McDonough
New Iberia (Iberia Parish)

PORK RIB JAMBALAYA

–2 pounds of trimmed pork ribs
–4 tablespoons of cooking oil
– 1 medium onion, chopped
–½ bellpepper, chopped
–½ cup of chopped green onion
–½ cup of chopped parsley
–2 cups of short-grain rice, uncooked
–Water

1. Brown ribs in oil until dark brown; remove ribs.
2. Saute onion; add bellpepper and cook a few minutes.
3. Add ribs, green onion, parsley and rice; add water to cover rice.
4. Cook over low heat in tightly covered pot until water is absorbed.
Serves four.

—Nora Courts
Lake Arthur (Jefferson Davis Parish)

STUFFED MIRLITONS A LA FRANCAISE

- –5 medium-size mirlitons (vegetable pears)
- –1/3 cup of grated fresh onion
- –2/3 cup of finely chopped green onion tops
- –3 garlic cloves, minced
- –¼ cup of snipped parsley
- –½ cup of bacon grease
- –½ cup of ground cooked ham
- –½ cup of raw shrimp, chopped fine
- –1 cup of cooked rice
- –½ teaspoon of salt
- –1/8 teaspoon of cayenne pepper
- –1 teaspoon of monosodium glutamate
- –1 egg, beaten
- –Buttered breadcrumbs

1. Cover mirlitons with water; boil until tender (about one hour). Cool; cut in half lengthwise. Scoop out pulp and reserve. Discard seeds and set shells aside for stuffing.
2. Saute onions, green onions, garlic and parsley in bacon grease. Add ham and shrimp; cook, stirring gently for five minutes.
3. Add mirliton pulp, rice and seasonings. Cook 10 minutes. Add more bacon grease if too dry. Remove from heat.
4. Add egg; return to heat; cook one minute.
5. Fill shells, sprinkle with buttered fresh breadcrumbs. Bake at 375 degrees for 15 to 20 minutes or until crumbs are browned.

Serves five.

—Mrs. Youngs Foreman
Indian Bayou (Vermilion Parish)

STUFFED BELLPEPPERS I

- –½ pound of ground meat (or shrimp, pork or veal may be used)
- –2 tablespoons of fat
- –1 onion, chopped
- –2 tablespoons of chopped bellpepper
- –1/3 cup of canned tomato (or 1 fresh tomato), peeled and chopped
- –1 cup of water
- –1 cup of cooked rice (or breadcrumbs)
- –Salt and pepper, to taste
- –6 whole bellpeppers
- –½ cup of buttered breadcrumbs

1. Brown meat in fat; add onion and chopped bellpepper. Cook until onions are tender.
2. Add tomato and water; cook until meat is tender. Add rice or breadcrumbs and seasonings, to taste.
3. Cut off stem ends of whole bellpeppers and remove seeds; boil bellpeppers for five minutes in lightly salted water; drain.
4. Stuff bellpepper with meat mixture; cover with buttered breadcrumbs.
5. Bake at 350 degrees for 20 minutes.

—Mrs. Francis Kerne
Thibodaux (Lafourche Parish)

STUFFED BELLPEPPERS II

—1½ pounds of ground meat
—½ cup of chopped onions
—½ cup of chopped green onions
—½ cup of chopped bellpeppers
—¼ cup of oil
—½ cup of Italian breadcrumbs
—Salt and pepper, to taste
—1 egg
—12 to 15 small bellpeppers
—Breadcrumbs
—Parmesan cheese
—Romano cheese
—Butter

1. Saute ground meat, onions, green onions and bellpeppers in oil until meat is brown.
2. Add Italian breadcrumbs, a small amount of water if needed and seasoning; let cool slightly.
3. Add egg and mix well.
4. Stuff mixture into bellpeppers and sprinkle with additional breadcrumbs, Parmesan cheese and Romano cheese; dot with butter.
5. Bake at 350 degrees 20 to 25 minutes or until tops are brown.

—Lucy Kliebert
Convent (St. James Parish)

CABBAGE-BEEF CASSEROLE I

—2 small cans of tomato juice (or 1 medium can)
—1 pound of ground meat
—1 cup of raw rice
—2 onions, chopped fine
—3 to 4 ribs of celery with leaves
—Red pepper and salt, to taste
—Garlic cloves, minced (to taste)
—1 bay leaf
—Green onion tops, chopped
—1 bellpepper, chopped
—Parsley, chopped
—1 head of cabbage
—¼ pound of butter, melted

1. Mix all ingredients except butter and cabbage.
2. Remove leaves of cabbage and par-boil; drain.
3. Place butter in bottom of baking dish; alternate layers of cabbage and meat mixture, using all ingredients.
4. Bake covered at 350 degrees for one and one-half hours.

—Mrs. W. F. Dunkleman
Thibodaux (Lafourche Parish)

STUFFED BELLPEPPERS III

—1 onion, chopped
—1 garlic clove, minced
—1 tablespoon of chopped celery
—2 tablespoons of bacon drippings
—2 green eggplants (one if it is large), peeled and diced
—1 tomato, peeled and chopped (or one-half cup of canned tomatoes)
—½ pound of ground beef, browned
—4 large bellpeppers
—½ cup of breadcrumbs or one cup of cooked rice

1. Saute onion, garlic and celery in bacon drippings.
2. Add eggplants and tomato; cook until tender over medium heat, stirring frequently.
3. Add browned ground beef and breadcrumbs or rice; mix well.
4. Stuff pepper and sprinkle tops with additional breadcrumbs. Bake at 350 degrees until peppers are tender.

Note: Shrimp or crab meat may be substituted for the beef.

—Mrs. Ludovic T. Patin
New Roads (Pointe Coupee Parish)

CABBAGE-BEEF CASSEROLE II

- 1 medium cabbage
- 1 pound of ground meat
- 1 cup of chopped onion
- 1 cup of chopped bellpepper
- 1 cup of chopped celery
- 1 can of Rotel tomatoes
- 1 cup of breadcrumbs

1. Chop and boil cabbage.
2. Fry ground meat; add onion, bellpepper, celery, cabbage and tomatoes.
3. Cook 45 minutes; add part of breadcrumbs to mixture.
4. Put in casserole and add remaining breadcrumbs on top; brown in oven at 350 degrees.

—Marie Guidry
Garyville (St. John the Baptist Parish)

ROLLED CABBAGE

- 10 cabbage leaves
- ½ cup of chopped shrimp
- ½ cup of breadcrumb stuffing mix
- 1/3 cup of milk
- ½ pound of ground beef
- Dash of salt and red pepper
- ½ cup of flour
- 3 tablespoons of butter

1. Boil cabbage leaves in salted water until tender; remove from water and put aside.
2. Peel, devein and chop shrimp.
3. Soak breadcrumbs in milk.
4. Mix ground meat, shrimp and breadcrumbs; season, to taste.
5. Mix well and make five meat rolls.
6. Roll lightly in flour and brown in melted butter in skillet.
7. Wrap each roll in two cabbage leaves and place in a two-quart dish.
8. Pour one and one-half cups of water in inner pan of electric rice cooker; put steam plate in place.
9. Put two-quart dish on steam plate, cover and turn rice pot on for 30 minutes; switch will go off after that time.

—Mrs. Luciella Gautreaux
Labadieville (Assumption Parish)

GRILLADES

- 1 garlic clove, mashed
- 1 tablespoon of oil
- 2 quarts of green onion tops, chopped
- 1 4- to 5-pound pork roast, cut into pieces ½-inch thick by 3 inches square
- 1 large onion, chopped
- Salt and pepper, to taste

1. Spread garlic on the sides and bottom of a large bowl. Pour oil in the bowl.
2. Place in layers the green onions and then about two inches of meat. Continue layers, using all the green onions and all the meat, ending with the green onions.
3. Cover tightly and keep in the refrigerator at least seven days.
4. Take out amount desired and place in a large pot with a small amount of oil. Add onions and some of the green onion tops. Season, to taste. Let brown, adding water as needed. Cook on low heat until tender.

—Mrs. Jessie Hoffpauir
Indian Bayou (Vermilion Parish)

COLONIAL HAM LOAF

–1 cup of breadcrumbs
–3 eggs
–½ cup of milk
–½ cup of brown sugar
–3 tablespoons of lemon juice
–2 teaspoons of dry mustard
–1 teaspoon of salt
–¼ teaspoon of pepper
–1 pound of lean ground pork
–1 pound of ground smoked ham

1. Combine breadcrumbs, eggs and milk; stir-in brown sugar, lemon juice, dry mustard, salt and pepper.
2. Add ground pork and ham; mix thoroughly.
3. Press mixture into loaf pan and bake at 350 degrees for one hour and 15 minutes.

—Mary Campbell
Ascension Parish

PORK FRICASSEE

–Water
–5 tablespoons of roux
–3 large onions, chopped
–3 pounds of pork steak
–Salt and pepper
–1 bunch of green onions, chopped

1. Add enough water to roux to make a thick gravy in skillet; add onion and pork and season, to taste.
2. Simmer until tender; add green onions and serve over rice.

—Manning "Pete" Broussard
Lafayette (Lafayette Parish)

TOURTIERE
(Pork Pie)

–2 pounds of ground lean pork
–½ cup of chopped onion
–1 cup of chopped celery
–1 garlic clove, crushed
–¼ cup of chopped parsley
–1 teaspoon of salt
–¼ teaspoon of leaf marjoram, crushed
–1/8 teaspoon of ground cloves
–1/8 teaspoon of ground mace
–½ teaspoon of ground pepper
–2 tablespoons of flour
–2 beef bouillon cubes
–1 cup of hot water
–Pastry for a 2-crust pie, unbaked (can use frozen pie shells)

1. Saute pork, onion, celery and garlic in a large skillet until pork is brown and vegetables are tender.
2. Stir-in parsley, salt, marjoram, cloves, mace and pepper; cover and simmer over low heat for 30 minutes.
3. Drain excess fat from skillet; blend flour into meat mixture. Add bouillon cubes dissolved in hot water.
4. Return to heat and bring mixture to a boil; simmer for one minute, stirring constantly. Remove from heat and set aside to cool.
5. Pile meat mixture in pie shell; top with other shell, seal and flute edges. (Brush with egg if desired.)
6. Bake at 400 degrees for 45 minutes or until golden brown.
Makes one nine-inch pie.
Serves six.

Can be eaten cold or warm.

—Mrs. Hazel Gourgues
Hahnville (St. Charles Parish)

FRESH PORK AND FRESH SAUSAGE TOMBOUILLE

- –1 cup of cooking oil
- –1 cup of flour
- –3 cups of onions, chopped
- –1 cup of green onion bottoms, chopped
- –½ cup of celery, chopped
- –1 cup of bellpeppers, chopped
- –1 tablespoon of garlic juice
- –1 cup of Rotel tomatoes
- –1 can of cream of mushroom soup
- –1 can of cream of celery soup
- –1 can of golden mushroom soup
- –1 small can of mushroom steak sauce
- –4 cans of tomato sauce
- –1 can of tomato paste
- –3 pounds of fresh pork
- –3 pounds of fresh sausage
- –1 medium can of mushroom stems and pieces
- –1 cup of green onion tops
- –½ cup of parsley

1. Using a two-gallon aluminum or stainless steel pot, make a light brown roux with oil and flour.
2. Add onions, green onion bottoms, celery, bellpeppers and garlic juice; smother for 15 minutes.
3. Mix Rotel tomatoes, cream of mushroom soup, cream of celery soup, golden mushroom soup, mushroom steak sauce, tomato sauce and tomato paste; pour into pan with smothered ingredients.
4. Fry pork and sausage until brown; combine with other ingredients that are cooking.
5. Cook for four hours on low heat.
6. Fifteen minutes before cooking is finished add mushroom stems and pieces, green onion tops and parsley.

Makes 18 to 20 servings.

Note: To get right texture, add water.

—Curtis "Chinee" Matherne
Grand Point (St. James Parish)

BARBECUED PORK WITH RICE

- –3 pounds of boneless pork cut in two-inch cubes
- –2 tablespoons of fat
- –Salt
- –Pepper
- –1 8-ounce can of seasoned tomato sauce
- –½ cup of water
- –½ cup of catsup
- –½ cup of chopped celery
- –1 medium onion, sliced
- –2 tablespoons of brown sugar
- –2 tablespoons of prepared mustard
- –1 tablespoon of worcestershire sauce
- –Hot cooked rice

1. Brown pork slowly on all sides in hot fat; season with salt and pepper.
2. Combine remaining ingredients except rice, pour over meat, cover and simmer (do not boil) until tender or about two hours.
3. Remove cover last 20 minutes and spoon off excess fat.
4. Mound hot rice in center of platter; circle with meat; ladle the sauce over meat and rice.

The meat and sauce can be baked in moderate oven (350 degrees) for two hours in a covered dish or pan.

—Anna Jones
Ascension Parish

STUFFED PORK ROAST

–1 large onion, chopped
–3 garlic cloves, minced
–½ cup of creamy onion dressing
–2 6-ounce packages of Italian salad mix
–1 small can of jalapeno peppers, chopped fine
–1 8-pound pork roast
–Salt and pepper, to taste

1. Combine onion, garlic, onion dressing, salad mix and jalapeno peppers (including the juice from the can).
2. Make deep incisions in pork roast. Stuff with above mixture, forcing all of the stuffing into the incisions.
3. Add salt and pepper to liquids remaining from stuffing. Rub over pork roast.
4. Cover and let stand overnight, turning occasionally.
5. To cook, place roast in roasting pan with a rack. Pour all drippings over roast. Cover and bake at 375 degrees for three to four hours or until meat thermometer registers 185 degrees.
6. Baste occasionally with pan drippings. Add water when necessary, to make a brown gravy. If needed, uncover and cook an additional 15 to 20 minutes to brown meat to desired color.

—Mrs. Amson Corner
Abbeville (Vermilion Parish)

OVEN BARBEQUE

–1 cup of ketchup
–½ cup of water
–¼ cup of wine vinegar
–¼ cup of chopped onion
–1½ tablespoon of worcestershire sauce
–1 teaspoon of dry mustard
–2 tablespoons of brown sugar
–Chicken, beef, game or other meat
–½ cup of sliced bellpepper

1. Cook all ingredients except bellpepper about five minutes.
2. Foil-line pan and place the meat you want in pan; cover with sauce and bellpepper.
3. Cover with foil; bake for one and one-half hours at 350 degrees.

—Mrs. Larry McNease
Grand Chenier (Cameron Parish)

LIVER AND ONIONS

–2 pounds of calf liver
–2 teaspoons of baking soda
–2 cups of boiling water
–1 teaspoon of salt
–½ teaspoon of pepper
–½ cup of flour
–½ cup of oil
–2 onions, chopped
–1 teaspoon of hot pepper sauce

1. Place liver in large flat pan; sprinkle with soda. Pour rapidly boiling water over liver; stir until well-mixed.
2. Pour off hot water; rinse liver well with cold water.
3. Sprinkle salt and pepper on liver; roll in flour.
4. Brown liver quickly in hot oil; remove liver from pan and pour oil out.
5. Replace liver in skillet, alternating with layers of onion. Sprinkle with pepper sauce; add enough water to make a gravy, one to two cups.
6. Cover and cook on low heat 15 to 20 minutes, stirring once or twice to prevent sticking.

—June Crain Harper
Grand Chenier (Cameron Parish)

ROUND STEAK ROLL I

–1 large round steak
–Salt and pepper, to taste
–¼ cup of chopped onion
–2 tablespoons of chopped bell-pepper
–2 tablespoons of chopped celery
–1 garlic clove, minced
–2 tablespoons of oleo
–¼ pound of ground beef
–¼ pound of ground pork
–½ cup of cooked rice

1. Pound steak to tenderize, and sprinkle with salt and pepper.
2. Set in refrigerator.
3. Saute vegetables in oleo to wilt; add beef and pork just to mix and lose some red color.
4. Mix rice into meat and vegetable mixture; spread over round steak and sprinkle again with salt and pepper.
5. Roll steak and secure ends with toothpicks.
6. Place in baking dish lined with foil; bake uncovered at 350 degrees for one and one-half to two hours.

—Mrs. John Hicks
Washington (St. Landry Parish)

CHOPPED STEAK WITH WILD PECAN RICE

–2 pounds of chopped steak
–3 tablespoons of whole black peppercorns, crushed
–Salt
–¼ cup of olive oil
–¼ cup of brandy
–½ pint of cream
–2 cups of wild pecan rice, cooked
–Chopped parsley

1. Form chopped steak into four patties; season the meat with peppercorns and salt.
2. Pan broil on both sides in a very hot skillet in olive oil; remove to a heated serving dish and keep warm.
3. Discard all but two tablespoons of oil and drippings, add brandy and flame for one minute; add cream, stir and heat.
4. When sauce thickens, pour over steak and pecan rice and garnish with chopped parsley.

—L.S. "Lee" Smith
New Iberia (Iberia Parish)

VEAL SCALLOPINE WITH SWEET PEPPERS

–1½ to 2 pounds of thin slices of veal taken from sirloin tip cut in 1/8-inch thick slices
–1 to 2 tablespoons of olive oil
–Salt and pepper, to taste
–¼ to 1/3 cup of dry white wine
–2 to 3 sweet bellpeppers, sliced in wedges
–¼ cup of grated Parmesan cheese
–Parsley
–Lemon

1. Saute the veal slices in olive oil at medium heat until tender and slightly brown; add salt, pepper and wine.
2. Stir and add bellpeppers; lower heat and stir constantly.
3. Cook until peppers are tender and still slightly crisp; spoon out onto platter and sprinkle with Parmesan cheese. Garnish with parsley and lemon wedges.
Serves four to six.

—Robert W. Benoit
New Iberia (Iberia Parish)

DAUBE

- 1 cup of oil
- Salt and pepper, to taste
- 1 round steak (1½ to 2 inches thick)
- 3 tablespoons of flour
- 3 medium onions, sliced
- 1½ cups of water

1. Heat oil in skillet and brown seasoned steak on both sides.
2. Sprinkle flour on one side of steak, turn and brown slightly.
3. Remove steak from skillet and saute onions.
4. Return steak to skillet, add water and cook on medium heat uncovered for 20 minutes, stirring.
5. Cook covered until tender; uncover and cook until gravy is thick and smooth.

Serves 8 to 10.

—Merlyn Vernon
Lutcher (St. James Parish)

ROLLED STEAKS

- 6 to 8 strip steaks (See note.)
- Yellow mustard
- Salt, pepper and garlic powder, to taste
- 6 to 8 strips of bacon
- 2 dill pickles, quartered
- 1 medium onion, sliced into strips
- 1 tablespoon of oil
- 2½ cups of water
- 2 tablespoons of flour
- 2 bouillon cubes

1. Lay steaks lengthwise, widest end toward you; coat each steak with mustard, salt, pepper and garlic powder.
2. Lay bacon strips lengthwise on each steak and place a pickle and onion strip on each steak.
3. Fold the end away from you and roll meat; secure ends with toothpick.
4. Brown meat in frying pan with oil.
5. Chop remaining onion strips and add to pan; continue cooking until onions are brown; add water and allow to simmer for one and one-half hours.
6. When meat is tender, remove meat and thicken drippings by adding flour and bouillon cubes; simmer for five minutes.

Note: Have butcher slice steaks from a rump roast or sirloin tip about ¼-inch thick, 6 or 8 inches long and 2½ or 3 inches wide.
Serves six.

—Mrs. Sybille Galliano
Houma (Terrebonne Parish)

OVEN POT ROAST

- 2- to 4-pound chuck roast
- 1 teaspoon of salt
- Dash of pepper sauce
- 1 garlic clove, finely chopped
- 1 onion, sliced
- 1 cup of sliced celery
- 3 or 4 medium potatoes, peeled and cut in chunks
- 3 or 4 medium carrots, cut in cubes

1. Season roast with salt and hot pepper sauce.
2. Put in covered pan and bake at 300 to 350 degrees for one hour.
3. Place garlic, onion and celery on top of meat; place potatoes and carrots around the meat.
4. Cover and bake about one hour or until done at 300 to 350 degrees.

—Mrs. Adela Jardell
Jennings (Jefferson Davis Parish)

ROUND STEAK ROLL II

- 1 round steak, ½-inch thick
- Salt and pepper, to taste
- 1 envelope of onion soup mix
- 1 bellpepper, chopped
- 1 onion, chopped
- Parsley, chopped
- 2 ribs of celery, chopped
- 1 tablespoon of shortening
- 2 cups of water
- 1 can of cream of mushroom soup
- 4 carrots, peeled and quartered
- 4 potatoes, peeled and quartered

1. Season steak with salt and pepper.
2. Mix onion soup, bellpepper, onion, parsley and celery; sprinkle on steak.
3. Roll steak as you would a jelly roll; use toothpicks to hold together.
4. Brown on all sides in shortening; add water and bring to a boil.
5. Add cream of mushroom soup and mix well; add carrots and potatoes around steak and cook in gravy until steak is tender and carrots and potatoes are done, about 45 minutes.

—Leola Broussard
Ascension Parish

BEEF A LA DEUTSCH

- 1½ pounds of beef top sirloin, cut in 1-inch strips
- 1 cup of mushrooms, sliced
- ½ cup of bellpepper, sliced
- ½ cup of onion, sliced
- 2 tablespoons of butter
- 1 quart of beef stock (can also use bouillon or consomme)
- ¼ cup of flour
- 1½ cups of sour cream
- Salt and pepper, to taste
- ¼ cup of chopped pimento

1. Saute beef, mushroom, bellpepper and onion in butter until meat is brown and onions are soft; add stock then simmer until meat is tender.
2. Mix flour with a little sour cream and stock; add this to the meat.
3. Cook until thick, season and remove from heat; add remaining sour cream and pimento and then bring to a boil.
4. Remove from heat 15 minutes before serving; keep covered.

Yields four large servings.

Very good over rice.

—Sharon Truxillo
St. Landry Parish

CHICKEN STEW

- 2 tablespoons of butter
- ½ cup of flour
- 1 onion, chopped
- 1 bellpepper, chopped
- 1 rib of celery, chopped
- ½ cup of chopped parsley
- 2 cups of water
- 1 chicken, cut up
- Salt and pepper, to taste
- 1 teaspoon of garlic salt

1. Make a roux with butter and flour in pot; add onion, bellpepper, celery and parsley; cook until wilted.
2. Add water, chicken and seasonings; cook about 25 minutes or until chicken is done.

Serve over rice.

—Mrs. Mary Colar
Franklin (St. Mary Parish)

COQ AU VIN WITH ALMOND RICE
(Chicken Cooked In Wine With Almond Rice)

–2 2½- to 3-pound fryers, cut into serving pieces
–¼ pound of oleo
–3 garlic cloves, mashed
–2 bay leaves
–2 ribs of celery, diced
–Salt and pepper, to taste
–1 bottle of dry red table wine
–4 to 5 slices of salt pork, finely diced
–8 to 10 very small white onions, peeled and left whole
–1 large can of mushrooms, drained
–1 tablespoon of brandy
–Almond Rice (Recipe follows)

1. Season and flour fryers; brown evenly in melted oleo. Remove chicken and drippings and place in a two- or three-quart casserole.
2. Add garlic, bay leaves, celery and seasoning; pour wine over all, cover tightly and place in preheated 350-degree oven for 30 minutes.
3. Brown salt pork in a separate skillet; reserve both salt pork and drippings.
4. After chicken has baked 30 minutes, add cooked salt pork, rendered fat from salt pork, onions, mushrooms and brandy; cover casserole tightly and return to oven for another 30 minutes or until chicken is fork-tender. Serve over Almond Rice.

ALMOND RICE
–½ cup of sliced almonds
–¼ cup of oleo
–¼ cup of chopped parsley
–Cooked rice

Brown almonds in oleo; add with parsley to cooked rice.

—Matt and Sarah Vernon
Eunice (St. Landry Parish)

STUFFED BREAST OF CHICKEN

–1 pound of ground meat
–1 beef bouillon cube
–¼ cup of chopped onions
–¼ cup of chopped green onions
–¼ cup of chopped celery
–¼ cup of chopped parsley
–2 garlic cloves, minced
–1/8 teaspoon of oregano
–½ teaspoon of red pepper
–Salt, to taste
–½ cup of breadcrumbs
–4 whole chicken breasts, halved and de-boned
–¼ pound of oleo, melted

1. Brown ground meat in a heavy pot; add beef bouillon cube, onions green onions, celery, parsley and garlic. Cook on low heat for 10 minutes.
2. Add oregano, red pepper, salt and breadcrumbs. A little water may be needed to make dressing moist.
3. On one piece of deboned chicken, place one-fourth cup of dressing and then another piece of deboned chicken; fasten securely with toothpicks.
4. Put melted oleo in an uncovered baking pan and place stuffed chicken on top of the oleo.
5. Bake at 350 degrees about one hour, basting often.
Serves four.

—Alzina Toups
Galliano (Lafourche Parish)

CHICKEN PAPRIKA

- ¼ cup of butter
- 8 small onions, chopped
- 2 tablespoons of Hungarian paprika
- 2- to 3-pound chicken, cut up
- Salt and pepper
- 1 cup of chicken broth
- 3 tablespoons of flour
- ½ cup of light cream
- ½ cup of sour cream

1. Heat butter; add onions and saute until golden, but not brown; add paprika.
2. Season chicken with salt and pepper; add to onions and cook over medium heat 15 minutes, turning once.
3. Add chicken broth; cover and cook 20 minutes or until tender.
4. Mix flour with light cream; add a little hot broth and add to pot; stir until it thickens.
5. Stir-in sour cream and reheat, but do not boil.

—L. S. "Lee" Smith
New Iberia (Iberia Parish)

CHICKEN CASSEROLE

- 1 fryer, cup up into pieces
- Salt and pepper
- Flour
- ¼ pound of oleo
- 2 tablespoons of flour
- 1 cup of chopped onions
- 1 large can of mushrooms
- Water

1. Season fryer with salt and pepper and dredge in flour.
2. Melt oleo in iron frying pan and brown chicken; arrange chicken in large casserole.
3. To the drippings add the two tablespoons of flour and brown; add onion, mushrooms and water to make enough gravy to cover the chicken.
4. Pour gravy over chicken, cover casserole and bake at 350 degrees for one hour and 15 minutes.

Serve with cooked rice.
Serves four.

—Billie McHugh
Loreauville (Iberia Parish)

POULET AUX CHAMPIGNONS
(Chicken With Mushrooms)

- 1 large fryer, cut in serving pieces
- Salt, black pepper and red pepper, to taste
- ½ cup of oil
- 2 cups of chopped onions
- 1 cup of chopped celery
- ½ cup of chopped bellpepper
- 2 garlic cloves, minced
- Thyme, to taste
- 1 teaspoon of worcestershire sauce
- 1 bay leaf
- Green onion tops, chopped
- Parsley, chopped
- 1 large can of mushrooms

1. Season chicken with salt and pepper; fry in oil in a heavy pot until chicken is brown on all sides.
2. Add onions, celery, bellpepper, garlic, thyme, worcestershire sauce and bay leaf; cover and cook over low heat for about an hour.
3. About five minutes before serving, add green onion tops, parsley and mushrooms.
4. Serve over rice.

—Aggie Holl
Lake Charles (Calcasieu Parish)

STUFFED CORNISH HENS

–4 cornish hens
–Salt and pepper
–½ cup of dry white wine
–½ cup of grape juice concentrate, thawed
–2 tablespoons of lemon juice
–1 tablespoon of grated lemon peel
–2 tablespoons of butter, melted
–1 package of long-grain wild rice mixture
–1 quart of chicken stock
–½ cup of diced celery
–¾ cup of diced onion
–¼ cup of diced bellpepper
–½ cup of chopped green onion
–2/3 cup of sliced water chestnuts, drained
–1 3-ounce can of chopped mushrooms, drained
–2 tablespoons of soy sauce
–Salt and pepper

1. Wash and dry hens; salt and pepper inside and out.
2. Combine wine, grape juice, lemon juice, lemon peel and butter for marinade; place hens in a bowl and pour marinade over them; cover.
3. Place in refrigerator, preferably overnight, turning hens at least three times.
4. Cook wild rice according to directions on the package, using chicken stock for liquid in place of water; when rice is done combine the remaining ingredients with the cooked rice. If the mixture is too dry add some of the stock.
5. Remove hens from the marinade and pat dry; loosely stuff hens with the rice mixture and place in a baking pan.
6. Cover with foil and bake at 375 degrees for one and one-half hours.
7. Baste every 30 minutes with marinade; remove foil after one hour.

—Fred Hoyer
New Iberia (Iberia Parish)

CHICKEN-ARTICHOKE CASSEROLE

–½ cup of oleo
–¼ cup of flour
–2 cups of milk
–Minced garlic
–Minced onion
–1 cup of grated cheddar cheese
–Red pepper
–Salt
–De-boned meat from one boiled chicken
–2 large cans of button mushrooms
–2 large cans of artichoke hearts
–Broth from boiled chicken
–Seasoned breadcrumbs

1. Make a cream sauce with oleo, flour, milk, garlic, onion and cheese. Season, to taste.
2. Add remaining ingredients (except breadcrumbs). Put combined mixture in casserole dish. Add broth to thin to preferred consistency.
3. Sprinkle with breadcrumbs and bake uncovered at 350 degrees for 30 minutes.

Note: Lobster or shrimp may be substituted for chicken.

—Mrs. Jake Miller
Lafayette (Lafayette Parish)

BARBECUED TURKEY

- –1 medium onion, chopped
- –4 garlic cloves, chopped
- –½ bellpepper, chopped
- –Salt and pepper
- –1 10- to 15-pound turkey, cut in half
- –Barbecue Sauce (Recipe follows)

1. Mix together onion, garlic, bellpepper, salt and pepper.
2. Cut slits in legs, thighs and breasts of turkey as deep as you can and stuff above seasonings into slits; rub more salt and pepper on turkey.
3. Wrap turkey in two layers of extra heavy-duty foil and refrigerate one or two days before barbecuing.
4. Cook turkey (still in foil) over hot coals for two hours, turning every 15 minutes on pit; remove turkey from foil and reserve the broth.
5. Continue cooking for another one and one-half hours, basting and turning every 15 minutes. Baste with the reserved broth and the oil from the top of the Barbecue Sauce. After the oil has been used, put the thick sauce on top of the turkey.

BARBECUE SAUCE

- –1½ pounds of oleo
- –2 medium onions, finely chopped
- –4 garlic cloves, finely minced
- –1 bellpepper, finely chopped
- –1 pint of barbecue sauce
- –¼ cup of worcestershire sauce
- –1 teaspoon of liquid smoke
- –2 tablespoons of brown sugar
- –2 cans of frozen limeade concentrate

1. Melt one-half pound of oleo in pan and cook onions, garlic and bellpepper until limp; add barbecue sauce and cook about 20 minutes.
2. Add worcestershire sauce, liquid smoke, sugar and limeade and cook about 10 more minutes; add remaining oleo and stir until melted, about 15 minutes.

—Jay Norris
New Iberia (Iberia Parish)

CHICKEN SPAGHETTI

- –¼ cup of barbeque-basting sauce
- –1 fryer, cut up
- –Salt and pepper, to taste
- –2 large onions, chopped
- –2 bellpeppers, chopped
- –2 cans of Rotel tomatoes
- –1 can of tomato sauce
- –1 jar of Ragu Wine spaghetti sauce

1. Heat barbeque-basting sauce in pot; add seasoned chicken and cook until lightly browned.
2. Remove chicken and saute onions and bellpeppers in the sauce; add tomatoes and tomato sauce.
3. Cook about three hours or until thick; return chicken to pot and add spaghetti sauce.
4. Cook until chicken is tender; serve over cooked spaghetti.

—Roland Romero
New Iberia (Iberia Parish)

TURKEY A LA KING

- –6 tablespoons of butter or oleo
- –1 large onion, chopped fine
- –3 ribs of celery, chopped fine
- –6 tablespoons of flour
- –3 cups of milk
- –1 chicken bouillon cube
- –1 small can of pimento, chopped fine
- –3 cups of chopped cooked turkey

1. Melt butter; add onion and celery and cook until transparent.
2. Add flour and mix well; add milk slowly and stir.
3. Add bouillon cube, pimento and turkey and simmer a few minutes until well-mixed and bubbly.

Serve over toast or in pattie shells. Serves six.

—Rea R. Gilbert
Lafourche Parish

STUFFED PEPPER MEAT LOAF

- –1 small bellpepper
- –2 eggs, slightly beaten
- –½ cup of milk
- –½ cup of fine dry breadcrumbs
- –½ cup (2 ounces) of shredded sharp American cheese
- –3 tablespoons of catsup
- –1 teaspoon of salt
- –1 teaspoon of worcestershire sauce
- –1/8 teaspoon of pepper
- –2 pounds of ground meat

1. Cut top from bellpepper, remove seeds and halve lengthwise. Cook, covered, in boiling water five minutes; set aside after draining.
2. Combine eggs, milk, breadcrumbs, cheese, catsup, salt, worcestershire and pepper; add ground beef and mix thoroughly. Stuff pepper halves with some of the meat mixture.
3. Pat half of the remaining meat in bottom of foil-lined 8x4x2-inch loaf pan. Place pepper halves, cut sides down, on meat. Carefully press remaining meat mixture over and around peppers to make a smooth loaf.
4. Bake, covered, at 350 degrees one and three-fourths hours; uncover, bake 15 minutes more. Spoon off excess fat as it accumulates.

Makes eight servings.

—Mrs. Elrita Howe
Luling (St. Charles Parish)

CARBENEAT

- –1 pound of carrots, cleaned and diced
- –1 quart of cut green beans
- –2 medium onions, chopped
- –1 pound of ground meat
- –1 teaspoon of salt
- –¼ teaspoon of sugar
- –½ cup of water

1. Put all ingredients in a four-quart pot; cook over medium heat until the carrots and beans are tender, 20 to 25 minutes.
2. Smother until water has evaporated.

Serves six to eight.

Note: With this recipe, you don't need any cooking oil; the fat from the ground meat provides all you need.

—LaVerne Bergeron
Montegut (Terrebonne Parish)

MEAT LOAF I

- –1 pound of ground meat
- –1 egg, well-beaten
- –1 teaspoon of salt
- –Dash of garlic salt
- –¼ teaspoon of black pepper
- –2 tablespoons of finely chopped onions
- –2/3 cup of milk
- –1 cup of toasted breadcrumbs

1. Combine ingredients in a large bowl; mix well.
2. Pack in a greased loaf pan.
3. Bake at 350 to 375 degrees for one hour.

—Mrs. Pearl Bueche
Ventress (Pointe Coupee Parish)

MEAT LOAF II

- – 1 pound of ground bottom round
- –½ pound of sausage meat
- –½ cup of milk
- –1 cup of cooked rice
- –1 small onion, minced
- –¼ cup of chopped bellpepper
- –1 egg, slightly beaten
- –1 teaspoon of salt
- –¼ teaspoon of pepper
- –Garlic powder, to taste
- –½ teaspoon of poultry seasoning
- –1 teaspoon of A-1 sauce
- –1/3 cup of warm water
- –1 tablespoon of Kitchen Bouquet
- –2 tablespoons of melted butter

1. Mix beef with sausage, milk, rice, onion, bellpepper, egg, salt, pepper, garlic powder, poultry seasoning and A-1 sauce; form into a loaf and place in a nine-inch loaf pan.
2. Bake at 325 degrees for one and one-half hours.
3. Combine water with Kitchen Bouquet and butter and use this to baste loaf occasionally.

Serves six.

—Hazard Guillot
Jennings (Jefferson Davis Parish)

PLANTATION CASSEROLE

- –2 cups of cooked chicken, ham or beef, chopped
- –1 cup of cooked peas, drained
- –1 17-ounce can of cream style corn
- –1/4 pound of American cheese, cubed
- –1 cup of chopped onion
- –1 cup of evaporated milk
- –1 tablespoon of worcestershire sauce
- –2 tablespoons of sugar
- –½ teaspoon of salt
- –1 cup of biscuit mix
- –½ cup of cornmeal
- –1 egg, beaten

1. Combine meat, peas, corn, cheese and onion, one-half cup of evaporated milk and worcestershire sauce.
2. Pour into a greased eight-inch baking dish and bake uncovered at 400 degrees for 10 minutes.
3. Combine remaining ingredients; stir-in one-half cup of evaporated milk.
4. Pour batter around edges of meat mixture, leaving center uncovered.
5. Bake uncovered for 20 minutes longer.

Serves six.

—Mrs. William Montet
Henry (Vermilion Parish)

EGGPLANT AND GROUND MEAT

- 1 pound of ground beef
- 1 teaspoon of salt
- Pepper, to taste
- 2 tablespoons of salad oil
- 1 medium eggplant
- 1/3 cup of flour
- ¼ cup of olive oil
- 2 cans of tomato sauce
- ½ to 1 teaspoon of oregano
- 1 tablespoon of Parmesan cheese
- 1 cup of grated cheddar cheese

1. Shape ground beef into thick patties.
2. Season with salt and pepper; brown in hot salad oil.
3. Slice eggplant into thick slices. (Do not remove skin.) Season with salt and pepper.
4. Coat eggplant with flour and brown in olive oil.
5. Place cooked eggplant slices in shallow baking dish; top each with browned meat patties.
6. Cover with tomato sauce.
7. Sprinkle oregano and Parmesan cheese over it all; top with grated cheddar cheese.
8. Bake uncovered at 300 degrees for 35 minutes.

Serves six.

—Mrs. Henry Jarreau
Lakeland (Pointe Coupee Parish)

POTATO-SAUSAGE CASSEROLE

- 1½ to 2 pounds of smoked pork sausage, sliced
- 2 to 3 pounds of white potatoes, peeled and sliced
- Salt and pepper
- 1 medium onion, sliced
- 1 bunch of green onions, chopped

1. In a large heavy casserole or oven-proof pot, place one-third of the sausage; layer one-half of the potatoes on top of the sausage and sprinkle with salt and pepper.
2. Layer one-half of the sliced onion and one-half of the chopped green onions on top of the sausage and potatoes.
3. Add one-third of the sausage, the remainder of the potatoes, salt and pepper, the remainder of the sliced onions, and the remainder of the chopped green onions.
4. Top the entire casserole with the remaining one-third of the sausage.
5. Cover tightly and bake at 350 degrees for one hour or until potatoes are done. Do not stir casserole during baking.

—Corinne Daigle
Brusly (West Baton Rouge Parish)

SPAGHETTI SAUCE
(Makes 13 quarts)

–1 pork chop
–3 pounds of onions, chopped
–5 bellpeppers, chopped
–15 to 20 garlic cloves, minced
–3 to 5 celery stalks, chopped
–1¼ to 1½ cups of olive oil
–90 ounces of tomato paste
–90 ounces of tomato sauce
–½ teaspoon of baking soda
–Salt and red pepper, to taste
–Basil leaves, to taste
–1 cup of chopped parsley
–1 cup of chopped green onions

1. Cook pork chop, onions, bellpeppers, garlic and celery in olive oil on low heat until wilted, two to three hours, in a covered pot, stirring occasionally.
2. Add tomato paste and tomato sauce and continue cooking for five to six hours, stirring occasionally.
3. Add water (according to desired thickness), baking soda, salt, red pepper and basil leaves and continue cooking three to four hours.
4. About one-half hour before sauce is finished, add parsley and green onions; cool and freeze sauce.
5. To serve, add one cup of water to each pint of sauce and allow to simmer with desired meat for one to two hours.

Makes about 13 quarts.

—George C. Veazey
Abbeville (Vermilion Parish)

HOT SAUSAGE PIE

–1 pound of hot pork sausage
–2 cups of canned tomatoes
–2 cups of whole-kernel corn, drained
–2 tablespoons of minced onion
–2 tablespoons of bacon drippings
–3 tablespoons of all-purpose flour
–1 teaspoon of sugar
–1 teaspoon of salt
–Breadcrumbs

1. Cook sausage slowly in heavy skillet until brown, crumbly and well-done.
2. Add tomatoes and corn; simmer for 10 minutes.
3. Saute onion in bacon drippings; mix flour, sugar and salt together, and blend with bacon drippings and onions. Add to sausage and vegetables; heat to boiling point.
4. Spoon in to two-quart baking dish and top with breadcrumbs.
5. Bake uncovered at 425 degrees for 20 minutes or until topping is browned. Serve hot.

Serves six to eight.

—Mrs. Ethel Tramonte
New Sarpy (St. Charles Parish)

STUFFED BREAD WITH STROGANOFF SAUCE

–2 13¾-ounce packages of hot roll mix
–1 cup of warm water
–5 eggs
–Filling (Recipe follows)
–Sauce (Recipe follows)

1. Remove package of yeast in roll mix and pour into a large bowl; stir-in water until yeast dissolves.
2. Stir-in four eggs and flour mix.
3. Turn out dough on floured surface and knead for five minutes; replace in bowl and let rise, covered in a warm place, until double in bulk.
4. Prepare Filling.
5. Knead dough again on floured surface.
6. Cut off a piece the size of a big apple; roll out into a 14-inch square and place on a greased cookie sheet.
7. Pile Filling down center of dough and pat with spoon until shape resembles a meat loaf; fold one side of dough lengthwise over Filling.
8. Brush dough with one beaten egg; fold other side of dough over, stretching it to cover top and sides.
9. Tuck dough flap and ends under loaf to seal; brush with more egg.
10. Roll out remaining dough to one-quarter-inch thickness; cut dough with sharp knife into one-half-inch strips.
11. Crisscross strips over loaf, tucking ends under loaf, and brush with more egg; let rise for 30 minutes.
12. Place loaf in preheated 350-degree oven for 35 minutes or until browned.
13. Prepare Sauce while loaf is baking.
14. Remove loaf from oven and cut into thick slices; spoon Sauce over loaf and serve piping hot.

FILLING

–3 cups of cooked bulk sausage
–1 10½-ounce can of cream of chicken soup
–4 cups of cooked rice
–½ cup of parsley, chopped
–¼ cup of green onions, chopped
–4 boiled eggs, chopped

In a large bowl, combine all Filling ingredients. Season with salt and pepper.

SAUCE

–½ cup of butter
–½ pound of fresh mushrooms, sliced
–¾ cup of flour
–3 cups of milk
–2 cups of sour cream
–Salt and pepper

1. Melt butter and saute mushrooms for five minutes; stir-in flour.
2. Gradually stir-in milk; stir over low heat until sauce bubbles and becomes very thick.
3. Stir-in sour cream; season with salt and pepper.

Serves 10.

—Leonard Bernard Jr.
Houma (Terrebonne Parish)

Seafood

CONTENTS

BAKED STUFFED FLOUNDER

–½ cup of chopped celery
–½ cup of chopped green onions, tops included
–1 garlic clove, minced
–8 tablespoons of butter
–1½ cups of moistened bread cubes
–½ pound of boiled shrimp, chopped
–½ pound of crab meat
–2 tablespoons of parsley, chopped
–1 egg, slightly beaten
–Salt, black pepper and red pepper, to taste
–4 flounders, medium-sized, or 2 fairly large ones

1. Saute celery, onion and garlic in four tablespoons of butter over low heat; add bread, shrimp, crab meat, parsley and egg, mixing well.
2. Season with salt and pepper.
3. Split thick side of flounder lengthwise and crosswise and loosen meat from bone of fish to form a pocket for stuffing; brush well with melted butter.
4. Salt and pepper and stuff pocket.
5. To bake, melt remaining four tablespoons of butter in a shallow baking pan; place fish in pan. Do not overlap.
6. Cover and bake at 375 degrees for 25 minutes or until fish flakes very easily with a fork. Remove cover; bake another five minutes. Serves four.

—Mrs. Ralph Marshall
Egan (Acadia Parish)

SNAPPER FILLET HOLLANDAISE

–6 red snapper fillets, with skin
–2 white onions, sliced thin
–4 lemons, sliced thin
–6 dashes of hot pepper sauce
–¼ pound of butter
–Salt, red pepper and white pepper
–1 pound of lump crab meat
–Hollandaise Sauce (Recipe follows)

1. Place first five ingredients in a large shallow baking dish; sprinkle with salt, red pepper and white pepper, to taste.
2. Place in 450-degree oven for 45 minutes or until well-browned.
3. Place fillets on separate plates with portions of lemon and onions; cover with lump crab meat.
4. Pour Hollandaise Sauce over all.

HOLLANDAISE SAUCE
–2 tablespoons of butter, melted
–4 teaspoons of flour
–1 cup of boiling water
–1 teaspoon of salt
–Juice of 1 lemon
–2 egg yolks, beaten

1. Stir all ingredients except yolks together in a sauce pan and cook over low heat until thickened.
2. Remove from heat and stir-in yolks while hot.

—Luther P. Tompkins
Lafayette (Lafayette Parish)

STUFFED RED SNAPPER CASSEROLE

–¾ pound of butter
–4 onions, chopped
–2 bellpeppers, chopped
–3 ribs of celery, chopped
–1 garlic clove, chopped
–1 pound of crab meat
–1 pound of shrimp, peeled and chopped
–1 cup of green onion tops, chopped
–1 cup of parsley, chopped
–1 cup of lemon juice
–1 cup of sherry wine
–2 cups of breadcrumbs
–3 tablespoons of worcestershire sauce
–1 tablespoon of hot pepper sauce
–Salt and pepper, to taste
–4 pounds of red snapper fillet
–1 large can of mushroom pieces and stems
–Paprika
–Parsley
–Lemon slices

1. In one-half pound of the butter saute the onions, bellpeppers, celery and garlic.
2. Add the crab meat and shrimp; let simmer for about 15 minutes.
3. Add the onion tops, parsley, one-half cup of the lemon juice, one-half cup of the sherry, breadcrumbs, worcestershire sauce, hot pepper sauce, salt and pepper; cook five minutes longer, remove from heat and set aside.
4. In an oblong two-quart buttered casserole dish layer two pounds of snapper fillet; season lightly.
5. Place the stuffing over the fish; place the mushrooms over stuffing and cover the stuffing completely with the remaining fish.
6. Add the remaining butter, cut in pieces, over the fish and the remaining lemon juice and sherry; season lightly with salt, pepper and paprika.
7. Bake at 350 degrees for one hour; garnish with parsley and lemon slices. When ready to serve cut in squares and serve as entree. Serves eight.

—Eugene A. Patout Sr.
New Iberia (Iberia Parish)

FISH IN BEER BATTER

–2 pounds of frozen or fresh fillets of trout, flounder, ling or ocean perch
–1 cup of flour
–1 teaspoon of salt
–1 tablespoon of paprika
–1 can of beer
–Lemon juice
–Oil for deep frying

1. Let fillets thaw, if frozen.
2. Combine flour, salt and paprika in a mixing bowl; gradually add beer, beating until batter is smooth.
3. Sprinkle fillets with lemon juice; dip lightly in additional flour, then draw fillets carefully through beer batter until completely coated.
4. Drop into hot oil 400 degrees and cook, turning once, about three to four minutes or until crackly brown. Drain on absorbent towels. Makes four to six servings.

—Mrs. Hayes Picou Sr.
Cameron (Cameron Parish)

BAKED STUFFED REDFISH

–1 6- to 8-pound redfish, cleaned, skinned and tenderloined
–Salt and pepper
–½ cup of cooking oil
–1 large onion, chopped
–½ cup of green onions, chopped
–½ cup of bellpepper, chopped
–1 large garlic clove, chopped fine
–1 pound of boiled and peeled shrimp
–3 boiled potatoes, mashed well
–1 cup of prepared breadcrumbs
–2 teaspoons of chopped parsley
–2 eggs, well-beaten

1. Wash fish and season well on inside with salt and pepper; set aside.
2. To make stuffing, saute onion, green onion, bellpepper and garlic in oil until soft; add shrimp and cook for five minutes on low heat.
3. Add potatoes, mix well and cook five more minutes.
4. Remove from heat, add breadcrumbs, parsley and salt and pepper, to taste.
5. When warm, add eggs and mix well.
6. Spread fish open on greased baking pan; place dressing in cavity of fish and close.
7. Cover with foil and bake at 350 degrees for one hour; remove foil and let brown slightly for 15 minutes.
8. Place fish in platter and garnish with lemons (sliced thin) and parsley.

Serves six to eight.

—Mrs. Mary Pryolo
Thibodaux (Lafourche Parish)

CATFISH FILLETS WITH MUSTARD SAUCE

–2 pounds of fresh catfish fillets
–1 quart of buttermilk
–½ cup of butter or oleo, melted
–1 tablespoon of onion juice
–1 tablespoon of garlic juice
–Salt and pepper, to taste
–1 cup of chicken fry mix
–1 cup of crushed potato chips
–Wedges of lemon
–Oil
–Poppy Seed Mustard Sauce (Recipe follows)

1. Soak fillets in enough buttermilk to cover for one hour.
2. Mix together butter, onion juice, garlic juice, salt and pepper.
3. Dip fish in butter mixture and coat fish with mixture of chicken fry mix and crushed potato chips.
4. Place in pre-heated electric skillet 350 to 375 degrees, with three tablespoons of oil; brown on one side, then turn carefully and brown on the other side, about five minutes total time. Do not over-cook.
5. Serve at once with lemon and Poppy Seed Mustard Sauce.

POPPY SEED MUSTARD SAUCE

–¾ cup of salad dressing
–2 tablespoons of prepared mustard
–½ teaspoon of poppy seeds

Combine all ingredients and mix well.

—Mrs. Louise Clement
Napoleonville (Assumption Parish)

BAKED STUFFED FISH FILLETS WITH TOMATO SAUCE

—2 tablespoons of chopped onion
—2 tablespoons of chopped celery
—2 tablespoons of chopped bell-pepper
—¼ cup of butter
—2 tablespoons of flour
—½ cup of milk or cream
—¼ teaspoon of salt
—1/8 teaspoon of pepper
—1/8 teaspoon of paprika
—2 teaspoons of worcestershire sauce
—2 drops of hot pepper sauce
—1 cup of cooked crab meat
—1 cup of cooked shrimp
—½ teaspoon of chopped parsley
—6 flounder or sole fillets (Bass fillets may be used.)
—Melted butter
—Tomato Sauce (Recipe follows)

1. Saute onion, celery and bell-pepper in butter; cook until ingredients are soft but not brown.
2. Stir-in flour and milk and cook and stir until thickened; remove from heat.
3. Stir-in seasonings, crab meat, shrimp and parsley.
4. Mound some stuffing on each fillet, roll up and secure with wooden picks; put roll-ups, leaving space between, into shallow greased baking dish.
5. Brush fish with melted butter. Bake at 350 degrees for 10 to 15 minutes.
6. Pour Tomato Sauce over top. Return to oven and bake 25 minutes.

TOMATO SAUCE

—4 cups of canned tomatoes
—1 teaspoon of salt
—½ teaspoon of thyme
—1 bay leaf, crumbled
—Black pepper and red pepper
—1 garlic clove, chopped
—2 tablespoons of butter
—1 tablespoon of flour

1. Combine tomatoes and seasonings in one tablespoon of the butter in saucepan; boil over medium heat until sauce is reduced to half, stirring occasionally.
2. In another saucepan melt remaining butter, blend-in flour and cook over low heat; mix with sauce and cook five minutes.

—Mrs. Opal Blood
Evangeline Parish

GRILLED RED SNAPPER STEAKS

—½ cup of oil
—½ teaspoon of oregano
—¼ cup of lemon juice
—¼ teaspoon of cumin
—½ teaspoon of salt
—3 pounds of red snapper fillet (or redfish or speckled trout) cut into steaks one inch thick

1. Mix oil, oregano, lemon juice, cumin and salt.
2. Marinate fish in sauce for 10 to 15 minutes.
3. Grill on a slow charcoal fire six to eight minutes or until fork easily penetrates fish. Extra sauce can be used as a baste.

—Josephine Hill
Ascension Parish

CRAWFISH PIE

–¾ medium bellpepper, chopped
–1 large onion, chopped
–2 ribs of celery, chopped
–¾ cup of butter
–6 tablespoons of crawfish fat (optional)
–1½ pounds of peeled crawfish tails
–½ cup of chopped green onions
–½ cup of minced parsley
–1½ teaspoons of salt
–½ teaspoon of black pepper
–1/8 teaspoon of red pepper
–½ teaspoon of garlic powder
–Cornstarch
–Dough for a double-crust pie

1. Saute bellpepper, onion and celery in butter until tender; add crawfish fat and simmer 10 minutes.
2. Add crawfish tails, green onions, parsley and seasonings. Thicken if necessary with a little cornstarch; let cook long enough to thicken gravy.
3. Place half of the pie crust dough in a nine-inch pie pan. Fill with the cooled filling. Place top crust on pie, moisten edges and seal edges. Cut two or three one-inch-long slits in the top crust.
4. Bake 10 minutes at 450 degrees; lower oven to 375 degrees and cook for 35 minutes longer or until crust is golden brown.

Note: Individual pies can be made using muffin pan with large cups. Bake as above.

—LSU Cooperative Extension Service,
Iberville Parish

CRAWFISH ETOUFFEE I

–3 large onions, chopped
–1 large bellpepper, chopped fine
–½ cup of Rotel tomatoes
–½ cup of chopped green onions
–¼ cup of minced parsley
–½ cup of oleo
–1 pound of crawfish tails with fat
–Salt and pepper, to taste

1. Saute onions, pepper, tomatoes, green onions and parsley in oleo for 10 minutes.
2. Add crawfish with fat and cover tightly; cook for 20 minutes. Add no water, as crawfish has enough liquid; season, to taste.
Serve over hot rice.

—Edlin Petitjean
Rayne (Acadia Parish)

CRAWFISH STEW

–3 tablespoons of fat
–2 small onions, chopped
–½ bellpepper, chopped
–2 ribs of celery, chopped
–1 garlic clove, minced
–2 tablespoons of flour
–½ cup of tomato sauce
–¼ teaspoon of hot pepper sauce
–1 tablespoon of worcestershire
–Salt and pepper, to taste
–1½ cups of water
–2 pounds of crawfish tails, cleaned and peeled

1. Heat fat; add onions, bellpepper, celery and garlic. Saute until clear.
2. Add flour, tomato sauce, seasonings, water and crawfish tails. Simmer on low heat for 30 minutes.
3. Serve on hot rice.

—Jeanette M. Guidry
Breaux Bridge (St. Martin Parish)

CRAWFISH ETOUFFEE II

–1 cup of chopped green onions
–1 cup of chopped celery
–¼ pound of oleo
–3 tablespoons of flour
–Crawfish fat
–1 can of chicken broth
–1 pound of crawfish tails
–Salt, black pepper and red pepper, to taste
–2 teaspoons of paprika
–Green onion tops, chopped
–Parsley, chopped

1. Saute onions and celery in oleo until wilted. Add flour and cook, but do not brown.
2. Add crawfish fat and chicken broth; simmer 20 minutes.
3. Add crawfish tails, salt, pepper and paprika; simmer 20 minutes more.
4. Before serving, add onion tops and parsley.

—Jeanette M. Guidry
Breaux Bridge (St. Martin Parish)

CRAWFISH ETOUFFEE III

–¼ cup of oleo
–1 large onion, chopped
–1 rib of celery, chopped
–1 garlic clove, minced
–1 pound of crawfish tails
–1 tablespoon of catsup or tomato sauce
–½ teaspoon of cornstarch
–½ of lemon, sliced
–Crawfish fat (if desired)
–¼ cup of chopped parsley
–Salt and pepper, to taste

1. Melt oleo; add onion, celery and garlic. Simmer until light brown.
2. Add crawfish tails, catsup, cornstarch (dissolved in one and one-half teaspoons of water), lemon slices and crawfish fat (if used). Bring to a boil; lower heat and simmer for about ten minutes or until done.
3. Add parsley; serve over cooked rice.
Serves three.

—Mrs. William P. Gilbert
Thibodaux (Lafourche Parish)

CRAWFISH SPAGHETTI

–2 large onions, chopped
–½ cup of chopped celery
–¼ cup of chopped bellpepper
–¼ cup of oil
–1 20-ounce can of tomatoes
–1 8-ounce can of tomato sauce
–1½ cups of water
–4 garlic cloves, minced
–½ cup of parsley, minced
–1 teaspoon of worcestershire sauce
–Salt and pepper, to taste
–2 to 3 pounds of cleaned crawfish tails
–½ cup of sherry
–1 pound of spaghetti
–Grated cheese

1. Saute onion, celery and bell-pepper in oil until brown and transparent; add tomatoes, tomato sauce, water, garlic, parsley and seasonings.
2. Simmer about three hours; add crawfish and sherry and simmer for 30 minutes.
3. Cook spaghetti and drain, but do not wash; add to crawfish sauce and mix well.
4. Put on platter and sprinkle with grated cheese.

—LSU Cooperative Extension Service, Iberville Parish

CRAWFISH CANTELONNI

–3 tablespoons of flour
–3 tablespoons of oil
–1 onion, chopped
–½ cup of chopped celery
–½ cup of chopped bellpepper
–1 garlic clove, chopped fine
–1 quart of chicken broth
–1 teaspoon of liquid crab boil
–Salt and pepper, to taste
–Chopped parsley
–Chopped green onion tops or chives
–4 cups of crawfish tails, whole
–1 package of cantelonni (or manicotti)
–Stuffing (Recipe follows)

1. Make a roux with flour and oil; add onion, celery, bellpepper and garlic. Cook until done.
2. Add chicken broth, liquid crab boil and seasonings; cook about 30 minutes.
3. Add parsley, green onion and crawfish tails; cook about five minutes until sauce starts to bubble. Set aside.
4. Cook cantelonni according to instructions on the package. Carefully stuff with Stuffing. Arrange in a lightly greased baking dish in a single layer. Pour the above sauce over the stuffed cantelonni.
5. Bake at 325 degrees, covered, for 25 to 30 minutes.

STUFFING

–2 tablespoons of flour
–4 tablespoons of oil
–1 large onion, chopped
–½ cup of chopped celery
–¼ cup of chopped bellpepper
–1 garlic clove, pressed
–4 cups of crawfish tails, parboiled and ground
–2 hard-boiled eggs, chopped fine
–Salt and pepper, to taste
–1 cup of seasoned breadcrumbs
–Chopped parsley, to taste
–Chopped green onion tops, to taste

1. Make a roux with flour and oil; add onion, celery and bellpepper, and saute. Add garlic and cook until done.
2. Add ground crawfish tails and eggs; cook until thick.
3. Add seasonings, breadcrumbs, parsley and green onions.

—Gene Knobloch
Thibodaux (Lafourche Parish)

CRAWFISH NEWBURG

–¼ cup of butter
–¼ teaspoon of salt
–½ teaspoon of white pepper
–¼ teaspoon of paprika
–¼ teaspoon of nutmeg
–1 tablespoon of flour
–1 cup of coffee cream
–2 pounds of cooked crawfish
–3 egg yolks, beaten
–2 tablespoons of dry sherry
–Pastry shells or hot rolls

1. Melt butter in sauce pan; add the seasonings and flour.
2. When smooth, add cream gradually; bring to a boil, stir-in the crawfish, and when thoroughly heated add the egg yolks and sherry.
3. Cook until thick, but do not boil.
4. Serve in pastry shells or on hot rolls.

Serves four.

—LSU Cooperative Extension Service,
Iberville Parish

CRAWFISH DOG

- 3 tablespoons of shortening
- 3 tablespoons of flour
- 1 medium onion, chopped
- ½ pound of crawfish tails, peeled and ground
- ½ cup of crawfish fat
- ¼ cup of water
- 1 teaspoon of red pepper
- 2 teaspoons of salt

1. Make roux with shortening and flour; cook until light brown.
2. Add onion; cook until done. Add crawfish and fat, water and seasoning. Cook 20 minutes and serve on open-face hot dog bun.

—Mim Blanchard
Breaux Bridge (St. Martin Parish)

CRAWFISH JAMBALAYA

- 1 tablespoon of flour
- 2 tablespoons of oil
- 1 cup of chopped onions
- 1 pound (2½ cups) of crawfish tails, peeled
- ¼ cup of crawfish fat
- 1 1/8 cups of raw long-grain rice
- ½ cup of chopped parsley (or 2 teaspoons of dehydrated parsley)
- ½ cup of chopped green onions
- ½ cup of chopped celery
- ½ cup of chopped bellpepper
- 2½ teaspoons of salt
- ½ teaspoon of black pepper
- 1/8 teaspoon of red pepper

1. Make a roux with flour and oil; add onions, stirring until onions are almost cooked.
2. Add one and one-half cups of cold water; simmer 30 minutes.
3. Add crawfish tails and fat; cook until crawfish turns pink, about 10 to 15 minutes. Add two cups less two tablespoons of water; bring to a boil.
4. Add remaining ingredients; stir to blend. Cook on low heat, covered, for about 30 minutes or until rice is tender.
5. Five minutes before serving, fluff up with a two-pronged fork. Serves four to five.

—LSU Cooperative Extension Service,
Iberville Parish

CRAWFISH BOUCHES

- 4 tablespoons of chopped onion
- 2 tablespoons of minced bell-pepper
- 3 tablespoons of minced celery
- 2 tablespoons of butter
- ¾ pound of peeled crawfish tails, chopped fine
- 1 teaspoon of salt
- ¼ teaspoon of red pepper
- 2 cups of cubed bread, cut in ½-inch cubes
- 1 egg
- 1 tablespoon of water
- 1 tablespoon of minced parsley
- Breadcrumbs
- Oil for frying

1. Saute onion, bellpepper and celery in butter until onions are transparent.
2. Add crawfish and seasonings; simmer 15 minutes. Remove from heat; cool.
3. Mix bread cubes with egg (which has been beaten with water); add to crawfish mixture along with parsley. Mix well.
4. Shape into patties 1½x2x1½ inches; coat with breadcrumbs.
5. Fry in deep oil at 350 degrees about two minutes until brown; drain.

—LSU Cooperative Extension Service,
Iberville Parish

CRAWFISH OMELETTE

- –1 pound of crawfish tails, peeled
- –¼ pound of butter
- –½ cup of chopped green onions
- –1 garlic clove, minced
- –½ cup of chopped parsley
- –8 eggs
- –Salt and pepper, to taste
- –½ teaspoon of worcestershire sauce

1. Saute crawfish in butter over low heat until tender, 10 to 15 minutes; add green onions, garlic and parsley.
2. Beat eggs with salt, pepper and worcestershire sauce; pour over crawfish, stirring gently.
3. When eggs are set, turn onto platter.

Serves five to six.

—LSU Cooperative Extension Service,
Iberville Parish

CRAWFISH PATRICE

- –1¼ cups of chopped onion
- –1 bellpepper, chopped fine
- –2 garlic cloves, minced
- –2 ribs of celery, chopped fine
- –¼ pound of oleo
- –2 pounds of crawfish tails, peeled
- –1 can of Rotel tomatoes
- –1 can of cream of mushroom soup
- –½ cup of water
- –4 slices of bread, soaked in water
- –2 cups of cooked long-grain rice
- –¼ cup of chopped parsley
- –Salt and red pepper, to taste
- –Buttered breadcrumbs

1. Saute onion, bellpepper, garlic and celery in oleo; add crawfish and tomatoes. Cook about 10 minutes.
2. Add soup and one half cup of water; cook five minutes.
3. Squeeze water from bread; add bread, rice, parsley and seasonings to crawfish mixture.
4. Pour into a lightly greased casserole; sprinkle with buttered breadcrumbs. Bake uncovered at 350 degrees for 30 minutes.

—Mrs. Pat Green
Breaux Bridge (St. Martin Parish)

CRAWFISH CASSEROLE I

- –1 cup of chopped onions
- –1 cup of chopped bellpeppers
- –3 garlic cloves, chopped
- –1 cup of chopped celery
- –1/4 pound of butter or oleo
- –1 can of cream of mushroom soup
- –1 can of cream of cheddar cheese soup
- –1/3 cup of chopped parsley
- –1 cup of chopped green onion tops
- –1 can of chopped pimento and juice
- –3 cups of cooked crawfish
- –2 cups of cooked rice
- –2 slices of toast, crumbled
- –2 tablespoons of hot sauce
- –¾ teaspoon of black pepper
- –1 teaspoon of salt
- –Italian breadcrumbs

1. Cook onions, bellpeppers, garlic and celery in butter until tender.
2. Add the soups, parsley, green onions and pimento, stirring gently while adding ingredients.
3. Stir-in crawfish, rice and toast; add seasoning; pour into casserole.
4. Sprinkle Italian breadcrumbs over casserole.
5. Bake uncovered at 350 degrees for 30 minutes.

—Mrs. Edith Fontenot
Crowley (Acadia Parish)

CRAWFISH CASSEROLE II

–½ cup of butter
–1 cup of finely chopped onions
–2 cups of crawfish fat (optional)
–½ cup of chopped bellpepper
–½ cup of chopped green onions
–2 pounds of crawfish tails
–½ teaspoon of freshly ground black pepper
–1 teaspoon of garlic powder
–½ teaspoon of red pepper
–Salt, to taste
–1 cup of mushroom stems and pieces
–¼ cup of finely chopped pecans (optional)
–¼ cup of chopped parsley
–2½ cups of breadcrumbs
–1 egg, beaten

1. Heat butter in skillet; add onions and saute slowly five minutes.
2. Add crawfish fat; cook for 10 minutes.
3. Add bellpepper, green onions and crawfish tails; cook five minutes.
4. Add seasonings, mushrooms, pecans and parsley; remove from heat and add two cups of breadcrumbs and well-beaten egg; stir to mix well.
5. Pour into a buttered casserole; top with remaining breadcrumbs.
6. Bake uncovered in pre-heated 300-degree oven for 25 minutes. Serves six.

—LSU Cooperative Extension Service,
Iberville Parish

BOILED CRAWFISH
(For 20)

See page 192

CRAB MEAT AU GRATIN I

–½ cup of chopped green onions
–2 tablespoons of chopped celery
–½ cup of chopped mushrooms
–3 tablespoons of butter
–1 cup of thick White Sauce (Recipe follows)
–1 pound of lump crab meat
–Salt and hot pepper sauce, to taste
–1 cup of American cheese, grated

1. Saute chopped green onions, celery and mushrooms in butter.
2. Add White Sauce, crab meat, salt and pepper.
3. Place in buttered baking dish, top with cheese and bake at 350 degrees until brown, about 20 to 25 minutes.
4. Garnish with black olive halves and wedges of lemon.

WHITE SAUCE
–¼ cup of butter
–¼ cup of flour
–1 cup of milk, scalded
–Salt and pepper, to taste

1. Melt butter in heavy saucepan; blend-in flour on low heat, stirring constantly until smooth.
2. Remove from heat; stir-in heated milk a little at a time.
3. Season, to taste; cook on low heat until thick and bubbly.

—Mrs. Martha Montrejean
Cut Off (Lafourche Parish)

CRAB MEAT AU GRATIN II

- –1 cup of flaked crab meat
- –1 tablespoon of butter
- –2 green onions, chopped
- –½ cup of hot Hollandaise Sauce (Recipe follows)
- –Parmesan cheese
- –Additional butter

1. Heat crab meat in butter with green onions and Hollandaise Sauce; place in individual baking dishes.
2. Top with Parmesan cheese and butter; bake at 375 degrees until brown.

HOLLANDAISE SAUCE

- –¼ pound of butter
- –4 egg yolks, beaten
- –2 teaspoons of lemon juice
- –White pepper and salt

1. Heat butter in top of double boiler over simmering water (not boiling).
2. Stir constantly while adding egg yolks; add lemon juice and seasonings.

—Sheila Bourgeois
Lutcher (St. James Parish)

CRAB MEAT PIE

- – 1 9-inch pie shell
- –1 cup of Swiss cheese, freshly grated
- –7½ ounces of crab meat, canned or frozen
- –2 green onions, chopped
- –2 eggs
- –¾ cup of milk or half-and-half
- –½ teaspoon of salt
- –¼ teaspoon of mustard
- –½ teaspoon of lemon peeling, grated
- –Sliced almonds or Chinese noodles

1. Bake pie shell for 10 minutes and cool.
2. Sprinkle grated cheese over pie shell, top with flaked crab meat and green onions.
3. Beat eggs; add milk with seasonings and mix together; pour mixture over other ingredients in pie-shell.
4. Top with almonds or crumbled Chinese noodles. Bake at 325 degrees about 55 minutes.

Makes four to five servings.

Note: For a more economical dish use white tuna and only one egg. Remember, the grated lemon peelings is the thing.

—Mrs. Camille Delarette
Plattenville (Assumption Parish)

CRAB CAKES

- –1 pound of crab meat
- –1 cup of mayonnaise
- –3 tablespoons of flour
- –¼ cup of finely chopped bell-pepper
- –¼ cup of finely chopped onion
- –Cracker crumbs
- –Oil

1. Mix first five ingredients together; form into patties and coat each patty with cracker crumbs.
2. Fry slowly in oil until brown; drain on paper towels.

—Irvin Arceneaux
Jennings (Jefferson Davis Parish)

STUFFED CRABS

—1 cup of chopped onions
—½ cup of chopped celery
—½ cup of chopped bellpepper
—2 garlic cloves
—¼ pound of oleo or ½ cup of oil
—½ teaspoon of worcestershire sauce
—1 pound of crab meat (about 10 crabs)
—Salt, black pepper and red pepper, to taste
—½ cup of chopped green onion tops
—1 tablespoon of chopped parsley
—2 stale hamburger buns (or 6 slices of stale bread)
—1 cup of evaporated milk
—3 eggs
—Breadcrumbs

1. Saute onion, celery, bellpepper and garlic in oleo or oil until wilted.
2. Add worcestershire sauce, crab meat and seasoning, to taste; cook over medium heat about 15 minutes, stirring constantly.
3. Add onion tops, parsley and bread which has been soaked in milk and eggs; mix well.
4. Fill 12 crab shells; top with breadcrumbs.
5. Bake 15 minutes at 375 degrees.

—Mary Campbell
Ascension Parish

STUFFED CRABS D'ABBEVILLE

—½ cup of creamy onion salad dressing
—1½ cups of chopped onion
—¼ cup of chopped celery
—¼ cup of chopped bellpepper
—1 cup of fresh peeled shrimp, ground
—2 jalapeno peppers, seeded and chopped fine
—1 can of cream of mushroom soup
—½ cup of sandwich spread with relish
—1 cup of cooked rice
—2 cups of fresh crab meat
—Green onion tops, chopped fine
—Parsley, chopped fine
—Salt and pepper, to taste
—1 cup of finely crushed potato chips

1. Heat one-fourth cup of the creamy onion salad dressing in a three-quart saucepan. Add onion, celery and bellpepper. Cook, stirring constantly, until wilted.
2. Add shrimp and jalapeno peppers, lower heat and cook until liquid is absorbed.
3. Add soup, sandwich spread, rice, crab meat, onion tops and parsley. Season, to taste. Mix well. Spoon mixture into crab shells or casserole.
4. Brush with remaining onion dressing and sprinkle with potato chip crumbs.
5. Bake at 350 degrees for 20 minutes or until browned.

—Mrs. Amson Corner
Abbeville (Vermilion Parish)

CRAB CASSEROLE I

- —1 cup of chopped onions
- —¾ cup of chopped celery
- —¼ cup of chopped bellpepper
- —¼ pound of butter or oleo
- —1 pint of crab meat
- —3 eggs, slightly beaten
- —Salt, red pepper and black pepper, to taste
- —½ cup of cornflakes crumbs

1. Cook chopped vegetables in butter until tender on medium heat; remove from heat and mix in crab meat, slightly beaten eggs and seasonings.
2. Add cornflakes crumbs, reserving enough to sprinkle on top of casserole; pour into casserole dish and sprinkle with remaining crumbs.
3. Bake uncovered at 350 degrees for about 20 minutes.

Note: This may be used to stuff crabs or bellpeppers.

—Grace B. Veazey
Abbeville (Vermilion Parish)

CRAB CASSEROLE II

- —1 bellpepper, chopped
- —1 large onion, chopped
- —½ pound of oleo
- —3 pounds of crab meat
- —8 slices of bread, soaked in milk
- —Salt and pepper, to taste
- —2 heaping tablespoons of mayonnaise
- —Breadcrumbs

1. Saute bellpepper and onion in oleo; add crab meat, bread, seasonings and mayonnaise.
2. Put in 10x16-inch casserole dish and top with breadcrumbs; add pats of butter on top.
3. Bake uncovered at 350 degrees for 30 minutes.

—Deanna Gondron
St. Martin Parish

CRAB CASSEROLE III

- —1 cup of chopped onion
- —1 rib of celery, chopped
- —¼ pound of oleo
- —½ cup of flour
- —1 13-ounce can of evaporated milk
- —2 egg yolks
- —1 teaspoon of salt
- —¼ teaspoon of black pepper
- —½ teaspoon of red pepper
- —1 pound of white crab meat
- —Chopped green onions, to taste
- —½ pound of cheddar cheese, grated

1. In blender, blend onions and celery. Saute in oleo in a skillet until soft.
2. Stir-in flour well, but do not brown. Pour in milk, stirring constantly. Add egg yolks, salt and peppers and cook five minutes until thick (if too thick, add a little milk).
3. Add crab meat and green onions; mix well. Pour the mixture in a greased casserole dish and sprinkle with cheese.
4. Bake uncovered at 375 degrees for 15 to 20 minutes or until cheese is melted and brown.

—Mrs. Camille Delorette
Napoleonville (Assumption Parish)

CRAB-STUFFED CREPES

- –3 eggs, beaten
- –1½ cups of milk
- –2 tablespoons of butter, melted
- –½ teaspoon of salt
- –1 cup of flour
- –Crab Filling (Recipes follows)
- –Swiss Cheese Sauce (Recipe follows)
- –1 cup of grated Swiss cheese

1. Place eggs, milk and butter in blender; add salt and flour (which has been mixed together) to blender and blend about one minute, until batter is smooth.
2. Place in refrigerator for at least two hours and as long as 12 hours before making crepes.
3. To cook crepes, pour three tablespoons of batter into a greased and heated crepe pan or small skillet; cook until done on one side. It is not necessary to cook crepes on both sides.
4. To assemble crepes, blend one-half of the Swiss Cheese Sauce with the Crab Filling; check for seasoning. Place a large spoonful of filling on each crepe and roll; place seam side down in a buttered large rectangular glass baking dish. This recipe makes enough crepes to fill two baking dishes.
5. Spoon remaining Sauce over crepes and sprinkle with one cup of grated Swiss cheese; dot with butter.
6. Bake at 400 degrees uncovered for 20 minutes, until hot and bubbly.
7. This dish may be frozen or refrigerated before serving. If refrigerated, remove 30 minutes before baking.

CRAB FILLING

- –¼ pound of butter
- –½ cup of green onions, minced
- –2 pounds of fresh lump crab meat
- –Salt and white pepper, to taste
- –Dash of garlic powder, if desired
- –½ cup of vermouth

1. Melt butter in skillet; stir-in green onions and crab meat.
2. Mix lightly and cook a few minutes; add seasonings, to taste.
3. Add vermouth and boil rapidly until liquid is almost evaporated.
4. Scrape from skillet into a bowl and set aside until ready to assemble crepes.

SWISS CHEESE SAUCE

- –2/3 cup of vermouth
- –¼ cup of cornstarch
- –¼ cup of milk
- –4 cups of heavy cream
- –Salt and white pepper, to taste
- –1½ cups of grated Swiss cheese

1. Add vermouth to the same skillet that the Filling was cooked in; boil rapidly untill vermouth is reduced to two tablespoons.
2. Remove from heat; stir-in cornstarch and milk (which have been mixed together).
3. Return to low heat and add cream slowly with salt and pepper; cook several minutes until slightly thickened.
4. Stir-in cheese and cook until melted and well-blended; check for seasoning.

Makes 24 crepes.

—Mrs. Blue Thibodaux
Plattenville (Assumption Parish)

CRAB MEAT IN WHITE SAUCE

- 1 pound of crab meat
- 1 onion, chopped
- 1 can of cream of mushroom soup
- ½ teaspoon of each of the following: garlic puree, salt, red pepper, celery flakes, hot pepper sauce, worcestershire sauce and parsley flakes
- ¼ pound of oleo
- ½ cup of flour
- ½ cup of milk

1. Combine crab meat, onion, soup and seasonings; mix well.
2. Make a white sauce by melting oleo and adding flour and then milk; cook until thick.
3. Combine white sauce with crab meat mixture; mix well. Cook on low heat for one hour.

Serves six to eight.

—Mrs. Ferdie Richard
Labadieville (Assumption Parish)

CRAB 'N' CHIPS

- ¼ pound of butter
- ¼ cup of chopped green onion
- 3 tablespoons of flour
- 2 cups of breakfast cream
- ½ cup of dry white wine (optional)
- ½ teaspoon of salt
- Dash of hot pepper sauce
- ½ pound of grated Swiss cheese
- 1 pound of crab meat
- 2 cups of crushed potato chips

1. Saute green onions in butter until wilted.
2. Add flour and cream to make white sauce; add wine, seasonings and cheese; stir until cheese is melted.
3. Fold in crab meat.
4. Top with crushed potato chips and bake uncovered at 350 degrees for 20 minutes.

Serves eight.

—Mrs. Gertrude S. Dumez
Houma (Terrebonne Parish)

CRAB ETOUFFEE

- ¼ cup of flour
- 1 cup of oil
- 2 medium onions, chopped fine
- 1 bellpepper, chopped fine
- ¾ cup of chopped celery
- 2 pounds of crab meat
- ¼ cup of onion tops and parsley, chopped
- ¼ cup of water
- Salt and pepper, to taste

1. Brown flour in oil; add onions, bellpepper and celery and cook until wilted.
2. Add crab meat, onion tops, parsley and water; bring to boil in uncovered pot on medium heat for 15 minutes.

Serve on cooked rice.

—Gerry Cormier
St. Martin Parish

STEAMED SHRIMP I

- ¼ cup of red wine vinegar
- ½ cup of olive oil
- 4 green onions, chopped
- 1 large onion, chopped
- ½ rib of celery, chopped
- 2 lemons, sliced thick
- Salt, pepper and garlic powder, to taste
- 4 pounds of raw shrimp, unpeeled but de-headed

1. Mix all ingredients together in large pot; stir well.
2. Cover and simmer about 45 minutes; stir often.

—Mrs. Gordon Martin
Grand Point (St. James Parish)

STEAMED SHRIMP II

- —½ pound of oleo
- —1 large onion, chopped
- —½ cup of chopped celery
- —½ cup of chopped bellpepper
- —1 tablespoon of worcestershire sauce
- —Salt and pepper, to taste
- —2 pounds of shrimp, unpeeled
- —1 bottle of beer

1. Place oleo in saucepan and melt over low heat.
2. Add chopped vegetables and seasonings and saute until tender.
3. Add shrimp and cool about five minutes.
4. Add beer; cover and steam about 15 to 20 minutes.

Serves five.

—Mrs. Agnes Jewell
Ventress (Pointe Coupee Parish)

SHRIMP AND SHELLS

- —3 eggs, hard-cooked and chopped
- —3 cups of peeled, deveined and boiled shrimp
- —1½ cups of cooked macaroni, shells or elbows
- —¼ cup of chopped celery
- —¼ cup of chopped bellpepper
- —¼ cup of chopped onion
- —1 teaspoon of chopped garlic
- —½ cup of mayonnaise
- —2 tablespoons of mustard
- —1 tablespoon of lemon juice
- —Salt and pepper, to taste

1. Mix eggs with shrimp; if shrimp are large, chop coarsely.
2. Add macaroni and remaining ingredients; mix well and serve on lettuce if desired.

—Mrs. Frank Daviet
Lockport (Lafourche Parish)

SHRIMP SPAGHETTI

- —¼ cup of flour
- —¾ cup of oil
- —2 cups of chopped onions
- —4 ribs of celery, chopped
- —1 bellpepper, chopped
- —2 cans of tomato paste
- —2 cans of tomato sauce
- —1 can of whole tomatoes
- —4 garlic cloves, minced
- —4 bay leaves
- —4 to 5 cups of water
- —1 large can of sliced mushrooms, drained (reserve liquid)
- —1 tablespoon of worcestershire sauce
- —Salt and pepper, to taste
- —½ cup of Parmesan cheese
- —½ cup of grated American cheese (optional)
- —3 pounds of shrimp, peeled, de-veined and seasoned
- —Cooked spaghetti

1. Brown flour in oil; add onions, celery, bellpepper and saute until onions are transparent.
2. Add tomato paste, tomato sauce and whole tomatoes, stirring well; simmer 10 minutes, stirring often.
3. Add garlic, bay leaves, water, liquid from mushrooms and worcestershire sauce; mix well. Season to taste with salt and pepper.
4. Bring to a boil; lower heat and simmer 45 minutes; add cheeses, shrimp and mushrooms. Adjust seasoning.
5. Bring to boil; lower heat and simmer 20 to 30 minutes until shrimp are cooked.
6. Serve over cooked spaghetti.

—Iris McClung
Gramercy (St. James Parish)

SHRIMP STEW OVER FRIED RICE

–3 slices of breakfast bacon, cut up fine
–1 medium-size onion, chopped fine
–3 garlic cloves, cut up fine
–4 8-ounce cans of tomato sauce
–½ cup of water
–1 tablespoon of sugar
–2 teaspoons of salt (more if desired)
–½ teaspoon of black pepper
–1 teaspoon of crushed red hot peppers (more if desired)
–4 bay leaves
–1 cup of chopped celery
–2 pounds of fresh shrimp, cleaned
–1 8-ounce can of mushrooms
–1 cup of chopped green onions
–Fried Rice (Recipe follows)

1. Brown bacon in dutch oven or pot; add onion and garlic, and saute.
2. Add tomato sauce, water, sugar, salt, pepper, hot pepper, bay leaves and celery; cook 25 minutes or until thick.
3. Add shrimp, mushrooms and green onions and cook 20 minutes.
4. Taste sauce to see if it is bitter; if so, add a little more sugar.
5. Serve over Fried Rice.
Serves six to eight people.

FRIED RICE
–3¼ cups of water
–2 teaspoons of salt (more if desired)
–¼ teaspoon of pepper
–½ teaspoon of garlic powder
–1/3 cup of cooking oil
–1½ cups of long-grain rice (do not wash)
–1 medium onion, sliced thin
–1/3 cup of bellpepper, sliced thin
–3 tablespoons of tomato sauce

1. Pour water in pot with tight cover; add salt, pepper and garlic powder and bring to a boil.
2. In a frying pan heat oil; add rice and stir until brown.
3. Add onion, bellpepper and tomato sauce; stir and add to boiling water.
4. Stir for 10 seconds, put lid on tight, turn down heat to simmer or low and cook 20 minutes.
5. Take off heat; do not open until ready to serve.

—Norman Wigle
Luling (St. Charles Parish)

SHRIMP FRIED RICE

–1 small bunch of green onions, chopped
–1 pound of shrimp, peeled and chopped fine
–2 tablespoons of oil
–Salt and pepper, to taste
–4 cups of cooked rice
–2 tablespoons of soy sauce

1. Cook onions and shrimp together in oil until done, about 10 minutes.
2. Add salt and pepper to taste (use a very small amount of salt), cooked rice and soy sauce, mixing well.

—Leola Cutno
Ascension Parish

SHRIMP WITH RICE

—½ cup of butter
—1 large onion, chopped
—1 cup of sliced mushrooms
—1 bellpepper, chopped
—1 1/4 cups of raw rice
—1 teaspoon of salt
—½ teaspoon of pepper
—1/4 teaspoon of thyme
—1/4 cup of wine (optional)
—3 cups of hot chicken stock
—2 tablespoons of chopped parsley
—½ bay leaf
—2 pounds of raw shrimp

1. In a large skillet, melt the butter; add onion, mushroom, bellpepper, rice, salt and pepper.
2. Cook, stirring until rice is brown.
3. Add thyme and wine and simmer five minutes.
4. Add chicken stock, parsley and bay leaf; cover and cook ten minutes, stirring occasionally.
5. Add shrimp and simmer ten to fifteen minutes, depending on size of shrimp. Remove bay leaf and serve.

—Mrs. Allie Bizette
Oscar (Pointe Coupee Parish)

SHRIMP IN WINE

—4 to 6 garlic cloves
—¾ pound of butter
—Salt and pepper
—1 pound of shrimp, de-headed but with shells on
—1½ cups of vermouth
—Lemon juice, to taste

1. Cut garlic into small pieces.
2. Melt butter in a skillet and add salt and pepper; add garlic and fry until brown.
3. Add shrimp and cook until they are pink, about 10 minutes.
4. Add vermouth and continue cooking for 12 minutes.
5. Add lemon juice.
6. The juice may be put in a small dish to sop with french bread or to dip shrimp in.

Shrimp are just like boiled ones with lots of seasoning.

—Brenda Hebert
Gibson (Terrebonne Parish)

SHRIMP STEW

—1 onion, chopped
—½ cup of chopped bellpepper
—½ cup of chopped celery
—4 tablesppons of oil
—1¾ pounds of shrimp
—3½ cups of water
—3 tablespoons of flour
—1 tablespoon of liquid brown gravy coloring (like Kitchen Bouquet)
—Salt and pepper, to taste

1. Saute onions, bellpeppers and celery in oil; add shrimp and simmer five minutes on a low heat.
2. Add three cups of the water and bring to a boil.
3. Mix flour and one-half cup of the water until it is smooth; add to the shrimp mixture.
4. Reduce heat and continue stirring until thoroughly mixed; add liquid brown gravy coloring and simmer 15 minutes.
Serves six.

—Mollie Prince
Ascension Parish

BAKED MARINATED SHRIMP

–½ pound of butter or oleo, melted
–¼ cup of olive oil
–Dash of hot pepper sauce
–2 tablespoons of worcestershire sauce
–1 tablespoon of rosemary
–½ teaspoon of thyme
–½ teaspoon of oregano
–½ teaspoon of basil
–2 bay leaves, crumbled
–1/8 teaspoon of crushed red pepper
–½ lemon, squeezed
–¼ cup of white wine
–3 garlic cloves, sliced
–1 teaspoon of sugar
–1 teaspoon of Accent
–2 large onions, quartered
–2 large bellpeppers, quartered
–2 ribs of celery, cut into chunks
–Salt, to taste
–2 pounds of large, raw, unpeeled shrimp
–Black pepper, to taste

1. Melt butter in a saucepan and remove from heat.
2. Combine with all other ingredients except shrimp and black pepper; pour mixture into shallow baking pan.
3. Place shrimp in sauce and cover with black pepper; mix well and refrigerate for several hours or overnight.
4. Stir occasionally to allow shrimp to be well-coated with marinade.
5. Preheat oven to 425 degrees and cook shrimp in marinade in pan uncovered for about 25 minutes or until shells are loosened around shrimp (depends on size of shrimp); stir twice while cooking. Remove from oven and serve with hot french bread.
Serves four to six.

—Linda F. Guidry
Grand Caillou (Terrebonne Parish)

BAKED SHRIMP

–5 pounds of shrimp with heads (medium preferred)
–3 tablespoons of salt
–6 lemons (approximately 1 cup of juice)
–¼ pound of butter, melted
–Pepper sauce and paprika, to taste

1. Wash shrimp well, arrange in shallow pan, 12x6x2.
2. Add remaining ingredients.
3. Cover with foil and bake at 350 degrees for 45 minutes.
4. About 20 minutes before shrimp are done, remove foil, stir and continue to bake with foil off the pan. Taste shrimp for doneness, as sometimes larger shrimp require longer baking.
5. The juice is served in a small bowl to each guest for dunking hot, buttered french bread.

—Georgiana Bourg
Donaldsonville (Ascension Parish)

BROILED SHRIMP

—1 pound of raw shrimp, peeled
—Salt and pepper, to taste
—¼ cup of butter
—Juice of one lemon
—Worcestershire sauce (optional)
—Parsley, chopped

1. Place seasoned shrimp in shallow pan; dot butter on top of shrimp and squeeze on juice of one-half lemon.
2. Place in broiler about four inches from heat source; broil for three minutes.
3. Turn each shrimp over. (If worcestershire sauce will be used, sprinkle on shrimp about two minutes before turning.)
4. After turning, squeeze juice of remainder of lemon on shrimp.
5. Broil about seven minutes or until brown.
6. Sprinkle parsley on shrimp after removing from heat.
Serve immediately.

—Mrs. Cleo Cheramie
Golden Meadow (Lafourche Parish)

SHRIMP FLAMBÉ

—1 small onion, chopped
—6 garlic cloves, minced
—¼ cup of butter
—1 pound of shrimp
—2 tablespoons of flour
—3 tablespoons of brandy
—¼ cup of vermouth
—¼ cup of water
—2 teaspoons of lemon juice
—4 slices of toast

1. Saute onion and garlic in butter until brown; add shrimp and sprinkle with the flour.
2. Cook until shrimp are pink, about 10 minutes; add brandy and flame.
3. Wait two minutes; add vermouth, water and lemon juice and stir; cook for five minutes.
Serve over toast.

—L.S. "Lee" Smith
New Iberia (Iberia Parish)

STUFFED SHRIMP

—1 cup of oil
—1 cup of chopped onion
—1 cup of chopped bellpepper
—1 cup of chopped celery
—1 pound of crab meat
—Salt and pepper, to taste
—Breadcrumbs
—1 pound of large shrimp, peeled (leave on tips of tails and last segment of shells)
—2 eggs
—1 cup of evaporated milk
—Corn flour
—Oil for frying

1. Saute in oil the onion, bellpepper and celery until tender.
2. Add crab meat, seasonings, a small amount of water and breadcrumbs to make a stiff dressing.
3. "Butterfly" shrimp by making a vertical cut in the back; stuff center with mixture, squeezing shrimp in hand to form a croquette. Freeze shrimp.
4. Mix eggs and evaporated milk; dip frozen shrimp into egg-milk mixture, then into corn flour.
5. Fry while frozen in deep oil until brown.

Note: Crabs and flounder can be stuffed with the same dressing.

—Mrs. Amelie Naquin
New Iberia (Iberia Parish)

SHRIMP ETOUFFEE I

- 2 large onions, chopped fine
- 1 large bellpepper, chopped fine
- ¼ pound of oleo
- 2 pounds of shrimp, peeled and deveined
- Green onions
- Salt and pepper, to taste

1. Saute onions and bellpepper in oleo until tender.
2. Stir-in shrimp; cook at medium heat until shrimp are done, 10 to 15 minutes. Add a small amount of water, as needed.
3. Add green onions; cook about five minutes. Season with salt and pepper. Serve over rice.

—Mrs. Libby Morell
Morgan City (St. Mary Parish)

SHRIMP ETOUFFEE II

- 1 medium onion, finely chopped
- 2 green onions, finely chopped
- 3 or 4 garlic cloves, minced
- ¼ cup of chopped celery
- ½ cup of butter
- 2 tablespoons of flour
- 2 ½ cups of water
- 1 10½-ounce can of tomato juice
- 1 tablespoon of worcestershire sauce
- Hot pepper sauce
- 1 teaspoon of salt
- 1 pound (3 cups) of cleaned raw shrimp

1. In a large skillet, saute onion, green onions, garlic and celery in butter until tender; add flour and cook and stir until lightly browned.
2. Add water, tomato juice, worcestershire sauce, hot pepper sauce and salt; simmer uncovered, stirring occasionally 25 minutes or until sauce is nearly of desired consistency.
3. Add shrimp and continue cooking 15 minutes.

Serve with parsley rice.
Serves four to six.

—Audie Watson
Egan (Acadia Parish)

SHRIMP AND CRAB MEAT ETOUFFEE

- 4 cups of onions, chopped
- ¼ pound of oleo
- 1 pound of shrimp, peeled and de-veined
- ½ pound of crab meat
- ½ cup of celery, chopped
- ½ cup of green onions, chopped
- 1 tablespoon of cornstarch
- ½ cup of water
- Salt and pepper, to taste
- ½ cup of parsley, chopped
- Cooked rice

1. Saute onions in oleo until brown; add shrimp and cook until done, about 10 minutes.
2. Add crab meat, celery, green onions, cornstarch and water; mix well.
3. Season to taste and cook 10 minutes more. Garnish with parsley. Serve over rice.

Makes six servings.

—Mrs. Luciella Gautreaux
Labadieville (Assumption Parish)

FRIED SHRIMP

–1 cup of all-purpose flour
–½ teaspoon of sugar
–½ teaspoon of salt
–1 slightly beaten egg
–1 cup of ice water (leave 1 or 2 cubes in)
–2 tablespoons of oil
–2 pounds of fresh, frozen shrimp, unpeeled

1. Combine ingredients, except shrimp; stir until smooth, then set in refrigerator or freezer to chill.
2. Peel shells from shrimp, leaving tail intact; "butterfly" shrimp by cutting lengthwise to tail.
3. Dry shrimp, dip into batter, fry in deep hot fat (350 to 400 degrees) till floating and golden brown (three to five minutes). Serve immediately.

Also good for frying soft- and hard-shelled crabs, eggplants, onions, etc.

—Carolyn Harper
Grand Chenier (Cameron Parish)

SHRIMP IN CRAB MEAT SAUCE

–3 large onions, chopped
–5 garlic cloves, minced
–½ pound of oleo
–1 quart of water
–Salt and pepper, to taste
–Hot pepper sauce
–2 cups of white wine
–2 cans of sliced mushrooms
–1/3 cup of soy sauce
–2 tablespoons of cornstarch
–2 pounds of peeled shrimp
–1 pound of white crab meat

1. Saute onions and garlic in oleo; add water, salt, pepper, hot pepper sauce, one cup of the wine, mushrooms, soy sauce and cornstarch (which has been diluted with a small amount of water).
2. Bring to a slow boil, add shrimp and crab meat and cook on medium heat for 20 to 25 minutes; add remaining cup of wine, stir and taste for seasoning. Remove from heat.
3. Let set for 10 minutes before serving.
Serves six.

—Eugene D. "Doc" Lanier
Lafayette (Lafayette Parish)

SHRIMP NEWBURG

–¾ pound of shrimp, cooked, cleaned and peeled
–¼ cup of butter or other fat
–2 tablespoons of flour
–¾ teaspoon of salt
–Dash of cayenne pepper
–Dash of nutmeg
–1½ cups of coffee cream
–2 egg yolks, beaten
–2 tablespoons of sherry
–Toast points

1. Cut large shrimp in half.
2. Melt butter; blend-in flour and seasonings.
3. Add cream gradually and cook until thick and smooth, two or three minutes, stirring constantly.
4. Stir a little of the sauce while still hot into egg yolks; add to remaining sauce, stirring constantly.
5. Add shrimp, and heat.
6. Remove from heat and slowly stir-in sherry. Serve immediately on toast points.
Serves six.

—Mrs. Irene Clause
Labadieville (Assumption Parish)

SHRIMP AND FLOUNDER

–2 pounds of peeled raw shrimp
–2 large onions
–1 bellpepper
–3 celery ribs
–3 green onions
–6 sprigs of parsley
–2/3 cup of cooking oil
–Salt, to taste
–Pepper, to taste
–Hot pepper sauce, to taste
–1½ cups of breadcrumbs
–2 large flounders, deboned
–4 tablespoons of oleo

1. Grind shrimp, onions, bellpepper, celery, green onions and parsley.
2. Heat cooking oil over medium heat, adding mixture and stirring often so it won't stick; cook one-half hour.
3. Remove from heat; add salt, pepper, hot pepper sauce and breadcrumbs.
4. Pile stuffing into flounders; raise sides, push into pockets with spoon and pack until all is used.
5. Place oleo over flounders and cover with foil.
6. Bake for 45 minutes covered and 15 minutes with foil removed in oven preheated to 375 degrees.
7. Re-cover with foil until ready to serve. (Covering keeps it moist.)

Note: Filling can be used to fill eight big bellpeppers.

—Mrs. Dot Detillier
Raceland (Lafourche Parish)

SHRIMP PIE

–1 medium onion, chopped
–1 medium bellpepper, chopped
–4 garlic cloves, minced
–3 small ribs of celery, chopped
–¼ pound of oleo
–2 pounds of peeled raw shrimp
–2 heaping tablespoons of flour
–1 can of mushroom soup
–1 small can of mushrooms (optional)
–Salt, to taste
–Red pepper, to taste
–½ cup of chopped green onion tops (optional)
–1 9-inch unbaked double pie crust

1. Wilt onion, bellpepper, garlic and celery in oleo.
2. Cut shrimp into bite-size pieces; add shrimp and cook until pink, five to ten minutes.
3. Add flour; blend and add soup (plus one small can of mushrooms, if desired), salt, pepper and green onion tops.
4. Simmer about 10 minutes; pour into crust and cover with top crust.
5. Bake at 400 degrees about 30 minutes or until crust is golden brown.

—Elza Stewart
Jennings (Jefferson Davis Parish)

SHRIMP STROGANOFF

–2 onions, minced
–¼ pound of butter
–1 to 2 pounds of raw shrimp, peeled and de-veined
–2 tablespoons of flour
–1 teaspoon of salt
–¼ teaspoon of red pepper
–1 garlic clove, mashed
–1 4-ounce can of button mushrooms, drained
–1 can of cream of mushroom soup
–1 cup of sour cream
–Hot rice
–½ cup of chives, chopped

1. Saute onions in butter until golden brown.
2. Add shrimp and cook until pink, about 10 minutes; stir-in flour and mix well.
3. Add salt, pepper, garlic, mushrooms and soup; simmer 15 to 20 minutes.
4. Add sour cream just before serving over hot rice. Garnish with chives.
Serves four to six.

—Hazel Delahoussaye
New Iberia (Iberia Parish)

SHRIMP BURGERS

–2 cups of fresh shrimp, peeled
–1 dozen sprigs of parsley
–1 medium onion, chopped
–1 medium bellpepper, chopped
–2 ribs of celery, chopped
–10 green onion tops, chopped
–2 eggs
–3 slices of stale bread, soaked in water
–½ cup of Italian-flavored breadcrumbs
–Salt and pepper, to taste
–1 tablespoon of garlic salt
–Flour
–Oil

1. Grind shrimp with parsley, onion, bellpepper, celery and onion tops.
2. Mix with eggs, soaked bread (squeeze water out) and breadcrumbs. Add seasoning, to taste.
3. Shape into burgers. Roll in flour and fry in one-half inch of oil. Cook on medium heat until brown.
Makes 12 large burgers.

—Mrs. S. E. Curole
Larose (Lafourche Parish)

SHRIMP CROQUETTES I

–1 tablespoon of butter or oleo
–1 tablespoons of flour
–¼ cup of milk or water
–1 cup of cooked shrimp, chopped
–1 teaspoon of lemon juice
–½ teaspoon of salt
–1/8 teaspoon of pepper
–Breadcrumbs
–1 egg
–1 tablespoon of cold milk

1. Make a cream sauce with butter, flour and milk.
2. Add shrimp, lemon juice, salt and pepper; mix with fork till well-blended, then refrigerate.
3. When cold, mold into desired shapes; roll in breadcrumbs, then in egg beaten with one tablespoon of cold milk, and again in breadcrumbs.
4. Fry in deep fat at 385 degrees until brown.
Serves four.

—Colette Foret
Lutcher (St. James Parish)

SHRIMP CROQUETTES II

- –1 quart of peeled and deveined shrimp
- –½ cup of chopped onions
- –½ cup of chopped parsley
- –½ cup of chopped bellpepper
- –2 eggs
- –2 tablespoons of flour
- –½ cup of breadcrumbs
- –Salt and pepper, to taste
- –Oil for frying

1. Grind shrimp in meat grinder or blender.
2. Combine shrimp and other ingredients; season, to taste.
3. Drop by the spoonful into hot oil; fry until brown on both sides.

Serves six.

—Mrs. Camille Delorette
Plattenville (Assumption Parish)

SHRIMP CASSEROLE

- –1 pound of boiled shrimp, peeled
- –2 cups of chopped celery
- –½ cup of canned chestnuts, sliced
- –2 boiled eggs, chopped
- –2 tablespoons of grated onion
- –¾ cup of mayonnaise
- –2 tablespoons of lemon juice
- –½ teaspoon of salt
- –½ cup of grated cheese
- –1 cup of crushed potato chips

1. Combine first five ingredients.
2. Mix mayonnaise, lemon juice and salt; stir into mixture.
3. Pour in baking dish and top with cheese and potato chips.
4. Bake uncovered at 400 degrees for 20 to 25 minutes.

—Mrs. Marilyn Hebert
Crowley (Acadia Parish)

SHRIMP BOULETTES

- –1 can of cream of shrimp soup
- –1 medium bellpepper, grated
- –2 tablespoons of minced onion tops
- –2 tablespoons of minced parsley
- –3½ cups of breadcrumbs
- –½ teaspoon of worcestershire sauce
- –1 teaspoon of Creole seasoning
- –Hot pepper sauce, to taste
- –Red pepper and black pepper, to taste
- –2 cups of chopped cooked shrimp
- –Breadcrumbs
- –3 eggs, beaten
- –Oil

1. Mix first ten ingredients in a mixing bowl. Shape mixture into boulettes.
2. Roll boulettes in breadcrumbs, dip in beaten eggs and then again in breadcrumbs. Place boulettes on a tray and chill until firm.
3. Reshape boulettes, roll in breadcrumbs and fry in hot fat until golden brown, or approximately three to five minutes.

Makes eight boulettes.

—Suzanne Lognion
Opelousas (St. Landry Parish)

OYSTER PIE I

- 4 tablespoons of flour
- 4 tablespoons of bacon drippings
- ¾ cup of chopped green onions
- 1 cup of oyster water
- 1¾ cups of oysters
- 1/3 cup of chopped parsley
- Salt and red pepper
- 2 9-inch unbaked pie shells
- 2 tablespoons of cream
- 2 tablespoons of oleo

1. Make a light roux with flour and bacon drippings; add green onions and cook until wilted.
2. Add oyster water and let boil; add oysters and cook until oysters begin to curl.
3. Add parsley, salt and red pepper; remove from fire.
4. Place contents in unbaked pie shell; top with second pie shell, prick and brush with cream and oleo.
5. Bake in preheated oven at 450 degrees for ten minutes; lower temperature to 350 degrees and bake for 30 minutes longer.

Serves four.

—Josie Chauvin
Norco (St. Charles Parish)

OYSTER PIE II

- French bread
- 2 jars of oysters, drained (save juice)
- 2 pounds of ground pork
- 3 pounds of ground beef
- 2 medium onions, chopped
- 1 cup of parsley, chopped
- Green onions (optional)
- Double Pie Crust (Recipe follows)

1. Soak about six inches of bread in oyster juice.
2. Cook pork, beef and onions in covered pan until grease is gone (about one hour).
3. Add parsley, oysters and soaked bread; mix well.
4. Place in prepared pie crust; top with second crust.
5. Bake at 350 degrees for 45 minutes to one hour.

DOUBLE PIE CRUST

- 2 cups of sifted regular flour
- ¾ cup of shortening
- 1 teaspoon of onion salt
- ¾ cup of cold water

1. Cut flour into shortening; add onion salt and water; mix well.
2. Divide into two balls; roll each to fit pie plate. Fit one in bottom of pie plate.

Serve with cranberry sauce.

—Shirley Faucheux
Paulina (St. James Parish)

OYSTERS EN BROCHETTE

- 1 or 2 large onions
- 2 apples
- 1 large bellpepper
- 2 ribs of celery
- 1 dozen oysters
- 1 pound of bacon
- Salt and pepper

1. Cut onions and apples into wedges; cut bellpepper into large strips; cut celery into two-inch sticks.
2. Wrap oysters in bacon.
3. Arrange onion, apple, celery, bellpepper and oysters on skewers. Salt and pepper, to taste.
4. Bake at 300 degrees until brown, about 20 to 30 minutes.

Makes four skewers.

—Mrs. Rose Broussard
Lafayette Parish

OYSTER AND SAUSAGE JAMBALAYA

—2 tablespoons of butter or oleo
—1 cup of chopped lean baked ham
—1 pound of lean pork, cut into cubes
—1 cup of chopped onions
—½ cup of chopped celery
—¼ cup of chopped bellpepper
—3 garlic cloves, minced
—1½ pounds of smoked sausage, fried and cut into ¼-inch slices
—2 teaspoons of salt
—1 teaspoon of monosodium glutamate
—½ teaspoon of cayenne pepper
—1 tablespoon of worcestershire sauce
—½ teaspoon of chili powder
—½ teaspoon of thyme
—1½ cups of raw long-grain rice
—3 cups of beef stock or 3 bouillon cubes dissolved in 3 cups of water
—1 pint of oysters, drained

1. In a heavy eight-quart pot, melt butter or oleo over low heat. Add ham, pork, onion, celery, bellpepper and garlic. Brown over low heat 15 minutes.
2. Add sausage slices and seasonings; mix thoroughly. Continue cooking for 20 minutes over low heat, stirring occasionally.
3. Add rice; cook five minutes over medium heat, scraping pot often. Add beef stock and oysters; mix gently.
4. Bring to a boil; cook uncovered five minutes; lower heat to low; cover and cook for 50 minutes; stirring occasionally to prevent sticking. Serves six.

—Mrs. Youngs Foreman
Indian Bayou (Vermilion Parish)

STUFFED OYSTERS

—1 pound of country-style sausage, crumbled
—1 pint of oysters, drained and chopped
—½ cup of minced parsley
—½ cup of chopped green onion tops
—4 hamburger or hot dog buns, dried in oven and crumbled
—4 tablespoons of butter or oleo
—Juice of one-half lemon
—Seasoned breadcrumbs
—12 to 14 medium-size oyster shells, cleaned and boiled for a few minutes

1. Brown sausage in a lightly greased fry pan.
2. Add oysters, parsley and green onion tops; cook 10 minutes.
3. Stir-in crumbled buns, butter and lemon juice; blend well. (Add some oyster juice if stuffing is not moist enough.)
4. Stuff into oyster shells; sprinkle with breadcrumbs.
5. Bake in a shallow pan at 250 degrees for 25 to 30 minutes.

Note: Do not add any other seasonings.

—LSU Cooperative Extension Service,
Terrebonne Parish

BROCCOLI AND OYSTERS AU GRATIN

- 1 package of frozen chopped broccoli
- 3 cups of cooked rice
- 1 pint of oysters, drained
- ¾ cup of sour cream
- 2 tablespoons of catsup
- ¼ cup of milk
- 2 teaspoons of sherry
- 2 teaspoons of lemon juice
- 1 teaspoon of cream-style horseradish
- 1½ teaspoons of worcestershire sauce
- 6 to 8 drops of hot pepper sauce
- 1½ teaspoons of onion salt
- ½ cup of buttered breadcrumbs

1. Cook broccoli; drain; toss lightly with rice.
2. Spoon into a greased casserole.
3. Arrange oysters on rice mixture.
4. Combine remaining ingredients except breadcrumbs and pour over oysters.
5. Sprinkle with the breadcrumbs. Bake uncovered at 350 degrees for 20 minutes.

Serves six.

—Martha Fontenot
Cameron (Cameron Parish)

BROILED OYSTERS

- 2 dozen oysters
- ¾ cup of chopped green onions
- 8 to 10 slices of bacon, fried crisp and crumbled
- 1 can of chopped mushrooms, drained
- ½ to ¾ cup of Parmesan cheese
- Salt, red pepper, black pepper and garlic powder, to taste
- 2 cups of grated Mozzarella cheese (approximately)

1. Lay oysters in the bottom of a skillet with a small amount of bacon grease. Broil until edges curl, about five minutes. Watch carefully!
2. Add green onions; return to broiler and broil until onions get hot, but not cooked.
3. Sprinkle evenly with bacon crumbs, mushrooms, Parmesan cheese and seasonings, to taste. Top with Mozzarella cheese.
4. Return to broiler until hot and cheese is melted.

—Mrs. Louise Watson
Napoleonville (Assumption Parish)

CRAWFISH- AND CRAB-STUFFED PEPPERS

- 8 to 10 medium bellpeppers
- 1 pound of peeled crawfish
- 1½ cups of chopped onions
- 1 cup of chopped celery
- 1 cup of crab meat (or 1 can of crab meat, drained)
- Salt and pepper
- 1½ cups of Italian breadcrumbs
- 1¼ cups of water

1. Cut tops off bellpeppers and clean; par-boil for 10 minutes.
2. Saute crawfish, onions and celery in oil (crawfish fat can be added here) until vegetables are tender; add crab meat, season to taste and cook five minutes.
3. Remove mixture from heat and gradually add breadcrumbs.
4. Stuff peppers with mixture; add water to bottom of baking dish and bake for 40 minutes at 375 degrees.

—Mrs. Mary Bell
New Iberia (Iberia Parish)

CREPE RICETTES

- –1 tablespoon of cooked rice
- –1¼ cups of flour
- –1½ cups of milk
- –2 eggs
- –2 tablespoons of sour cream
- –1/8 teaspoon of salt
- –Rice-Shrimp Filling (Recipe follows)
- –Sour Cream Sauce (Recipe follows)

1. Mix rice, flour, milk, eggs, sour cream and salt in blender for 45 seconds. For best results, let batter set for two hours.
2. To cook crepes, pour three tablespoons of batter into a greased and heated crepe pan or small skillet. Cook until done on one side. (It is not necessary to cook crepes on both sides.) Crepe should be light and thin.
3. To assemble crepes, place a small amount of the Rice-Shrimp Filling on each crepe. Fold crepes around filling.
4. Serve with Sour Cream Sauce on top of each crepe.

RICE-SHRIMP FILLING

- –1 cup of cooked rice
- –¾ cup of boiled, chopped shrimp
- –1/3 cup of chopped onions
- –1/3 cup of chopped pickles
- –1 egg, boiled and chopped
- –1 tablespoon of lemon juice
- –2 tablespoons of mayonnaise
- –Salt and pepper, to taste

1. Mix all ingredients for filling in a large bowl.
2. Place in refrigerator until ready to serve.

SOUR CREAM SAUCE

- –8 ounces of sour cream
- –4 tablespoons of vinegar
- –2 teaspoons of sugar
- –½ teaspoon of salt

1. Beat all ingredients for sauce until smooth and creamy.
2. Refrigerate until ready to serve.

—Penny Winston
New Iberia (Iberia Parish)

STUFFED TOMATOES

- –6 large firm tomatoes
- –1 medium onion, chopped
- –½ cup of chopped celery
- –1 garlic clove, chopped
- –¼ cup of chopped bellpepper
- –2 tablespoons of oil
- –1 5-ounce can of shrimp
- –6 to 8 slices of stale french bread
- –Salt and pepper, to taste
- –Parsley
- –½ cup of buttered breadcrumbs

1. Wash tomatoes; remove a thin slice from the stem end and carefully scoop out pulp.
2. Saute the tomato pulp, onion, celery, garlic and bellpepper in oil until transparent; add shrimp and mix well with seasoning.
3. Dampen bread with a little warm water, enough to crumble well, and add to mixture; cook until well-blended. Salt and pepper, to taste. Add parsley.
4. Fill the tomato cup with the stuffing; cover with buttered breadcrumbs and bake in a moderate oven in a greased baking dish for 30 minutes.

Note: Fresh shrimp or oysters may be used in place of canned shrimp.

—Mrs. William P. Gilbert
Lafourche Parish

STUFFED MIRILITONS OR EGGPLANTS

- —4 mirlitons or eggplants
- —1 cup of soft breadcrumbs
- —1 large onion, finely chopped (or 3 or 4 green onions, chopped)
- —1 garlic clove, minced
- —3 tablespoons of oleo
- —Salt, to taste
- —Black pepper or red pepper, to taste
- —1 teaspoon of chopped parsley
- —1 sprig of thyme
- —½ pound of shrimp, coarsely chopped
- —½ cup of buttered breadcrumbs or seasoned Italian breadcrumbs

1. Simmer mirlitons in salted water until tender. Cut each in half, remove seeds and carefully spoon out pulp. Reserve shells. Chop pulp; add breadcrumbs.
2. Saute onion and garlic in oleo over medium heat until tender (five minutes).
3. Stir-in pulp, salt and pepper; continue cooking for five minutes, stirring often.
4. Add parsley, thyme and shrimp; mix thoroughly. Cook about 10 minutes.
5. Fill shells and cover with breadcrumbs. Bake in oven 375 degrees about five minutes.

Serves eight.

—Mrs. P. J. Aucoin Jr.
Thibodaux (Lafourche Parish)

SEAFOOD DELIGHT

- —1 package of frozen broccoli
- —1 can of cream of mushroom soup
- —½ cup of milk
- —1½ cups of shrimp, cooked and peeled
- —1 cup of crab meat (or lobster)
- —1 tablespoon of sherry
- —Salt and pepper, to taste
- —2 teaspoons of Parmesan cheese
- —Paprika
- —¼ cup of breadcrumbs

1. Cook broccoli according to directions on package; drain and place in a greased casserole.
2. Blend soup and milk; heat. Add shrimp, crab meat, sherry and seasonings; heat for a few minutes.
3. Spoon soup mixture over broccoli; sprinkle with cheese, paprika and breadcrumbs.
4. Bake at 375 degrees for 25 minutes until brown.

—Mrs. Olin Desonier
Franklin (St. Mary Parish)

BAKED EGGPLANT WITH SHRIMP

- —4 medium eggplants, peeled and cubed
- —2 pounds of raw shrimp, peeled
- —1 onion, chopped
- —5 tablespoons of oil
- —1 egg, beaten
- —Salt and pepper, to taste
- —Breadcrumbs

1. Boil eggpant until tender; drain.
2. Saute shrimp and onion in oil; add to boiled eggplant.
3. Add egg and seasonings to the eggplant. (This keeps the eggplant from turning dark.)
4. Heat a few minutes then put in baking dish; sprinkle with breadcrumbs.
5. Bake uncovered at 350 degrees for 10 minutes.

—Celine Oubre
Garyville (St. John the Baptist Parish)

SHRIMP/EGGPLANT DRESSING OR CASSEROLE

–2 to 3 eggplants
–Hot water
–Salt
–1 cup of water
–Red pepper and black pepper
–1 pound of peeled shrimp, cut up
–Oleo
–1 medium onion, chopped
–½ cup of chopped celery
–1 medium bellpepper, chopped
–5 cups of cooked rice
–Breadcrumbs

1. Peel and cut up eggplants (throw away seeds if large); put in hot water with a little salt and soak for 30 minutes (throw away this water).
2. Put eggplant in pot with one cup of water and cook down, leaving some liquid to help moisten dressing; set aside.
3. Season shrimp; saute in a small amount of oleo until shrimp turn pink, about 10 minutes, and set aside.
4. Saute onion, celery and bellpepper in more oleo and add to shrimp; combine shrimp mixture, eggplant and rice, mixing well.
5. Pour into a buttered baking dish; sprinkle top with breadcrumbs.
6. Bake uncovered for 25 to 30 minutes at 350 degrees.

Note: Great for stuffing bellpeppers and tomato shells. Sauted seasoned ground beef can be substituted for shrimp.

—Ellis Cormier
Jennings (Jefferson Davis Parish)

CAJUN COUNTRY CASSEROLE

–4 ounces of creamcheese
–4 tablespoons of butter
–1 pound of cleaned shrimp
–1 cup of chopped onions
–½ cup of chopped bellpepper
–½ cup of chopped celery
–1 can of golden mushroom soup
–1/4 cup of pimentos
–1 tablespoon of garlic salt
–1 teaspoon of hot pepper sauce
–½ teaspoon of red pepper
–1 pint of crab meat
–2 cups of cooked rice
–½ cup of buttered breadcrumbs
–1/4 cup of grated cheddar cheese

1. Melt creamcheese and two tablespoons of butter in double boiler.
2. Melt remaining two tablespoons of butter in skillet and saute shrimp until they turn pink, in 10 to 15 minutes.
3. Add vegetables and continue to saute until vegetables are slightly wilted.
4. Add melted creamcheese, butter and soup; mix well.
5. Add pimentoes, seasonings, crab meat and rice; mix well and place in a two-quart casserole.
6. Top with breadcrumbs and cheddar cheese.
7. Bake uncovered at 350 degrees 20 to 30 minutes until bubbly; garnish with cherry tomatoes and parsley.
Serves eight.

—Shari Beard
Sweetlake (Cameron Parish)

SEAFOOD CASSEROLE

- 3 tablespoons of butter
- 2 tablespoons of flour
- 2 cups of milk
- 3 eggs, well-beaten
- 1 teaspoon of salt
- Dash of nutmeg
- ¼ cup of sherry
- 1 dozen fresh oysters
- 2 cups of shrimp, peeled and de-veined
- 1 cup of crab meat
- ½ cup of breadcrumbs
- Parsley, chopped
- Paprika

1. Melt butter; add flour, milk, eggs, salt and nutmeg, stirring well. Cook until thick; add sherry. Set aside.
2. Mix oysters, shrimp and crab meat together in a two and a half-quart casserole dish; pour above sauce over seafood.
3. Sprinkle with breadcrumbs, parsley and paprika.
4. Bake uncovered at 325 degrees for 25 minutes.

Note: Oysters may be omitted, in which case more shrimp should be added.

—Mrs. Oscar Prejean
Lafourche Parish

CASSEROLE SPECIAL

- 1 can of crab meat
- 1 pound of raw shrimp, chopped
- 2 medium-size eggplants, boiled and chopped
- 1 large onion, diced
- 1 large bellpepper, chopped
- 1 8-ounce carton of sour cream
- Salt, pepper and hot sauce, to taste
- 1 cup of grated cheddar cheese
- 1 package of plain crackers, crumbled

1. Mix together crab meat, shrimp eggplants, onion, bellpepper, sour cream and seasonings.
2. In a buttered casserole dish, alternate layers of above mixture with grated cheese and cracker crumbs two or three times.
3. Bake uncovered at 400 degrees for about 25 minutes.

—Mrs. Al Fusilier
Ville Platte (Evangeline Parish)

SEAFOOD-CHEESE CASSEROLE

- 1 onion, chopped
- 1 small bellpepper, chopped
- 1 cup of chopped green onions
- 1 rib of celery, chopped
- ¼ pound of butter
- 1 cup of oysters
- 1 pound of shrimp, peeled and de-veined
- ¾ pound of Velveeta cheese
- 1 small can of evaporated milk
- 1 can of lump crab meat
- 1 cup of breadcrumbs
- Salt, red pepper and black pepper, to taste

1. Saute onion, bellpepper, onion tops and celery in butter; add oysters and shrimp and simmer water out of them.
2. Melt cheese in milk; add to mixture.
3. Fold-in crab meat; season to taste and pour into casserole.
4. Top with breadcrumbs; bake for 20 minutes at 350 degrees.

—Mrs. Roland J. Trosclair Jr.
Cameron (Cameron Parish)

Wild Game

CONTENTS

ALLIGATOR SAUCE PIQUANTE

–½ cup of flour
–1 cup of cooking oil
–1 large onion, chopped
–1 garlic clove, chopped
–½ bellpepper, chopped
–1 large can of tomatoes
–1 can of tomato sauce
–3 cups of water
–1 pound of alligator, cut into one-inch cubes
–Salt and pepper, to taste
–½ cup of onion tops, chopped

1. Cook flour in oil until medium brown; add onion and cook until onion wilts.
2. Add garlic, bellpepper, tomatoes, tomato sauce and water. Cook over low heat for 30 minutes.
3. Add meat, salt and pepper and onion tops; continue cooking until meat is tender, about 30 to 45 minutes.

—John Prescott
Johnson Bayou (Cameron Parish)

FRIED ALLIGATOR

–1 5-pound piece of alligator tail, rinsed and chopped into pieces
–1 small bottle of hot pepper sauce
–½ teaspoon of salt
–Juice of 2 or 3 lemons
–½ cup of water
–1 potato, boiled
–1 small bellpepper
–1 garlic clove
–Salt and pepper, to taste

1. Marinate alligator in hot pepper sauce, salt, lemon juice and just enough water to cover; place in refrigerator for 48 hours.
2. Drain.
3. Grind alligator with potato, bellpepper, garlic, salt and pepper.
4. Form into patties.
5. Drop into hot oil until golden brown.

Note: Instead of grinding, pieces may be rolled in flour or cornmeal and fried.

—Roland Perry
Cameron (Cameron Parish)

ALLIGATOR MEATBALLS

–2 pounds of alligator tail, ground
–2 teaspoons of salt
–1 teaspoon of red pepper
–1 egg, beaten
–¼ cup of milk
–½ cup of breadcrumbs
–Juice of one lemon
–½ cup of chopped green onions
–2 tablespoons of chopped parsley
–1 cup of flour
–1 cup of cornmeal

1. Mix alligator with salt, red pepper, egg, milk, breadcrumbs, lemon juice, green onions and parsley. Shape into small balls.
2. Mix flour and cornmeal; roll alligator meatballs in mixture and fry in deep fat at 350 degrees until brown.

—Mrs. Roland Primeaux
Creole (Cameron Parish)

ALLIGATOR STEW

–½ cup of cooking oil
–1 quart of alligator meat, cut in small pieces about ½-inch thick
–½ cup of chopped onions
–½ cup of chopped green onions
–½ cup of chopped bellpeppers or banana peppers
–½ cup of chopped celery
–2 tablespoons of minced parsley
–1 10-ounce can of Rotel tomatoes
–Salt and pepper, to taste

1. Put oil and alligator meat in pot and brown lightly; add chopped vegetables, minced parsley and Rotel tomatoes and season to taste with salt and pepper.
2. Cover pot and cook over medium heat for 30 to 40 minutes, stirring occasionally.

—Mrs. Charles W. Hebert
Sweet Lake (Cameron Parish)

POT-ROASTED DOVES

–12 doves
–Salt, garlic powder and pepper, to taste
–½ cup of oil
–2 large onions, chopped
–1½ cups of water
–1 bunch of green onion tops, chopped

1. Season doves with salt, garlic powder and pepper; brown in oil.
2. Add onions and saute until wilted; add water and cook until doves are tender, 30 to 45 minutes.
3. Add green onion tops and serve over rice.
Serves six.

—Manning "Pete" Broussard
Lafayette (Lafayette Parish)

DOVE A LA PAPIOT

–12 dove or quail
–Salt
–Pepper
–3 onions, chopped
–Parsley, chopped
–Onion tops, chopped
–2 bellpeppers, chopped
–1½ pounds of sausage
–12 bacon strips
–Cooking sherry

1. Clean birds and season well with salt and pepper.
2. Fill cavities with onion, parsley, onion tops and bellpepper.
3. Cut sausage into small pieces and add this to birds' cavities.
4. Wrap birds with bacon strips and bake at 375 degrees for 60 to 65 minutes, applying sherry sparingly over birds every 15 minutes.

—Betty Andrepont
St. Landry Parish

ROASTED DUCK

–2 ducks
–Salt and pepper, to taste
–½ cup of orange juice
–2 onions, chopped
–1 cup of chopped celery
–1 cup of wine

1. Season ducks inside and out with salt and pepper; mix orange juice with onions and celery.
2. Stuff ducks with the mixture and bake at 400 degrees, basting with wine, until ducks are tender, an hour and a half or two, depending on size.
Serves six.

—Irvin Arceneaux
Jennings (Jefferson Davis Parish)

SMOTHERED DOVES I

- —12 young doves, washed and dried
- —Salt, black pepper and red pepper, to taste
- —12 slices of bacon
- —½ cup of chopped onion
- —½ cup of water

1. Season doves with salt and pepper.
2. Wrap each dove individually with a slice of bacon and secure with a toothpick through the breast.
3. Brown slowly in a heavy roasting pan; remove from pan.
4. Saute onion until soft and slightly brown in pan; add water.
5. Return doves to pan; cover tightly and simmer two hours, turning once. Add additional water in small amounts as needed.

Serves four to six.

—Mrs. Stephen "Gaynell" Ardizone
Jeanerette (Iberia Parish)

SMOTHERED DOVES II

- —1 garlic clove, chopped
- —4 stalks of celery, chopped
- —5 medium onions, chopped
- —4 green onions, chopped
- —½ bunch of parsley, chopped
- —½ pound of butter
- —Salt, pepper, cayenne pepper
- —14 to 16 dove
- —7 or 8 slices of bacon
- —2 large cans of mushrooms with juice
- —1 can of consomme
- —1 bay leaf
- —Gravy flour

1. Into a large pot put the chopped garlic, celery, onions, green onions, parsley and butter; simmer over low heat.
2. Salt and pepper the doves; stuff each with one-half slice of bacon.
3. Place doves in pot; add mushrooms with juice, consomme and bay leaf.
4. Cover and cook on a low heat one hour and 45 minutes; remove cover and thicken gravy with flour.
5. Serve over rice.

—Mrs. John Prescott
Johnson Bayou (Cameron Parish)

SOLID GOLD DUCK

- —2 wild ducks
- —2 cups of wine
- —Salt and pepper, to taste
- —1 cup of chopped onion
- —½ cup of chopped bellpepper
- —½ cup of chopped celery
- —1 cup of diced potatoes
- —1 box of frozen mustard greens (or chopped spinach)
- —2 tablespoons of butter
- —Bacon slices
- —1 cup of orange juice

1. Marinate ducks overnight in wine (wine vinegar and salt may be used instead).
2. Salt and pepper ducks inside and out.
3. Saute onion, bellpepper, celery, potato and mustard greens in butter; stuff cavity of ducks.
4. Brush ducks with additional butter and lay bacon slices over breasts; place in heavy pot, breasts up.
5. Bake covered at 300 degrees for two hours, basting every 15 minutes with orange juice; remove cover during the last 15 minutes to brown bacon.

—Dezere M. Richard
Sweetlake (Calcasieu Parish)

WILD DUCK SAUCE PIQUANTE I

–3 wild ducks, cut into serving pieces
–¾ cup of olive oil
–1 small bottle of worcestershire sauce
–4 large onions, finely chopped
–1 large bellpepper, finely chopped
–5 stalks of celery, finely chopped
–5 to 6 garlic cloves, minced
–1 large bunch of green onions, chopped
–1 bunch of parsley, minced
–½ cup of diced ham
–¾ bottle of cooking sauterne
–5 ground artichokes, peeled and sliced (or 5 to 6 turnips, cubed; or 1 small can of water chestnuts, drained and sliced)
–Salt, black pepper, red pepper and hot pepper sauce, to taste

1. Soak ducks overnight in a solution of vinegar and water.
2. Brown seasoned ducks in olive oil; add worcestershire sauce, chopped vegetables and about one-half of the green onions and parsley. Stir well and cook slowly until vegetables are wilted.
3. Add ham, sauterne and about four cups of boiling water; cover and cook over low heat until tender, about one and one-half hours.
4. Add ground artichokes about 45 minutes before ducks are done; if using turnips, add about 30 minutes before ducks are done; and if using water chestnuts, add just before serving.
5. Add remaining green onions and parsley just before serving.

—Matt and Sarah Vernon
Eunice (St. Landry Parish)

WILD DUCK SAUCE PIQUANTE II

–3 ducks, cut in serving pieces
–Lemon juice
–Worcestershire sauce
–Vinegar
–Hot pepper sauce
–Season salt
–4 onions, finely chopped
–Oil
–1 bellpepper, finely chopped
–4 celery stalks, finely chopped
–1 8-ounce can of tomato sauce
–1 6-ounce can of tomato paste
–5 garlic cloves, minced
–1 bunch of green onions, chopped
–1 bunch of parsley, chopped
–1 can of mixed vegetables, drained
–1 can of cream of mushroom soup
–1 can of mushrooms

1. Sprinkle ducks with lemon juice, worcestershire sauce, vinegar, hot pepper sauce and season salt, and marinate overnight.
2. Saute onions in a heavy iron pot in a small amount of oil until wilted; add bellpepper, celery, tomato sauce, tomato paste and enough water to keep it from sticking.
3. Cook covered for about two and one-half hours, stirring often to prevent sticking.
4. In another skillet, brown ducks in a small amount of oil; add the ducks to the tomato gravy.
5. Cook slowly for one and one-half hours; add remaining ingredients and simmer until ducks are tender.
6. Season to taste and serve over rice.

—Hilman "Buster" Matherne
Luling (St. Charles Parish)

WILD DUCK AND OYSTER GUMBO

(For those who don't like "wild" taste).

- 4 teal or 2 large ducks, skinned and quartered
- 3 to 4 quarts of boiling water
- ¾ cup of oil
- ¾ cup of flour
- 1 large onion, chopped fine
- 3 quarts of water
- 2 tablespoons of salt
- 1 teaspoon of black pepper
- 1 teaspoon of red pepper
- ¼ cup of chopped parsley
- ¼ cup of chopped onion tops
- 2 dozen oysters
- Filé, to taste

1. Boil duck pieces in unseasoned water for about one hour to reduce "wild" taste. Drain and rinse the coating which will have formed on the meat. Reserve meat.
2. Prepare a dark brown roux, using the flour and oil. (This gives the gumbo its body and rich color.)
3. Saute onion in roux until tender.
4. Add duck; smother together, covered, for a few minutes. Add water a little at a time so that it mixes well with the roux. Add seasonings. Cover and simmer slowly for two to three hours (depending on the size and type of duck) until meat if fork tender.
5. Check for seasoning. About 10 minutes before serving, add parsley, onion tops and oysters.

Season each serving bowl with one-half teaspoon of filé, if desired.

—Mrs. Isby "Julaine" Schexnayder
New Iberia (Iberia Parish)

BAKED MALLARD DUCKS

- 4 mallard ducks
- Vinegar
- Salt
- Red pepper, to taste
- Bacon drippings
- 4 small onions
- 1 apple, quartered
- 1 stalk of celery, cut in four pieces
- 1 can of chicken broth
- 1 cup of red wine
- 1 bunch of green onions, chopped
- 1 can of water chestnuts, sliced
- ½ pound of fresh mushrooms
- Parsley, chopped

1. Soak ducks in vinegar, salt and water to cover one-half day.
2. Rub ducks well with salt, red pepper and bacon drippings.
3. Place one onion, one apple quarter and one piece of celery into the cavity of each duck; place ducks in a roasting pan large enough to hold the ducks without stacking them.
4. Add chicken broth, one soup can of water and red wine.
5. Bake at 300 degrees for four hours, turning after two hours.
6. Remove ducks from pan; add green onions, water chestnuts, mushrooms and parsley to duck gravy. Boil on top of the stove until gravy is reduced by one-half.

Serves six to eight.

—Dianne Moss
New Iberia (Iberia Parish)

TEAL JAMBALAYA

- 2 onions, chopped
- 3 tablespoons of cooking oil
- 3 teal, cut into serving pieces
- Onion tops, to taste
- Parsley, to taste
- Garlic powder, to taste
- Water, as needed
- 1½ cups of rice, uncooked
- Salt and pepper, to taste

1. Saute onion in oil until dark brown.
2. Add teal and brown.
3. When browned, add onion tops, parsley, garlic powder and water; let simmer until teal is tender, about an hour and a half.
4. Add rice and let simmer until rice is cooked, 20 to 30 minutes, adding water if needed.

—Mrs. Susan Benoit
Creole (Cameron Parish)

WILD DUCK JAMBALAYA

- 2 ducks, cut in pieces
- 1 pound of ham, cubed (or sliced smoked sausage)
- 6 tablespoons of olive oil
- 2 tablespoons of butter or oleo
- 3 medium onions, chopped
- 2 garlic cloves, minced
- 1½ bellpeppers, chopped
- 2 tablespoons of chopped celery
- 4 tablespoons of chopped parsley (optional)
- 8 cups of canned chicken broth
- 2 bay leaves
- Salt and hot pepper sauce, to taste
- Pinch of thyme
- 4 cups of raw rice

1. Lightly brown ducks and ham or sausage in olive oil and butter; add onions, garlic and bellpeppers, and saute for a minute or two, stirring constantly.
2. Add all other ingredients except the rice and simmer 45 minutes to an hour.
3. Wash rice and add to simmering mixture; cook about 15 minutes covered tightly. Rice should be done, but not too soft. Add more of the chicken broth if necessary. Serves eight.

—Mrs. Charles F. Hebert
Cameron (Cameron Parish)

BAKED WILD DUCKS

- 2 ducks
- Salt and pepper
- 2 medium onions
- 1 celery stalk
- ¼ cup of oil
- 1 cup of water
- 1 cup of sherry
- 1 tablespoon of flour
- ¼ cup of water
- 3 tablespoons of chopped parsley

1. Season ducks with salt and pepper inside and out; stuff cavity of each duck with one-half of an onion and one-half of a stalk of celery.
2. Brown in an open heavy roasting pan at 400 degrees in oil; add remaining onion, chopped, to pan and wilt.
3. Add one cup of water and sherry; reduce heat to 350 degrees, cover and cook until tender, about two hours or more, depending on size.
4. Baste and add more liquid if needed; make a paste with flour and one-fourth cup of water and add to the drippings to make gravy. Add parsley.

—Louis "Billy" Fontenot
Jennings (Jefferson Davis Parish)

GLAZED DUCKS

- 6 ducks
- Salt and pepper
- Apples, oranges, onions, celery (all sliced)
- Small amount of butter
- 2 cups of vermouth
- 3 ounces of brandy
- 1 small can of orange juice
- 3 tablespoons of worcestershire sauce
- Orange slices

1. Wash and clean ducks; salt and pepper well inside and out.
2. Stuff with slices of apples, oranges, onions and celery.
3. Brown in melted butter.
4. Place ducks in baking pan breast side up; add vermouth and small amount of water.
5. Cover and bake at 275 degrees for two and one-half to three hours; remove ducks from pan and allow to cool; save liquids.
6. De-bone ducks and place in casserole dish; add reserved liquid, brandy, orange juice and worcestershire sauce.
7. Cover with orange slices; bake uncovered at 200 degrees for 45 to 60 minutes.

Serve over rice.

—Mrs. Norman Davidson
Cameron Parish

STUFFED TEAL

- 6 teal
- Salt, red pepper and black pepper
- 1½ cups of finely chopped bellpepper
- 1½ cups of finely chopped onions
- 1 pound of smoked sausage
- 1 cup of cooking oil

1. The day before cooking, wash and season ducks well with salt, black pepper and red pepper; combine the bellpepper and onions and season lightly with salt, black pepper and red pepper.
2. Make a pocket in each duck breast and stuff with vegetable mixture.
3. Slit sausage lengthwise and cut into one-inch pieces; lodge firmly into pocket.
4. The next day, heat oil in a heavy pot; place ducks in the pot and brown slowly, adding a little water occasionally. Do not cover during this process.
5. When the ducks are brown, some of the sausage may be added to the gravy if desired; lower the heat and cover.
6. Continue to add water occasionally. Cook until tender, an hour to an hour and a half.

—Mrs. Burton Daigle
Creole (Cameron Parish)

STUFFED POT-ROASTED WILD DUCK

- –4 teal
- –Salt, red pepper and garlic powder, to taste
- –3 large onions
- –2 large Irish potatoes, peeled and cubed
- –6 slices of bacon, cut in pieces
- –Lemon juice
- –Oil
- –1 bunch of green onion tops, chopped

1. Season ducks well inside and out with salt, red pepper and garlic powder.
2. Cube two of the onions and mix together with cubed potatoes, bacon and seasoning; stuff the ducks with this mixture and skewer ducks closed with toothpicks.
3. Sprinkle ducks with lemon juice and let set overnight.
4. Brown ducks in a small amount of oil; add enough water to cover and the remaining onion, chopped.
5. Cook over medium heat until tender, an hour to an hour and a half. Serve over rice.

Serves four.

—Manning "Pete" Broussard
Lafayette (Lafayette Parish)

DUCK FRICASSEE

- –2 mallard ducks, cut up
- –Salt and black pepper, to taste
- –¼ cup of brandy
- –1 cup of dry red wine
- –2 large onions, coarsely chopped
- –1 tablespoon of minced parsley
- –½ teaspoon of thyme
- –½ teaspoon of marjoram
- –¼ teaspoon of allspice
- –1 bay leaf, broken into quarters
- –3 tablespoons of butter
- –3 tablespoons of olive oil
- –1 garlic clove, minced
- –½ pound of fresh mushrooms, sliced
- –¾ cup of beef stock (or canned beef broth)

1. Season ducks with salt and pepper.
2. Combine brandy, red wine, onions, parsley, thyme, marjoram, allspice and bay leaf in a large glass bowl; mix well. Add duck, turning to coat pieces well. Cover bowl with plastic wrap and refrigerate at least five hours, turning duck several times.
3. Remove duck from marinade, letting excess liquid drain back into bowl. Brown duck in a mixture of butter and olive oil over medium heat, about 15 to 20 minutes.
4. Add garlic, mushrooms, one-half cup of the marinade and the beef stock; cook over medium heat until liquid simmers, then cover skillet, reduce heat to low and cook until duck is tender, one to one and one-half hours. Spoon some of the sauce over duck when serving.

Serves four or five.

—Sue McDonough
New Iberia (Iberia Parish)

SMOTHERED FROG LEGS

- 6 pair of frog legs
- 2 tablespoons of butter
- Salt and pepper, to taste
- 4 onions, sliced
- 6 whole tomatoes, fresh or canned
- 1 bay leaf
- 1 sprig of thyme
- ¼ cup of chopped parsley
- 2 garlic cloves, pressed
- 4 bellpeppers, diced
- 1 cup of water or stock

1. Slowly brown frog legs in butter; add salt, pepper and onions and cook until brown.
2. Add tomatoes, bay leaf, thyme, parsley and garlic; cover and cook slowly for 30 minutes.
3. Add bellpeppers and water or stock; continue to smother until frog legs are tender, 45 minutes to an hour.

—Mrs. John Prescott
Johnson Bayou (Cameron Parish)

STUFFED QUAIL

- 6 quail
- Salt and pepper, to taste
- 1/4 cup of vegetable oil
- 3 tablespoons of sherry
- 1 pound of ground lean pork
- ½ cup of minced onion
- 3 tablespoons of chopped bell-pepper
- 1 small garlic clove, chopped
- 1/4 teaspoon of cayenne
- 1½ cups of cooked rice
- 1 can of drained mushrooms
- 6 slices of bacon

1. Sprinkle quail with salt and pepper to taste, then saute in oil.
2. Add sherry and cook 20 minutes over low heat.
3. In another pan, brown pork; add onion, bellpepper, garlic and cayenne.
4. Cook until pork is done, about 30 minutes.
5. Add rice and mushrooms; mix well and stuff quail.
6. Wrap each quail with bacon slices.
7. Place in covered baking dish and bake for one hour at 350 degrees.

—Mrs. John Prescott
Johnson Bayou (Cameron Parish)

SMOTHERED QUAIL

- ½ cup of cubed bacon
- Salt and pepper
- 8 quail
- 6 tablespoons of flour
- 1 medium onion, chopped
- 2½ cups of canned chicken broth
- Pinch of thyme
- ½ bay leaf
- 1 tablespoon of parsley, chopped

1. Saute bacon until brown and remove from skillet.
2. Put lightly peppered and salted quail in drippings and when browned, remove; add flour and onion, and stir a minute.
3. Add remaining ingredients and return bacon and quail to gravy; cover and simmer 20 to 30 minutes, turning occasionally until done. Add more chicken broth if needed.

Serve with white rice.

—Mrs. Charles F. Hebert
Cameron (Cameron Parish)

QUAIL SUPREME

–Salt
–Pepper
–12 quail (or 8 to 10 chicken breasts)
–Paprika
–Garlic powder
–2 packages of dehydrated onion soup
–1 medium onion, chopped
–2 slices of uncooked bacon, cut into pieces
–2 cans of cream of mushroom soup
–1 4-ounce can of stems and pieces of mushrooms
–2 tablespoons of dehydrated parsley
–1 teaspoon of Kitchen Bouquet
–1 chicken bouillon cube, dissolved in ¾ cup of water
–1/4 cup of wine

1. Salt and pepper each quail or piece of chicken; sprinkle each with small amounts of paprika and garlic powder.
2. Place one-half of the quail or chicken on bottom of a four-quart casserole dish; add one package of onion soup, one-half of the chopped onion, one slice of the bacon pieces, one can of cream of mushroom soup, one-half can of mushrooms, one tablespoon of dehydrated parsley, and sprinkle with one-half teaspoon of Kitchen Bouquet.
3. Place second half of quail or chicken on top of this and repeat layers.
4. Combine chicken bouillon mixture with wine and pour over casserole ingredients.
5. Cover casserole and cook at 350 degrees for one and one-half to two hours.

—John Daigre
Lafayette (Lafayette Parish)

RABBIT AND OKRA GUMBO

–1 large wild rabbit
–Salt and pepper
–Hot pepper sauce
–Worcestershire sauce
–1 pound of smoked sausage
–Oil
–1 cup of flour
–3 medium onions, chopped
–2 ribs of celery, chopped
–2 garlic cloves, chopped
–1 medium bellpepper, chopped
–1 whole green onion and tops, chopped
–2 quarts of water
–2½ cups of smothered okra
–1 tablespoon of gumbo filé

1. Season rabbit with salt, pepper, hot sauce and worcestershire sauce, to taste; set aside.
2. Fry sausage until brown; add enough oil to the sausage grease to make two-thirds cup; add flour and make a dark brown roux.
3. Add chopped seasonings and cook until wilted and soft.
4. Add rabbit; cook about 20 minutes.
5. Add water and bring to a boil; add sausage and cook on low heat for about two hours.
6. Add okra and continue cooking until tender.
7. Remove from heat, add filé and serve over rice.
Serves about eight.

—Mrs. Rene LeBlanc
New Roads (Pointe Coupee Parish)

RABBIT IN TOMATO GRAVY

–1 large rabbit
–Oil
–2 onions, chopped
–3 to 4 garlic cloves, minced
–1 large can of tomatoes
–½ can of tomato paste
–Parsley and green onions, chopped
–1 can of sliced mushrooms
–Salt and pepper, to taste

1. Fry rabbit in a small amount of oil until brown; remove from pan.
2. Saute onions and garlic with tomatoes and tomato paste; add about a cup of water when the mixture starts to stick.
3. Cook until thick, about an hour and a half.
4. Add rabbit and cook until rabbit is tender, an hour to an hour and a half; add parsley, green onions and mushrooms. Season to taste.

—Mrs. Carmen Brady
Hahnville (St. Charles Parish)

RABBIT SAUCE PIQUANTE

–2 young rabbits
–Salt and red pepper
–1 cup of oil
–½ pound of oleo
–2 onions, chopped
–2 cans of mushroom sauce
–3 cups of water
–1 bunch of green onion tops, chopped

1. Cut and season rabbits; brown in oil.
2. Remove rabbits and oil, leaving the drippings, and add oleo; brown oleo in the drippings.
3. Add onions and saute; add mushroom sauce, water and the rabbits to the pot and simmer until rabbits are tender, one to one and one-half hours.
4. Add green onion tops and serve over rice.

—Jim Picheloup
New Iberia (Iberia Parish)

MARINATED RABBIT WITH SOUR CREAM

–2½-pound rabbit, cut into pieces
–1¼ cups of water
–¾ cups of vinegar
–1 onion, sliced
–3 bay leaves
–10 whole cloves
–2 teaspoons of salt
–½ teaspoon of pepper
–1/3 cup of all-purpose flour
–1/3 cup of oil
–2 tablespoons of brown sugar
–1 cup of sour cream

1. Place rabbit in bowl and cover with mixture of water and vinegar; add onion, bay leaves, cloves, one teaspoon of salt and pepper. Cover tightly and refrigerate two to three days.
2. Remove rabbit and coat with mixture of flour and salt.
3. Heat oil in heavy skillet; fry rabbit until golden brown, turning frequently.
4. Gradually add one cup of strained vinegar mixture and brown sugar. Cover and simmer until tender, about one hour.
5. Add sour cream just before serving. Heat, but do not boil.

—Carolyn Gibbs
Sweetlake (Cameron Parish)

ROASTED SQUIRREL

–½ pound of smoked bacon, cubed
–4 squirrels, cut in pieces
–2 medium onions, chopped
–1 stalk of celery, chopped
–4 cups of chicken broth
–Salt, to taste
–Pinch of thyme
–Dash or two of hot pepper sauce

1. Brown bacon; remove and set aside.
2. Brown squirrel in drippings left from browning bacon; remove and set aside.
3. Add onions and celery to drippings and saute two minutes.
4. Add squirrel and bacon and enough chicken broth to cover bottom of pot; add seasonings. Cover and cook on a low heat, adding broth a little at a time as it needs replacing until squirrels are tender, about an hour.
Serves four.

Note: This is an ideal way to cook older squirrels that are tough. Rabbit may be cooked in this manner also.

—Mrs. Charles F. Hebert
Cameron (Cameron Parish)

SQUIRREL SAUCE PIQUANTE

–2 squirrels, cut up
–Salt, red pepper and black pepper
–Shortening
–2 medium onions, chopped
–½ cup of chopped bellpeppers
–1 tablespoon of flour
–½ cup of tomato sauce
–Water

1. Rub squirrels well with salt and pepper.
2. Cover bottom of Dutch Oven with one-fourth inch of shortening; when heated, brown pieces of meat well on all sides.
3. Remove meat; lower heat to medium and saute onions, bellpepper and flour in same pan until brown.
4. Return squirrel to the pan; add tomato sauce and enough water to cover the meat.
5. Cover with tight-fitting lid; simmer and hour and a half or until meat is tender. Serve over rice.

Note: Rabbit may be substituted for squirrel. As a variation, add one-half pound of pure pork sausage, fresh or lightly smoked, cut in one-inch pieces, with the onions and bellpeppers.

—Paul Huval
Cecilia (St. Martin Parish)

TURTLE SOUP

–2 pounds of turtle meat, chopped
–3 tablespoons of oil
–3 tablespoons of flour
–2 large onions, chopped
–1 cup of chopped celery
–½ cup of chopped bellpepper
–2 garlic cloves, minced
–1 cup of tomato sauce
–Water
–½ lemon, sliced
–4 bay leaves
–Parsley
–½ cup of sherry
–1 tablespoon of worcestershire sauce
–3 hard-cooked eggs
–Salt and pepper, to taste

1. Season turtle meat with salt and pepper; fry in oil until brown. Remove from fat. Add flour, browning slowly until golden.
2. Add onions, celery, bellpepper and garlic; cook until tender.
3. Return turtle meat to the pot; add tomato sauce and one cup of water; cook about 30 minutes.
4. Add lemon, bay leaves and two quarts of water; simmer for one hour or until soup has reduced to desired thickness.
5. Add parsley, sherry and worcestershire sauce.
6. Place slices of hard-cooked eggs (sprinkled with paprika) on soup plates before serving.
Serves six.

—Mrs. Edward Hebert Jr.
Thibodaux (Lafourche Parish)

VENISON DELIGHT

–2 to 3 pounds of venison meat, cut into 2-inch squares
–1 cup of flour
–2 tablespoons of lard
–1 can of mushroom sauce
–1 can of onion soup
–1 16-ounce can of tomatoes
–1 onion, chopped

1. Roll meat in flour and brown in skillet with lard; pour off most of the grease.
2. Mix remaining ingredients together and pour over meat; bake at 350 degrees for 45 minutes to one hour.
Serves six.

—Edward L. Reed
Jennings (Jefferson Davis Parish)

VENISON STEW

–2 pounds of boneless venison stew meat
–Oil
–1 cup of chopped bellpepper
–½ cup of chopped celery
–¼ cup of parsley
–1 cup of chopped onion
–Salt, pepper and garlic powder, to taste
–2 cans of golden mushroom soup
–1 soup can of burgandy wine
–2 packages of frozen stew vegetables (or fresh whole onions, carrots and small potatoes)

1. Brown stew meat in black iron pot in a small amount of oil.
2. Add seasonings, soup, wine and vegetables.
3. Cover and bake at 200 degrees for no less than eight hours.

—Mrs. Clifford Keowen
Church Point (Acadia Parish)

CAMP JAMBALAYA

–Salt, red pepper and black pepper
–10 doves (or quail or blackbirds)
–¼ cup of oil
–2 medium onions, chopped
–2 cups of chopped green onions
–1 cup of chopped bellpepper
–½ cup of chopped parsley
–2 cups of raw rice

1. Season birds heavily with salt and pepper. Add birds to oil in deep pot; let birds cook uncovered over medium heat, stirring occasionally, until they begin to fry.
2. Stir well and add one-half cup of water to pot. Continue cooking; when water cooks away, add another one-half cup of water and stir well. This may be done four to five times until a thick brown gravy forms when water is added.
3. Add onions; continue adding water and cooking down two more times.
4. Add one quart of water; cover and simmer until birds are tender. Taste liquid and adjust seasonings.
5. Add green onions, bellpepper and parsley; bring to a boil. Add rice. (There should be twice as much water as rice. Add water if necessary.)
6. Cover and simmer until rice is done, in about 15 minutes. Stir if rice has a tendency to stick.

—Editors of Cameron Parish Fur and Wildlife Festival Cookbook, Cameron (Cameron Parish)

VENISON ROAST

–1 venison roast, preferably leg
–½ pound of bacon, cut in pieces
–Salt and pepper, to taste
–2 garlic cloves
–3 tablespoons of bacon drippings
–1/4 pound of butter
–1 medium carrot, chopped
–1 rib of celery, chopped
–2 medium onions, chopped
–½ bellpepper, chopped
–2 tablespoons of minced parsley
–1 large bay leaf, halved
–1 pinch of thyme
–1 teaspoon of tarragon
–2 tablespoons of dried, minced onion
–2 packages of instant beef broth
–1 cup of dry sherry
–1 cup of burgundy wine
–Chicken broth
–Cornstarch
–Mushrooms (optional)

1. Cut slits in roast; insert bacon in slits.
2. Salt and pepper roast; halve garlic cloves and stuff into meat.
3. Brown roast in bacon drippings, using oven-proof covered dutch oven.
4. While roast is browning, melt butter in saucepan and add rest of ingredients, except chicken broth, mushrooms and cornstarch; simmer for about ten minutes.
5. Pour over roast, cover and bake at 325 degrees until roast is tender, about two hours.
6. Add chicken broth if drippings are not sufficient to make gravy; thicken gravy with cornstarch and add mushrooms.
Serves six to eight.

—Mrs. Maybelle C. Prather
Houma (Terrebonne Parish)

Dressings & Casseroles

CONTENTS

SHRIMP, GROUND MEAT AND EGGPLANT DRESSING

–1 pound of ground meat (can be a mixture of beef and pork)
–¼ cup or more of cooking oil
–1 or 2 large eggplants, peeled and cubed
–1 large onion, chopped
–¾ cup of chopped bellpepper
–½ cup of chopped celery
–2 pounds of raw shrimp, peeled
–¼ cup each of parsley and onion tops
–1½ cups of cooked rice
–1 dozen boiled shrimp, for decoration
–12 bellpepper rings
–Seasonings, to taste

1. Brown ground meat in oil; add eggplant, onion, bellpepper and celery. Cook about 20 minutes.
2. Add shrimp; continue cooking. Add a little water occasionally to keep ingredients from sticking.
3. Add parsley and onion tops. When shrimp are tender, after 10 to 15 minutes, add hot cooked rice and mix thoroughly.
4. Pour into casserole dish and garnish with peeled boiled shrimp and bellpepper rings. Place one shrimp inside each bellpepper ring for pretty decorations.

—Mrs. Donald Dugas
Henry (Vermilion Parish)

EGGPLANT DRESSING

–3 large eggplants, peeled and cubed
–1 large onion, chopped
–2 tablespoons of shortening
–1 link of smoked sausage, ground
–Salt and pepper, to taste
–3 cups of cooked rice or cornbread

1. Place eggplant in cool salt water to prevent discoloration.
2. Saute onion in shortening; add ground sausage. Cook together for five minutes.
3. Add drained eggplant, salt and pepper. Cook about 10 minutes or until eggplant becomes soft and tender.
4. Mix with rice or cornbread.

Note: Do not use an iron pot for this recipe.

—Lammie Normand
Marksville (Avoyelles Parish)

CABBAGE-CRAWFISH DRESSING

–2 small heads of cabbage, cut into small pieces
–½ cup of oil
–Salt, black pepper and red pepper, to taste
–1 teaspoon of soda
–1 large onion, chopped
–½ bellpepper, chopped
–1 rib of celery
–1 pound of crawfish tails
–2 cups of cooked rice

1. Cook cabbage in oil with seasonings and soda until tender, 10 to 15 minutes.
2. Grind onion, bellpepper, celery and crawfish together; add to cabbage. Smother until brown, about 20 minutes, adding a little water at a time.
3. When cooked, mix-in rice.

—Mrs. Emery Wiltz
Henderson (St. Martin Parish)

CORNBREAD DRESSING

- 1½ pounds of ground beef
- Salt, black pepper and red pepper, to taste
- 1 large onion, chopped
- ½ cup of chopped bellpepper
- 1/3 cup of chopped celery
- 1 teaspoon of garlic powder
- ¼ cup of oil
- ½ pound of liver, ground
- 2 cups of water
- 2 cans of mushroom sauce
- ½ cup of chopped green onion tops
- 1 cup of olives, stuffed with pimentoes, chopped
- Cornbread, broken up (Recipe follows)

1. Season ground beef with salt, black pepper and red pepper. Place in heavy pot with onion, bellpepper, celery, garlic and oil; cook until onions and bellpeppers start to brown.
2. Add liver; stir well and cook a few minutes. Add water and mushroom sauce; simmer a few minutes more.
3. Add green onion tops, olives and broken-up Cornbread; mix well. Add extra water or gravy if too dry.

CORNBREAD

- 2 cups of yellow cornmeal
- ½ cup of flour
- 2 eggs
- 2 teaspoon of baking powder
- 1 teaspoon of sugar
- 1¼ cups of buttermilk
- 1 teaspoon of salt

1. Mix all ingredients in a mixing bowl.
2. Pour into a greased pan and bake at 425 degrees for 25 to 30 minutes.
3. Remove from pan and cool before breaking up and adding to dressing.

—Mrs. Jessie Hoffpauir
Indian Bayou (Vermilion Parish)

BREAD DRESSING

- ½ pound of butter
- 2 onions, chopped
- 1 bellpepper, chopped
- 2 ribs of celery, chopped
- 1 cup of chopped green onion
- 4 to 6 garlic cloves, minced
- 1 pound of ground pork
- ½ pound of ground beef
- 2 loaves of stale french bread
- Water
- 2 eggs
- ½ cup of chopped parsley
- ½ teaspoon of Accent
- Salt and pepper, to taste

1. Melt butter in large skillet; add next five ingredients and saute until limp.
2. Add meat and cook until it turns color.
3. Grate or crumble bread; add to meat and vegetables.
4. Add enough water to moisten mixture but not enough to make it soggy.
5. Beat eggs and add to bread mixture.
6. Add parsley, Accent and salt and pepper to taste. Mix well with fork.
7. Put mixture in a casserole and bake uncovered in medium oven (about 350 degrees) for about an hour or until the top browns.

—Keith Courrege
New Iberia (Iberia Parish)

CRAWFISH-CORNBREAD DRESSING

- –1 tablespoon of corn oil oleo
- –1 large white onion, diced into ½-inch pieces
- –1 large bellpepper, diced in ½-inch pieces
- –Crawfish fat
- –2 pounds of crawfish tails
- –Salt and pepper, to taste
- –1 tablespoon of cornstarch
- –1/4 cup of chopped parsley
- –1/4 cup of chopped green onion tops
- –Cornbread (Recipe follows)

1. Melt oleo; add onion and bellpepper and saute on low heat to a golden brown.
2. Add crawfish fat and cook five minutes; add one-half cup of water.
3. Add crawfish tails, cover and cook for 30 minutes; salt and pepper to taste.
4. Mix cornstarch with one-quarter cup of water; add parsley and onion tops and cook five minutes.
5. Mix with Cornbread.

CORNBREAD

- –3 teaspoons of baking powder
- –2 eggs
- –½ cup of salad oil
- –1 cup of flour
- –1 cup of cornmeal
- –1/4 cup of sugar
- –½ teaspoon of salt

1. Preheat oven to 375 degrees.
2. Blend all ingredients; pour into greased baking pan.
3. Cook to golden brown at 350 degrees about 20 minutes.

Serves eight.

—Mr. and Mrs. W.R. "Bill" Angelle
Lafayette (Lafayette Parish)

RICE DRESSING I

- –2 tablespoons of flour
- –2 tablespoons of vegetable oil
- –1 cup of chopped onions
- –1 cup of chopped celery
- –½ cup of chopped bellpepper
- –2 garlic cloves, minced
- –½ pound of lean ground beef
- –½ pound of lean ground pork
- –½ pound of chicken giblets, chopped
- –2 teaspoons of salt
- –¾ teaspoon of black pepper
- –¾ teaspoon of red pepper
- –1 cup of chicken broth or water
- –3 cups of hot cooked rice
- –1 cup of sliced green onion tops

1. Brown flour in oil until it is a deep red-brown, stirring constantly to prevent burning.
2. Add onion, celery, bellpepper and garlic; cook until vegetables are tender.
3. Stir-in beef, pork, giblets and seasonings. Continue cooking until meat loses its color.
4. Blend-in broth; cover and simmer 25 minutes.
5. Stir-in rice and onion tops. Cook five minutes longer.

Mixture should be slightly moist.
Makes six servings.

—The Rice Council of America

RICE DRESSING II

–Giblets from 1 or 2 fryers
–½ pound of pork
–½ pound of beef
–Enough oil to grease bottom of skillet
–1 large onion, chopped
–1 cup of chopped celery
–2 garlic cloves, minced
–1 bellpepper, chopped
–3 cups of water
–2 small cans of mushrooms
–1½ cups of raw rice
–Salt and pepper, to taste

1. Grind giblets, pork and beef.
2. Fry in oil until partially cooked; add onion, celery, garlic and bellpepper.
3. Cook slowly about one hour.
4. Add water, mushrooms and rice; salt and pepper to taste.
5. Cook slowly in covered pot until rice is done, 15 to 20 minutes.

Note: You may also use parsley and bay leaf with the above seasonings.

—Mrs. John R. Smith
Torbert (Pointe Coupee Parish)

CRAWFISH-RICE DRESSING

–1 pound of cleaned crawfish tails
–1/4 bellpepper
–½ onion
–2 garlic cloves
–3 tablespoons of cooking oil
–1 small can of mushrooms
–1 cup of cooked rice
–Breadcrumbs

1. Grind up crawfish, bellpepper, onion and garlic.
2. Saute in oil until well done.
3. Add mushrooms and rice; mix.
4. Season to taste with salt and pepper.
5. Place in casserole and sprinkle with breadcrumbs.
6. Bake uncovered at 375 degrees for 25 to 30 minutes.

—Mrs. John Landreneau
Mamou (Evangeline Parish)

RICE-SEAFOOD CASSEROLE OR DRESSING

–½ cup of diced celery
–½ cup of diced onions
–½ cup of diced bellpepper
–¼ cup of oil
–1 can of Rotel tomatoes
–1 can of cream of mushroom soup
–1 can of crab meat (or 1 pound of fresh crab meat)
–1 pound of raw shrimp, peeled
–2 cups of cooked rice
–Green onion tops, chopped
–Parsley, chopped

1. Saute celery, onion and bellpepper in oil for 10 to 15 minutes, or until wilted.
2. Add Rotel tomatoes and soup and simmer for five minutes or more.
3. Add crab meat and shrimp and simmer for another five minutes.
4. Fold-in cooked rice, onion tops and parsley.
5. For a casserole, pour in baking dish and bake uncovered for 25 minutes at 350 degrees.
6. For a dressing, leave it in the pot on top of the stove, cover and put on a low heat for about 10 minutes.

—Mrs. Donald Dugas
Henry (Vermilion Parish)

OYSTER-RICE DRESSING

- –Giblets from fowl, chopped
- –1 package of frozen fowl livers, parboiled and chopped
- –2 tablespoons of fat
- –2 large onions, chopped
- –3 ribs of celery, chopped
- –1 small bellpepper, chopped
- –Oysters, as many as desired (25 to 100)
- –1 bay leaf
- –Cornmeal for frying oysters
- –¼ cup of chopped parsley
- –½ cup of green onion tops
- –Salt, red pepper, black pepper, sage and thyme, to taste
- –1½ cups of cooked rice
- –1 egg, beaten

1. Fry giblets and livers in fat; add onions, celery and bellpepper and cook until done. Add one cup of liquid (using oyster juice as part) and bay leaf and cook covered on low heat until tender, about one hour for turkey or half an hour for chicken.
2. Roll oysters in cornmeal and fry; drain. Add oysters, parsley and green onion tops to liver mixture.
3. Season highly; add cooked rice and beaten egg. Mix well.

Serves about 10.

—Mrs. Joseph Weldon
Thibodaux (Lafourche Parish)

AVOYELLES DIRTY RICE

- –1 bunch of green onions, chopped
- –½ bellpepper, chopped
- –2 ribs of celery, chopped
- –½ pound of chicken livers and gizzards, mixed
- –½ pound of calf's liver
- –¼ pound of ground beef
- –3 tablespoons of oil
- –Salt and pepper, to taste
- –3 cups of cooked rice
- –1 tablespoon of dry parsley
- –1 tablespoon of chives

1. Grind vegetables and meats.
2. Put oil in a heavy pot with lid. Add ground vegetables and meats. Cover pot. Simmer on low heat for one and one-half hours. Season to taste.
3. Mix rice and vegetable-meat mixture together. Stir thoroughly. Add dry parsley and chives.

—Mr. Teska Moreau
Marksville (Avoyelles Parish)

BAKED RICE

- –1 pound of sausage
- –2 cups of raw rice
- –2 cans of beef broth
- –¼ pound of oleo
- –4 tablespoons of chopped celery
- –4 tablespoons of chopped parsley
- –4 tablespoons of chopped green onions
- –4 tablespoons of chopped bell-pepper
- –1 can of water
- –1 teaspoon of worcestershire sauce

1. Brown sausage; add washed rice and all other ingredients to pot.
2. Bake in oven uncovered at 350 degrees, until all liquid is out of bottom, about 30 minutes.
3. Stir and cover, place on top of stove and cook 5 to 10 minutes.

—Mrs. Elma Vicknair
Norco (St. Charles Parish)

DIRTY RICE

- –2 medium onions, chopped
- –2 ribs of celery, chopped
- –4 green onions, chopped
- –3 tablespoons of oil
- –¼ pound of chicken livers, chopped or ground
- –¼ pound of chicken gizzards, chopped or ground
- –½ pound of ground meat
- –2 tablespoons of parsley, chopped
- –1 beef bouillon cube, dissolved in ½ cup of hot water (or ½ cup of beef bouillon soup)
- –1 tablespoon of worcestershire sauce
- –Salt, red pepper and black pepper, to taste
- –3 cups of cooked rice

1. Saute onions, celery and green onions in oil until soft, at least 10 minutes.
2. Add liver, gizzards, ground beef and parsley.
3. After browning meat thoroughly add beef bouillon liquid and seasonings; cover and simmer over low heat for 30 minutes. Remove from heat; add to rice and mix well.

—Mrs. Landen Alexander
Brusly (West Baton Rouge Parish)

EGGPLANT CASSEROLE

- –2 medium eggplants, peeled and sliced
- –1 large onion, chopped
- –1 bellpepper, chopped
- –1 bunch of green onion tops, chopped
- –1 garlic clove, minced
- –4 tablespoons of butter
- –Salt and black pepper, to taste
- –½ pound of ground beef, browned
- –6 crackers, crushed and toasted in 2 tablespoons of butter

1. Place vegetables and seasoning in heavy covered pan containing two tablespoons of water and four tablespoons of butter; let cook, stirring and mashing occasionally. Uncover when mixture is very moist. Cook and stir uncovered until all vegetables are soft and blended.
2. Add browned ground beef and two-thirds of the toasted crackers.
3. Place in casserole or in ramekins and sprinkle remaining crackers on top. Bake at 350 degrees for one-half hour.

This may be prepared the day before and run in oven just before serving.

—Kate Lee Long
New Roads (Pointe Coupee Parish)

CUCUMBER CASSEROLE

- –3 or 4 large cucumbers
- –½ pound of ground meat
- –1 onion, chopped
- –Green onions
- –Parsley
- –Breadcrumbs

1. Peel cucumbers and put through meat grinder or blender.
2. Fry meat, onion, cucumbers, green onions and parsley; simmer until done.
3. Put in casserole dish; sprinkle with breadcrumbs.
4. Bake uncovered at 350 degrees for 15 minutes.

—Maude Milano
Ascension Parish

EGGPLANT-BEEF CASSEROLE

- 2 tablespoons of butter
- 2 medium onions, chopped
- 1 garlic clove, minced
- 1½ pounds of ground beef
- 1 tablespoon of tomato paste
- 3 tablespoons of chopped parsley
- ½ cup of dry white wine
- Salt and pepper, to taste
- 3 large eggplants, sliced 3/8-inch thick but not peeled
- 4 tablespoons of olive oil
- 1 egg, beaten
- Breadcrumbs
- Grated Parmesan cheese
- Butter
- Cream Sauce (Recipe follows)

1. Saute onions and garlic in butter. Add ground beef and saute until onions and beef are browned.
2. Add tomato paste, parsley, wine and seasonings to taste. Cover skillet and simmer slowly until meat is well-cooked and the juices have almost been absorbed.
3. Fry eggplant in olive oil in another skillet until golden brown.
4. Add beaten egg to meat mixture along with three tablespoons of breadcrumbs. Mix well.
5. Sprinkle the bottom of a buttered casserole with breadcrumbs. Place one-third of the eggplant over crumbs. Top with one-half of the meat mixture, and liberally sprinkle meat with grated Parmesan cheese. Place another third of the eggplant, remaining meat, more cheese and then top with the remaining third of the eggplant.
6. Pour Cream Sauce over the entire casserole; sprinkle with more Parmesan cheese and breadcrumbs. Dot with butter.
7. Bake uncovered at 350 degrees for 45 minutes or until golden brown.

CREAM SAUCE

- 1¾ cups of milk
- 3 tablespoons of melted butter
- 1 egg yolk
- ¼ cup of sherry
- 2 tablespoons of flour
- Salt and pepper, to taste
- Pinch of nutmeg

1. Bring milk to a boil; add melted butter, egg yolk and sherry.
2. Thicken with the flour and season with salt, pepper and nutmeg, stirring constantly to keep mixture smooth.

—John R. Thistlethwaite
Opelousas (St. Landry Parish)

VEGETABLE PEAR (MIRLITON) CASSEROLE

–6 medium vegetable pears (mirlitons)
–½ cup of chopped onion
–½ cup of chopped celery
–2 to 3 tablespoons of butter
–2 cups of chopped shrimp
–1 cup of grated American cheese
–2 tablespoons of sugar
–¼ teaspoon of garlic salt
–1 teaspoon of salt
–1 teaspoon of Accent
–Toasted breadcrumbs

1. Boil vegetable pears until tender, 25 to 30 minutes; cut in half, peel, mash and drain.
2. Saute onion and celery in butter; add mashed vegetable pears, shrimp, cheese and seasoning; mix well and cook for 10 minutes.
3. Place in casserole dish and top with toasted breadcrumbs.
4. Bake uncovered at 350 degrees about 20 minutes.

—Mrs. C. J. Lousteau
Addis (West Baton Rouge Parish)

ZUCCHINI AND SHRIMP CASSEROLE

–6 strips of bacon
–2 onions, chopped
–½ cup of bellpepper, chopped
–1/4 cup of green onions, chopped
–4 zucchini
–2 pounds of peeled raw shrimp
–Salt and pepper, to taste
–1½ cups of Italian breadcrumbs

1. Fry bacon until crisp; remove bacon and set aside.
2. Saute onions, bellpepper and green onions in bacon drippings.
3. Wash and cut zucchini in cubes, removing any seeds, and add to above mixture; cook uncovered for 20 minutes.
4. Add shrimp, salt and pepper; cook 10 minutes more.
5. Add one cup of breadcrumbs; mix well.
6. Pour mixture into a buttered two-quart casserole dish.
7. Mix crumbled bacon with the rest of the breadcrumbs and sprinkle on top; dot with butter.
8. Bake uncovered at 350 degrees for 20 minutes.

Serves six to eight.

—Mrs. Zelda Musso
Thibodaux (Lafourche Parish)

BAKED SPAGHETTI AND CHEESE CASSEROLE

–6 tablespoons of butter
–3 tablespoons of flour
–½ teaspoon of salt
–Dash of black pepper
–1½ cups of milk
–10 ounces of sharp cheddar cheese, grated
–10 to 12 ounces of thin spaghetti, boiled in salted water
–1 single pack of saltine crackers, crushed

1. Melt three tablespoons of the butter in a saucepan; add flour, salt and pepper; mix well. Gradually add milk, stirring until thick; add cheese and stir until melted.
2. Combine cheese sauce with spaghetti; place in a greased 8x12-inch pan or casserole dish. Sprinkle with cracker crumbs that have been mixed with remaining three tablespoons of butter (melted).
3. Bake uncovered at 325 degrees about 20 minutes, until bubbly and brown.

—Mrs. Elizabeth Hebert
Jeanerette (Iberia Parish)

Breads & Cereals

CONTENTS

ASPHODEL BREAD

–5 cups of biscuit mix
–¼ cup of sugar
–½ teaspoon of salt
–2 envelopes of dry yeast
–2 cups of warm milk
–4 eggs
–Pinch of cream of tartar

1. Into a large bowl sift biscuit mix, sugar and salt.
2. In a separate bowl, sprinkle dry yeast over warm milk to soften; stir the mixture until the yeast is dissolved.
3. Beat eggs thoroughly with cream of tartar; combine the yeast and egg mixtures and add to the dry ingredients, stirring the dough until it is well-mixed. This produces a sticky dough that is not too thick.
4. Cover the top of the bowl securely with plastic wrap and let the dough stand in a warm place, away from drafts, until it doubles in size.
5. Stir the dough thoroughly and pour it into two oiled loaf pans, 8½x4½x2½ inches; let the dough stand in a warm place until it reaches the tops of the pans.
6. Bake the bread at 350 degrees for 25 to 30 minutes, or until it tests done and is well-browned. This bread is best when served hot.

Recipe can be halved to make one loaf.

—Mrs. I. J. Guerin
Port Allen (West Baton Rouge Parish)

DILLY CASSEROLE BREAD

–1 package of dry yeast
–¼ cup of warm water
–1 cup of creamed cottage cheese
–2 tablespoons of sugar
–1 tablespoon of minced onion
–1 tablespoon of melted oleo
–2 teaspoons of dill seeds
–1 teaspoon of salt
–¼ teaspoon of soda
–1 egg
–2¼ to 2½ cups of all-purpose flour

1. Soften yeast in warm water; set aside.
2. Heat cottage cheese to lukewarm; combine cottage cheese, sugar, onion, melted oleo, dill seeds, salt, soda and egg in a large bowl.
3. Stir-in yeast; add flour to make a stiff dough and beat well.
4. Cover and let rise in a warm place until doubled in bulk, about 50 or 60 minutes; stir down dough.
5. Spoon-in to a well-greased two-quart round baking dish; let rise in a warm place until doubled in bulk, about 30 minutes.
6. Bake at 350 degrees for 30 or 40 minutes or until golden brown.

—Claudia Huye
Lafayette Parish

BROWN BREAD

–1 package of active dry yeast
–¼ cup of warm water
–¼ cup of brown sugar
–¼ cup of light molasses
–1 tablespoon of salt
–2 tablespoons of shortening, melted
–1½ cups of hot water
–2½ cups of white all-purpose flour
–3 tablespoons of sesame seeds
–3½ to 4 cups of sifted all-purpose flour

1. Heat oven to 350 degrees; soften yeast in one-fourth cup of warm water.
2. In large bowl, combine sugar, molasses, salt and shortening; add one and one-half cups of hot water and stir until sugar dissolves. Cool to lukewarm.
3. Stir-in two and one-half cups of white flour and beat well; add softened yeast and sesame seeds, mixing well.
4. Stir-in enough flour to make moderately stiff dough; knead on well-floured surface till smooth and satiny, about 15 minutes.
5. Place in lightly greased bowl, turning once to grease surface; cover and let rise till double, one and one-half to two hours.
6. Punch down; turn out on lightly floured surface and divide into two portions. Shape each into a smooth ball; cover and let rest 10 minutes.
7. Pat dough into two round loaves and place on greased baking sheet or into two loaf pans; cover and let rise until double, one and one-half to two hours.
8. Bake at 350 degrees about 45 minutes to an hour. For a soft crust, brush with melted butter.

—Mrs. Gabe Speyrer
Opelousas (St. Landry Parish)

SAUSAGE SPOON BREAD

–½ pound of sausage meat
–¼ cup of finely chopped onion
–1 cup of finely chopped celery
–2½ cups of milk
–1 cup of enriched white cornmeal
–2 tablespoons of butter or oleo
–1 teaspoon of salt
–3 eggs, separated

1. In a 10-inch skillet, brown the sausage; remove with a slotted spoon.
2. In the sausage drippings, cook the onion and celery until wilted.
3. Scald one and one-half cups of milk; mix remaining cup of milk with the cornmeal and gradually stir-in to scalded milk.
4. Cook, stirring often, until thickened, about five minutes.
5. Remove from heat and stir-in the butter, salt, egg yolks and sausage mixture.
6. Beat egg whites until stiff, and fold into mixture; turn-in to a buttered shallow one and one-half quart baking dish, mounding slightly in center.
7. Bake in preheated oven at 375 degrees 40 to 45 minutes. Serve at once.

Makes six servings.

—Mrs. Charles R. Perkins
Cameron (Cameron Parish)

ZUCCHINI BREAD

—2 eggs
—1¾ cups of sugar
—2 teaspoons of vanilla
—¾ cup of oil
—3 cups of grated zucchini
—2½ cups of flour
—1½ cups of regular wheat germ
—2½ teaspoons of baking powder
—1 teaspoon of salt
—2 teaspoons of cinnamon
—1 cup of chopped nuts (optional)

1. Beat eggs; beat-in sugar, vanilla and oil and stir-in zucchini.
2. Mix together flour, wheat germ, baking powder, salt, cinnamon and nuts; gradually stir-in to egg mixture.
3. Turn in to two greased and floured bread pans; bake at 350 degrees for about one hour.
4. Cool 10 minutes in pans; then remove from pans and cool on wire rack.

—Mrs. Avis Schonlau
Lafayette Parish

BEER BISCUITS

—1 12-ounce bottle of hot beer
—3 cups of biscuit mix
—2 tablespoons of sugar

1. Mix ingredients.
2. Drop in a well-greased muffin tin.
3. Bake at 375 degrees until brown.

You can let the biscuits rise in muffin tin from 20 minutes to around one hour before baking. They are light, puffy and fluffy.

—Joyce Arceneaux
Jennings (Jefferson Davis Parish)

HOMEMADE BISCUITS

—3 cups of all-purpose flour
—1 tablespoon of baking powder
—1 teaspoon of salt
—2/3 cup of shortening
—Milk

1. Mix dry ingredients together; cut shortening into dry ingredients.
2. Add enough milk to make a sticky dough.
3. Roll out on floured board to a thickness of about one-fourth to one-half inch; cut with round biscuit cutter.
4. Dot each biscuit with shortening, about the size of a "BB."
5. Bake at 425 degrees for about 10 minutes.

—Corinne Daigle
Brusly (West Baton Rouge Parish)

ANGEL BISCUITS

—5 cups of flour
—3 tablespoons of sugar
—3 teaspoons of baking powder
—1 teaspoon of salt
—1 teaspoon of soda
—¾ cup of shortening
—1 package of dry yeast
—½ cup of warm water
—2 cups of buttermilk

1. Mix dry ingredients; cut-in shortening.
2. Dissolve yeast in water; add to dry ingredients with buttermilk; let rise.
3. Roll dough to three-fourths-inch thickness and cut out.
4. Bake at 450 degrees for 10 to 12 minutes.

—Emily Washington
Moreauville (Avoyelles Parish)

HOMEMADE ROLLS

- 6 cups of flour
- ½ cup of sugar
- 2 teaspoons of salt
- 2 packages of yeast
- ½ cup of butter or oleo, softened
- 2 cups of warm water

1. Combine two cups of the flour with sugar, salt, yeast and butter in a large bowl, mixing well.
2. Gradually add warm water and stir well. Mix-in one cup more of the flour, making a thick batter.
3. Mix-in the remaining three cups of flour, kneading until well-mixed.
4. Grease top of dough, cover and let rise one hour and 45 minutes.
5. Shape dough into rolls and place into greased baking pans; let rise again about one hour and 30 minutes.
6. Bake for 20 minutes at 375 degrees.

Makes about 36 rolls.

—Jeanette M. Guidry
Breaux Bridge (St. Martin Parish)

CORNBREAD

- 2 cups of cornmeal
- 2 cups of flour
- 2 cups of milk (or buttermilk)
- 4 eggs
- ½ cup of oil
- 1 cup of sugar (less if desired)
- 8 teaspoons of baking powder
- 1 teaspoon of salt

1. Mix all ingredients together.
2. Bake at 350 degrees for 30 minutes in a 13x9x2-inch pan.

—Hazel Delahoussaye
New Iberia (Iberia Parish)

SPOON ROLLS

- 2 cups of warm water
- 4 tablespoons of sugar
- 1 package of yeast
- ½ cup of cooking oil
- 1 egg, beaten
- 4 cups of self-rising flour

1. Mix ingredients as listed; let set covered for one hour in refrigerator.
2. Spoon into greased muffin tins; bake in 450-degree oven until light brown.

Makes about 24 rolls. Can be doubled.

—Mrs. Marion Spears
Addis (West Baton Rouge Parish)

CRACKLIN' CORNBREAD

- 3 tablespoons of oil or lard
- 1 to 2 cups of cracklings (to taste)
- 1½ cups of cornmeal
- ½ cup of flour
- ½ teaspoon of baking soda
- ½ teaspoon of salt
- 2 tablespoons of sugar
- 1 egg
- ¾ cup of milk

1. Heat oil in iron skillet until hot.
2. Mix all other ingredients together in a bowl; pour into hot skillet.
3. With a spoon, dip oil from sides of skillet and drop it on cornbread, making little puddles all over the top.
4. Bake at 375 to 400 degrees until golden brown and crusty.

For variations, try adding a cup of whole-kernel corn or one-third cup of onions or onion tops.

—Jerry Coldiron
Ville Platte (Evangeline Parish)

COUCHE COUCHE

–¼ cup of oil
–2 cups of cornmeal
–1½ teaspoons of salt
–1 teaspoon of baking powder
–¾ cup of milk
–¾ cup of water

1. Using heavy iron pot, heat oil.
2. Mix dry ingredients; add milk and water. (Batter will be soft.)
3. Pour batter in hot oil; let crust form on bottom before stirring. Put on low heat and stir occasionally, until couche couche is cooked, about 15 minutes.
4. Serve in bowl with milk and sugar, as a cereal.

—Mrs. Ralph Gonsoulin
New Iberia (Iberia Parish)

CORN PONES A LA AVOYELLES

–1½ cups of cornmeal
–3 tablespoons of all-purpose flour
–1½ tablespoons of baking powder
–1 teaspoon of salt
–2/3 cup of hot water
–1½ cups of shortening

1. Mix all dry ingredients. Add hot water, mixing well.
2. Immediately make patties.
3. Fry patties in deep, hot shortening until golden brown on each side.

—Julie McGee
Marksville (Avoyelles Parish)

HUSH PUPPIES

–1½ cups of yellow cornmeal
–¼ cup of sugar
–1 cup of flour
–½ teaspoon of Accent
–½ teaspoon of black pepper
–1 teaspoon of salt
–3 teaspoons of baking powder
–2 eggs, beaten
–½ cup of onion, chopped fine
–Milk

1. Combine dry ingredients; add eggs, onion and enough milk to make a thick batter.
2. Drop by the spoonful in four inches of hot deep fat and fry until golden brown; drain on paper towels.

—Tom Foret III
Lutcher (St. James Parish)

HUSH PUPPIES WITH SHRIMP

–2 cups of yellow cornmeal
–1 cup of flour
–3 tablespoons of baking powder
–1 teaspoon of salt
–2 tablespoons of sugar
–2 eggs
–1 large onion, chopped fine
–1 cup of partially boiled shrimp, chopped fine
–Water

1. Mix ingredients, adding enough water for a stiff batter. Batter should not be too soft.
2. Drop by the spoonful into hot fat and fry until golden brown.

—Robinetta Burg
Cameron (Cameron Parish)

SWEET POTATO BREAD AND MUFFINS

–½ cup of butter or oleo
–½ cup of shortening
–2 2/3 cups of sugar
–4 eggs
–2 cups of cold, mashed sweet potatoes
–3½ cups of sifted flour
–1 teaspoon of salt
–1 teaspoon of ground cinnamon
–1½ teaspoons of ground nutmeg
–2 teaspoons of baking soda
–1 cup of chopped walnuts
–2/3 cup of cold, strong, dark coffee

1. Cream butter, shortening and sugar; add eggs, one at a time, mixing well after each addition.
2. Blend-in sweet potatoes.
3. Sift together dry ingredients; add nuts.
4. Stir into creamed mixture alternately with cold coffee.
5. Pour batter into two greased 9x5x3 loaf pans and eight greased muffin pan cups.
6. Bake at 375 degrees for one hour for loaves and 25 minutes for muffins or until they test done in the center.
7. Cool 10 minutes, remove from pans and cool completely.

—Mrs. Charles F. Hebert
Cameron (Cameron Parish)

BLUEBERRY MUFFINS

–1½ cups of sifted flour
–½ cup of sugar
–2 teaspoons of baking powder
–½ teaspoon of salt
–¼ cup of soft shortening
–1 egg
–½ cup of milk
–1 cup of fresh or fresh frozen blueberries (¾ cup if canned berries are used)

1. Preheat oven to 400 degrees.
2. Sift dry ingredients together in mixing bowl; add shortening, egg and milk and beat with mixer at low speed only until blended. Do not overbeat.
3. Gently fold-in the blueberries with spatula; fill greased muffin tins two-thirds full and bake at 400 degrees until golden brown, for 20 to 25 minutes.

Yields 12 medium-size muffins.

—Karen Martin
Maringouin (Iberville Parish)

PAIN PERDU (Lost Bread)

–3 eggs
–¼ cup of sugar
–½ teaspoon of salt
–2 cups of milk
–12 slices of bread

1. Beat eggs, sugar and salt; add milk.
2. Dip slices of bread into mixture and fry in slight amount of hot fat until delicate brown on both sides.
3. Serve hot; sprinkle with powdered sugar or serve with syrup.

—Dot Robert
Iberville Parish

PEANUT BUTTER BREAD

–2 cups of flour
–3 teaspoons of baking powder
–½ teaspoon of baking soda
–½ teaspoon of salt
–¼ cup of oleo
–¾ cup of chunky peanut butter
–¾ cup of sugar
–1 egg
–1 teaspoon of vanilla
–1 cup of milk

1. Sift flour, baking powder, soda and salt on wax paper.
2. In medium-size bowl beat together oleo and peanut butter until blended; beat-in sugar, then egg and vanilla.
3. Add flour mixture, using pastry blender, mixing in until fine crumbs form; add milk and stir just until mixture is moistened.
4. Turn into a greased loaf pan (9x5x3); bake in preheated 350-degree oven for 55 to 60 minutes.
5. Place loaf in pan on wire rack and let stand five minutes; with a small spatula loosen edges, turn out on a wire rack, turn right side up, and cool. Store wrapped in transparent plastic wrap or foil.

—Ruth C. Hernandez
Lake Charles (Calcasieu Parish)

PUMPKIN-NUT BREAD

–2 cups of sifted flour
–2 teaspoons of baking powder
–½ teaspoon of baking soda
–1 teaspoon of salt
–1 teaspoon of cinnamon
–½ teaspoon of nutmeg
–1 cup of solid-packed pumpkin
–1 cup of sugar
–½ cup of milk
–2 eggs
–¼ cup of softened butter
–1 cup of chopped pecans

1. Sift together first six ingredients.
2. Combine pumpkin, sugar, milk and eggs in mixing bowl; add dry ingredients and butter and mix until well-blended.
3. Stir-in nuts; spread in well-greased loaf pan (9x5x3).
4. Bake in 350-degree oven for 45 to 55 minutes or until toothpick inserted in center comes out clean.
Makes one loaf.

Note: For two loaves, use one 16-ounce can of pumpkin and double remaining ingredients. Bread may be frozen.

—Mrs. David Middlebrooks Jr.
Pitreville (Acadia Parish)

BANANA BREAD

–6 bananas, mashed
–2 cups of sugar
–1 cup of shortening
–4 eggs, beaten
–2½ cups of flour
–2 teaspoons of soda
–1 teaspoon of salt
–½ teaspoon of ginger
–1 teaspoon of cinnamon

1. Combine bananas, sugar and shortening; add eggs one at a time.
2. Sift dry ingredients; add above mixture to this, stirring just until moistened.
3. Bake 45 to 50 minutes at 375 degrees.

—Linda Gentry
Lake Charles (Calcasieu Parish)

DOUGHNUTS

- –1 cup of sugar
- –2 eggs
- –4½ cups of all-purpose flour
- –3 tablespoons of baking powder
- –1 teaspoon of salt
- –¼ teaspoon of nutmeg
- –¼ teaspoon of cinnamon
- –1/8 teaspoon of mace
- –1 cup of milk
- –2 tablespoons of shortening, melted
- –Oil for frying

1. Blend sugar and eggs.
2. Sift flour and measure; add baking powder, salt and spices; sift again.
3. Add alternately with milk to sugar mixture. Stir-in melted shortening.
4. Put part of dough on to lightly floured board; if too soft to handle, knead-in small amounts of flour. Roll out to about one-half inch thick. Cut doughnuts round, using sharpened cutter. (Flour cutter before cutting to prevent sticking.)
5. Fry in deep fat heated to proper temperature (365 to 375 degrees).

—Alvina Rivet
Morganza (Pointe Coupee Parish)

BLUE CHEESE FRENCH BREAD

- –2 1-pound loaves of french bread
- –1 cup of soft butter or oleo
- –½ cup of crumbled blue cheese
- –4 tablespoons of grated Parmesan cheese

1. Heat oven to 350 degrees.
2. Cut loaves diagonally into one-inch slices.
3. Mix thoroughly butter and blue cheese; spread part of butter mixture on slices.
4. Reassemble loaves; spread top of loaves with remaining butter mixture and sprinkle with Parmesan cheese.
5. Wrap loaves securely in 28x18-inch piece of heavy-duty aluminum foil; heat 20 minutes.

Makes about 36 pieces.

—Carolyn and Anthony Musso
Gramercy (St. James Parish)

CHEESE GRITS

- –1 cup of quick-cooking grits
- –4 cups of water
- –¼ pound of oleo
- –½ pound of grated cheddar cheese
- –1 well-beaten egg
- –¼ teaspoon of pepper
- –1 teaspoon of salt
- –Paprika

1. Cook grits in water according to directions on box; add oleo and cheese and stir until melted.
2. Add beaten egg, and salt and pepper, to taste.
3. Put in a greased casserole and bake uncovered at 350 degrees for 30 minutes. Sprinkle paprika on top.

Serves six.

—Lorraine V. Oubre
Lutcher (St. James Parish)

Cakes, Cookies & Candies

CONTENTS

COCONUT CAKE

–2½ cups of cake flour
–3 teaspoons of baking powder
–1 teaspoon of salt
–1/4 pound of butter or oleo
–1½ cups of sugar
–2 eggs, unbeaten
–1 teaspoon of vanilla
–1 cup of milk
–Filling and Frosting (Recipe follows)

1. Sift flour, baking powder and salt together.
2. Cream butter and sugar; add eggs and vanilla to sugar mixture.
3. Add dry ingredients alternately with milk, finishing with dry ingredients. Beat two minutes after first addition, then one minute after each other addition.
4. Pour into greased and floured nine-inch pans for two layers or eight-inch pans for three layers.
5. Bake at 350 degrees for 25 to 30 minutes.
6. Cool before finishing with Filling and Frosting.

FILLING AND FROSTING

–2 cups of coconut (fresh is best)
–1 cup of sugar
–1 cup of evaporated milk
–4 tablespoons of butter or oleo
–½ cup of sugar

1. Cook first four ingredients for 10 minutes on low heat.
2. Use one-third of mixture for filling.
3. Brown the remaining one-half cup of sugar and add to remaining two-thirds of mixture; use this for top and sides of cake.

—Mrs. A J. Roy
New Roads (Pointe Coupee Parish)

GATEAU SUISSE
(Swiss Cake)

–2 cups of all-purpose flour
–1½ cups of sugar
–3½ teaspoons of baking powder
–1 teaspoon of salt
–½ cup of shortening
–1 cup of milk
–1 teaspoon of vanilla
–3 eggs
–Frosting (Recipe follows)

1. Heat oven to 350 degrees. Grease and flour two cake pans.
2. Measure all ingredients into large mixer bowl; blend one-half minute on low speed, scraping bowl constantly. Beat three minutes at high speed.
3. Bake 30 to 35 minutes or until wooden pick inserted in center comes out clean. Cool. Spread Frosting on sides, top and middle.

FROSTING

–2 2/3 cups of confectioners sugar
–2/3 cup of soft butter
–2 ounces of melted unsweetened chocolate, cooled
–¼ teaspoon of vanilla
–2 tablespoons of milk

1. In small mixing bowl, blend sugar, butter, chocolate and vanilla on low speed.
2. Gradually add milk; beat until smooth and fluffy.

Enough frosting for two nine-inch layers or three eight-inch layer cakes.

—Venita J. Cambre
Reserve (St. John the Baptist Parish)

WHISKEY CAKE

–3 eggs
–1 pound of white sugar
–½ pound of butter
–½ pound of brown sugar
–3 cups of flour
–½ teaspoon of mace
–½ pint of bourbon whiskey
–½ cup of broken pecans

1. Mix eggs and white sugar; beat well.
2. Cream butter with brown sugar.
3. Combine egg mixture with butter mixture.
4. Sift-in flour and mace, alternating with whiskey; add nuts.
5. Bake in a tube pan at 300 degrees for one and one-half hours.

Note: This cake should have a moist, crumbly texture, similar to a macaroon. Wrap in foil and store in cool place. Do not freeze. This cake will keep two or three weeks.

—Mrs. Lawrence Pourciau
New Roads (Pointe Coupee Parish)

COFFEE CAKE

–1½ cups of cake flour
–¾ cup of sugar
–2½ teaspoons of baking powder
–¾ teaspoon of salt
–¼ cup of shortening
–¾ cup of milk
–1 egg
–Streusel Filling (Recipe follows)

1. Blend all ingredients thoroughly with fork in large mixing bowl except Streusel Filling. Beat vigorously for 30 seconds.
2. Spread half the batter in greased layer pan. Sprinkle with half of Streusel Filling.
3. Spread remaining batter over filling and top with remaining Streusel Filling. Bake 25 to 30 minutes or until inserted pick comes out clean. Serve warm.

STREUSEL FILLING
–½ cup of packed brown sugar
–2 teaspoons of cinnamon
–½ cup of finely chopped nuts
–2 tablespoons of butter or oleo, melted

Mix together.

—Mrs. Ambrose Bodin
Franklin (St. Mary Parish)

OLD-FASHIONED SYRUP CAKE

–½ cup of sugar
–½ cup of butter or oleo
–2 cups of syrup
–2 eggs
–2 cups of flour
–1 teaspoon of salt
–½ teaspoon of soda
–½ cup of buttermilk
–2 teaspoons of vanilla

1. Mix sugar, butter and syrup together; add eggs and mix well.
2. Add flour, salt and soda, alternating with buttermilk; add vanilla.
3. Bake in a greased and floured tube pan at 350 degrees for 45 minutes to one hour.

—Jeanette M. Guidry
Breaux Bridge (St. Martin Parish)

LOUISIANA FIG CAKE

–1 large egg
–2 tablespoons of sugar
–1 teaspoon of vanilla
–½ cup of salad oil
–1¼ cup of flour
–½ teaspoon of baking powder
–½ teaspoon of salt
–1 pint of fig preserves

1. Grease and flour a 9x9x2-inch pan; preheat oven to 350 degrees.
2. Place the egg, sugar and vanilla in a mixing bowl and beat slightly with a spoon; add the salad oil and beat again.
3. Sift the dry ingredients all at once and add together; add the fig preserves to the stiff batter and stir.
4. Pour into the prepared pan, smooth and bake for 35 to 40 minutes.

—Mrs. Meredith Hebert
New Iberia (Iberia Parish)

FRUIT CAKE

–12 eggs
–1 pound of butter
–2 1/3 cups of sugar
–4 cups of cake flour
–1 tablespoon of salt
–1 tablespoon of cinnamon
–1 tablespoon of cloves
–1 tablespoon of mace
–2 pounds of candied fruits, chopped
–2 pounds of raisins
–1 pound of pecans, chopped
–1 pound of mixed nuts, chopped
–1 pound of dates
–1 cup of honey
–1 cup of whiskey
–2 cups of applesauce
–Juice from 16-ounce can of crushed pineapple (do not use the pineapple)
–1 tablespoon of baking soda
–1 cup of water
–1 quart of fig preserves
–Glaze (Recipe follows)

1. Cream eggs, butter and sugar together.
2. Sift flour with salt, cinnamon, cloves and mace three times.
3. Mix candied fruits, raisins, pecans, nuts and dates together in a bowl; add one-half of the flour mixture to the fruits and nuts; set aside.
4. Mix the remaining one-half flour mixture with honey, whiskey, applesauce and pineapple juice; set this batter aside.
5. Add baking soda to water and mix.
6. Pour baking soda mixture into batter and mix well.
7. Add floured fruits and nuts and fig preserves to batter, mixing well.
8. Pour into three tube pans that have been lined with greased paper; bake three to four hours at 300 degrees.

GLAZE
–1 egg
–1 tablespoon of water

1. Blend ingredients together.
2. Ten minutes before cake is done, brush top of cake with mixture.
3. Bake 10 minutes longer at 275 degrees.

—Mrs. Whitney Broussard
New Iberia (Iberia Parish)

CARROT CAKE

- 1 cup of oil
- 1½ cups of honey
- 6 tablespoons of wheatgerm
- 1 cup plus 10 tablespoons of whole wheat flour
- 1 teaspoon of salt
- 2 teaspoons of cinnamon
- 4 eggs
- 2 teaspoons of baking powder
- 2 teaspoons of baking soda
- 3 cups of shredded carrots
- Frosting (Recipe follows)

1. Mix all ingredients for cake together and pour into three eight-inch pans; bake at 350 degrees for 35 to 45 minutes.
2. Cool and frost.

FROSTING

- 8 ounces of creamcheese
- ¼ pound of oleo
- 1 teaspoon of vanilla
- 1 box of powdered sugar

Beat creamcheese and oleo together till fluffy; beat-in vanilla and powdered sugar.

—Anne Broussard
St. Martinville (St. Martin Parish)

KUMQUAT CAKE

- 1 cup of seeded kumquats
- 1 cup of raisins
- 1/3 cup of nuts
- 1 cup of sugar
- 2 cups of flour
- 1 teaspoon of soda
- 1 teaspoon of salt
- ½ cup of shortening
- 1 cup of milk
- 2 eggs
- Topping (Recipe follows)

1. Grind together kumquats, raisins and nuts; save juice for Topping.
2. Sift together sugar, flour, soda and salt into a mixing bowl.
3. Add shortening and three-fourths cup of milk; beat two minutes at medium speed.
4. Add eggs and one-fourth cup of milk and beat two minutes.
5. Fold-in ground kumquats, raisins and nuts.
6. Pour in greased and floured pan 12x8x2 inches or 9x13x2 inches.
7. Bake at 350 degrees for 40 to 50 minutes.

TOPPING

- 1/3 cup of sugar
- 1 teaspoon of cinnamon
- 1/4 cup of chopped nuts
- 1/3 cup of juice from grinding fruit

Mix ingredients; spread on hot cake. Serves about 20.

—Louise Arceneaux O'Grady
Welsh (Jefferson Davis Parish)

CAJUN CAKE

–2 cups of flour
–1½ cups of sugar
–2 teaspoons of baking soda
–2 small cans of crushed pineapple, with juice
–2 eggs
–Icing (Recipe follows)

Mix all ingredients well; bake in a square pan for 30 minutes at 350 degrees. Cool and ice cake.

ICING
–½ can of evaporated milk
–¼ pound of butter or oleo
–¾ cup of sugar
–1 package of coconut
–½ cup of chopped pecans

Cook evaporated milk, butter and sugar until very thick. Add coconut and pecans.

—Thelma Smith
Rayne (Acadia Parish)

JELLY ROLL

–4 eggs
–1 cup of sugar
–1 teaspoon of vanilla
–1 cup of flour
–1 teaspoon of baking powder
–Dash of salt
–Powdered sugar
–Jelly

1. Beat eggs, sugar and vanilla together; add flour, baking powder and salt, mixing well.
2. Line jelly roll pan with waxed paper. Pour in batter.
3. Bake at 375 degrees for 10 to 13 minutes.
4. Turn from pan at once onto waxed paper sprinkled well with powdered sugar. (Put newspaper under waxed paper.) Spread with jelly, then roll, then wrap in waxed paper and cool.

—Audrey Bourgeois
Gramercy (St. James Parish)

CARROT-PINEAPPLE CAKE

–2 cups of sugar
–1 cup of oil
–3 eggs
–1 can of crushed pineapple
–1½ cups of chopped pecans
–2 cups of grated carrots
–2 teaspoons of vanilla
–2 teaspoons of soda
–½ teaspoon of salt
–1 teaspoon of cinnamon
–3 cups of flour
–Glaze (Recipe follows)

1. Mix sugar, oil and eggs.
2. Add remaining ingredients except flour; mix well.
3. Add flour; mix well.
4. Bake in greased bundt pan at 350 degrees for one hour. Let cool about 10 minutes; take out of pan and pour Glaze on it.

GLAZE
–3 tablespoons of frozen orange juice
–3 tablespoons of brown sugar

Mix together and bring to a boil until sugar is melted.

—Mrs. Ambrose Bodin
Franklin (St. Mary Parish)

1-2-3 PERSIMMON FRUITCAKE

GROUP 1
- 3 cups of sugar
- 3 cups of flour
- 2 teaspoons of baking powder
- ½ teaspoon of salt
- 1 teaspoon of soda
- 2 teaspoons of ground ginger

GROUP 2
- 3 eggs
- 1½ cups of mashed persimmons
- 1 8-ounce can of drained, crushed pineapple
- 2 tablespoons of soft shortening

GROUP 3
- 1 cup of floured raisins
- 1 cup of floured candied mixed fruit

1. Mix ingredients of Group 1 in bowl.
2. Make hole and add Group 2.
3. Fold in Group 3.
4. Bake in floured bundt pan at 350 degrees for one hour.

—Mrs. Marion Zachary
Erwinville (West Baton Rouge Parish)

PERSIMMON CAKE

- ½ cup of oleo
- 2 cups of sugar
- 1 egg
- 1¾ cups of sifted cake flour
- 1 teaspoom of soda
- ¼ teaspoon of salt
- 1 teaspoon of cinnamon
- 1 teaspoon of cloves
- 1 cup of dates or raisins, chopped
- 1 cup of pecans, chopped
- 1 cup of persimmon pulp

1. Cream oleo and sugar; add egg and beat one minute.
2. Sift flour, soda, salt, cinnamon and cloves together; stir-in dates and pecans.
3. Heat persimmon pulp to boiling; add to creamed mixture alternately with dry ingredients, beating well after each addition.
4. Bake in two greased and floured pans at 375 degrees for 25 to 30 minutes, or in bundt pan for 45 minutes to an hour.

—Ethel L. Watts
Hackberry (Cameron Parish)

CHRISTMAS CAKE

- ½ pound of butter
- ½ pound of oleo
- 3½ cups of light brown sugar
- 6 eggs
- 4 cups of plain flour
- 1 teaspoon of baking powder
- 1 pound of raisins
- 3 cups of nuts (walnuts and pecans)
- ½ cup of brandy (peach or apricot)

1. Mix ingredients in a very large bowl in the order given.
2. Pour batter into a well-greased and -floured tube pan.
3. Bake at 350 degrees for two hours or more.

—Cookie Hutcherson
Houma (Terrebonne Parish)

MILK CHOCOLATE CAKE

–½ cup of butter or shortening
–1½ cups of sugar
–2 eggs
–2 cups of cake flour
–½ teaspoon of salt
–1 cup of buttermilk
–1 teaspoon of vanilla
–2 heaping tablespoons of cocoa, mixed with a little hot water (or 2 squares of bitter chocolate, melted)
–1 teaspoon of baking soda
–1 tablespoon of vinegar
–Chocolate Icing (Recipe follows)

1. Cream shortening; add sugar.
2. Add eggs one at a time, beating thoroughly after each egg.
3. Mix-in the flour and salt (sifted together) alternately with buttermilk (to which the vanilla has been added).
4. Beat cocoa or melted chocolate into batter thoroughly.
5. Dissolve soda in vinegar and add by hand to batter. Pour into two greased layer pans.
6. Bake at 325 degrees for about 25 minutes.
7. Cool before frosting with Chocolate Icing.

CHOCOLATE ICING
–1 box of powdered sugar
–6 tablespoons plus 1 teaspoon of oleo
–2 tablespoons of cocoa
–1 teaspoon of vanilla
–About 3 tablespoons of milk

1. Combine sugar and oleo; add cocoa, vanilla and enough milk to spread nicely.
2. Mix well before spreading on cooled cake.

—Mrs. F. A. Busch
Thibodaux (Lafourche Parish)

CHRISTMAS LOAF CAKE

–1 8-ounce package of creamcheese
–1 cup of oleo
–1½ cups of sugar
–1½ teaspoons of almond flavoring
–4 eggs
–2¼ cups of sifted cake flour
–1½ teaspoons of baking powder
–¾ cup (8 ounces) of red cherries, drained and chopped
–½ cup of chopped pecans
–Glaze (Recipe follows)
–Candied red cherries and green cherries, halved
–Pecan halves

1. Blend creamcheese, oleo, sugar and almond flavoring.
2. Add eggs, one at a time; mix well.
3. Add two cups of sifted flour with the baking powder.
4. Combine remaning one-fourth cup of flour with chopped cherries and chopped pecans; fold into batter.
5. Pour into a greased tube pan; bake at 325 degrees for one hour and 20 minutes.
6. Drizzle Glaze over cake while still hot. Decorate with cherry halves and pecan halves.

GLAZE
–1½ cups of powdered sugar
–2 tablespoons of milk

Mix together.

—Mrs. Ralph Gonsoulin
New Iberia (Iberia Parish)

CHOCOLATE PECAN LOG

–3 eggs
–1 cup of sugar
–3 tablespoons of cold water
–1 cup of flour
–1 teaspoon of baking powder
–1/3 teaspoon of salt
–Powdered sugar
–2 tablespoons of rum (or rum flavoring)
–Pecan Filling (Recipe follows)
–Chocolate Frosting (Recipe follows)
–Chopped pecans

1. Line the bottom of a jelly roll pan with waxed paper; grease paper, then flour.
2. Beat eggs until thick and creamy in a medium-size bowl; gradually add sugar while continuing to beat.
3. Add water and flour, baking powder and salt that have been sifted together; pour batter into pan.
4. Bake at 425 degrees for 12 to 15 minutes.
5. Turn out onto kitchen towel that has been liberally sprinkled with powdered sugar; peel off waxed paper and trim one-fourth inch from all sides.
6. Sprinkle the rum or flavoring over cake; roll cake and towel starting from short end.
7. When cool, unroll and spread with Pecan Filling; roll cake up again.
8. Place seam side down and frost with Chocolate Frosting; sprinkle with chopped pecans.

PECAN FILLING

–2 cups of ground pecans
–1 cup of granulated sugar
–2 tablespoons of butter or oleo
–1 cup of evaporated milk
–1 tablespoon of cornstarch
–1 teaspoon of vanilla flavoring

1. In saucepan mix pecans, sugar, butter and milk; cook and stir over medium heat until mixture cooks down a little.
2. Mix cornstarch with a small amount of cold water until smooth; add to pecan mixture and cook until mixture becomes thick.
3. Cool slightly; add vanilla flavoring.

CHOCOLATE FROSTING

–2/3 cup of sugar
–1/3 cup of water
–2 egg yolks
–½ cup of butter or oleo, softened
–1 ounce of unsweetened chocolate, melted and cooled
–1 tablespoon of rum (or rum flavoring

1. In small saucepan heat sugar and water to boiling and cook to soft-ball stage.
2. In mixer bowl, beat egg yolks till thick; very gradually, add the hot syrup, beating constantly.
3. Continue beating until mixture is cool; beat-in softened butter or oleo, one tablespoonful at a time.
4. Add unsweetened chocolate and rum or rum flavoring.

Note: There will be frosting left over to use again.

—Mrs. John Hicks
Washington (St. Landry Parish)

CHOCOLATE-PECAN SUPREME CAKE

–½ cup of shortening
–1½ cups of sugar
–2 eggs
–1 teaspoon of vanilla flavoring
–1 teaspoon of butter flavoring
–5 tablespoons of chocolate malt mix
–2½ cups of sifted cake flour
–1 cup of milk with a couple of squeezes of lemon juice
–1 teaspoon of soda
–1 tablespoon of vinegar
–Filling (Recipe follows)
–Frosting (Recipe follows)

1. Cream shortening, sugar, eggs and flavorings; add malt mix to mixture.
2. Alternately add flour and milk to mixture. Mix soda and vinegar in small cup and add to batter. Blend only–do not over-beat.
3. Bake in four thin layers about 15 minutes at 350 degrees. Don't over-bake. May bake in oblong pans.
4. Put together with Filling between the layers and frost entire cake with Frosting.

FILLING
–1 large can of evaporated milk
–1 cup of sugar
–1 cup of butter
–3 egg yolks
–2½ cups of coconut
–2 cups of pecans or walnuts, chopped

1. Cook milk, sugar, butter and egg yolks until thick.
2. Add coconut and pecans or walnuts.

FROSTING
–1 pound of powdered sugar, sifted
–3 tablespoons of evaporated milk
–3 eight-ounce packages of cream-cheese, softened
–1 cup of coconut

1. Cream sugar, milk and cream-cheese.
2. Add coconut.

Note: Cake is best when put in refrigerator and left overnight or at least a few hours. This cake freezes very well; wrap it in wax paper, then in aluminum foil.

—Joyce A. LeBlanc
Lafayette (Lafayette Parish)

GERMAN CHOCOLATE CAKE

–1 4-ounce package of German sweet chocolate
–½ cup of boiling water
–1 cup of butter or oleo
–2 cups of sugar
–4 egg yolks, unbeaten
–1 teaspoon of vanilla
–2½ cups of sifted cake flour
–½ teaspoon of salt
–1 teaspoon of baking soda
–1 cup of buttermilk
–4 egg whites, stiffly beaten
–Coconut-Pecan Frosting (Recipe follows)

1. Melt chocolate in boiling water; cool.
2. Cream butter and sugar until fluffy; add egg yolks, one at a time, and beat well after each addition.
3. Add melted chocolate and vanilla; mix well.
4. Sift together flour, salt and soda; add alternately with buttermilk to chocolate mixture, beating after each addition until smooth.
5. Fold-in beaten egg whites; pour into three eight- or nine-inch layer pans lined with paper (wax paper or parchment paper).
6. Bake at 350 degrees for 30 to 40 minutes; cool. Frost tops only, with Coconut-Pecan Frosting.

COCONUT-PECAN FROSTING
–1 cup of evaporated milk
–1 cup of sugar
–3 egg yolks
–½ cup of butter or oleo
–1 teaspoon of vanilla
–1 cup of flaked coconut
–1 cup of chopped pecans

1. Combine evaporated milk with sugar, egg yolks, butter and vanilla; cook and stir over medium heat until thickened, about 12 minutes.
2. Add coconut and pecans; beat until thick enough to spread.

—Lucille Demary
Hathaway (Jefferson Davis Parish)

BROWNIES

–2/3 cup of sifted all-purpose flour
–½ teaspoon of baking powder
–1/4 teaspoon of salt
–1/3 cup of butter
–2 squares of chocolate or 1/4 cup of cocoa
–1 cup of sugar
–2 eggs, well-beaten
–½ cup of broken nuts (optional)
–1 teaspoon of vanilla

1. Sift together flour, baking powder and salt.
2. Melt butter and chocolate over hot water.
3. Gradually add sugar to eggs, beating thoroughly.
4. Blend-in chocolate mixture and flour; add nuts and vanilla.
5. Spread in greased 8x8-inch pan.
6. Bake for 25 minutes at 350 degrees.

—Kathy deVeer
Ascension Parish

DOBERGE CAKE

- 3 cups of sifted cake flour
- 1/4 teaspoon of salt
- 3 teaspoons of baking powder
- 1 cup of oleo
- 2 cups of sugar
- 4 eggs
- 1 cup of milk
- 1 teaspoon of vanilla
- 1 teaspoon of butter flavoring (optional)
- Filling (Recipe follows)
- Chocolate Frosting (Recipe follows)

1. Sift flour, salt and baking powder together.
2. Cream oleo and sugar together; add whole eggs, one at a time, beating well after each addition.
3. Add milk and flour alternately to egg mixture; add flavorings.
4. Bake in three or four well-greased cake pans at 375 degrees for 20 to 25 minutes; cool.
5. Split each layer; spread with the Filling and frost top and sides with Chocolate Frosting.

FILLING

- 4 squares of unsweetened chocolate (or 4 one-ounce packets of no-melt unsweetened chocolate)
- 1 quart of milk
- 1/2 cup of flour
- 1 1/2 cups of sugar
- 2 eggs, beaten

1. Melt chocolate or use no-melt chocolate; add milk and bring to a boil.
2. Combine flour and sugar in a bowl and stir-in a small amount of hot liquid; add beaten eggs.
3. Blend into remaining liquid; cook until very thick; cool.

CHOCOLATE FROSTING

- 1/4 cup of butter
- 4 squares of unsweetened chocolate
- 2 cups of sifted confectioners sugar
- 1/2 cup of boiling water

Melt butter and chocolate on lowest heat possible; blend-in sugar and water and beat until smooth; cool.

—Mrs. Francis Kerne
Thibodaux (Lafourche Parish)

PECAN FINGERS

- 3/4 cup of shortening (use 1/2 oleo)
- 3/4 cup of confectioners sugar
- 1 1/2 cups of flour
- 2 eggs
- 1 cup of brown sugar, packed
- 1/2 teaspoon of baking powder
- 1/2 teaspoon of salt
- 2 tablespoons of flour
- 1/2 teaspoon of vanilla
- 1 cup of chopped pecans

1. Cream shortening and sugar; blend-in flour.
2. Press evenly in bottom of ungreased 13x8x2-inch pan. Bake 12 to 15 minutes at 350 degrees.
3. Mix remaining ingredients; spread over baked layer and bake 20 minutes longer.
4. Cool and cut into 30 bars.

—Cheryl Bordelon
St. Martin Parish

PRALINE COOKIES I

- 1 cup of light brown sugar
- 1 tablespoon of flour
- 1/3 teaspoon of salt
- 1 egg white, beaten
- 1 teaspoon of vanilla
- 2 cups of pecans

1. Mix sugar, flour and salt; sift.
2. Add beaten egg white, vanilla and pecans.
3. Drop by the teaspoonful on cookie sheet heavily greased with shortening.
4. Bake at 275 degrees for 35 minutes. Remove from cookie sheet before cookies are cold.

—Mrs. A. A. Smith
New Roads (Pointe Coupee Parish)

PRALINE COOKIES II

- 1 cup of butter (do not substitute)
- 1 cup of brown sugar
- 1 cup of chopped pecans
- Honey graham crackers

1. Bring butter, brown sugar and nuts to a boil; lower heat and cook five to ten minutes.
2. Spoon over 8x10-inch cookie sheet that has been covered with graham crackers.
3. Cook in 350 degree oven for five minutes; cool slightly and cut into squares.

—Charla Jo Blake
Cameron (Cameron Parish)

SAND TARTS

- 1 cup of butter or oleo, softened
- ½ cup of granulated sugar
- 2 teaspoons of vanilla extract
- 2 cups of sifted all-purpose flour
- 1½ teaspoons of baking powder
- 1 to 2 cups of finely chopped pecans

1. Cream butter and sugar; add remaining ingredients.
2. Roll into crescents and bake on ungreased cookie sheet at 325 degrees for 20 minutes.
3. Roll in powdered sugar after tarts have cooled.

—Nell Coco
Marksville (Avoyelles Parish)

NO-BAKE BRANDY BALLS

- 1 13¾-ounce pack of graham cracker crumbs, (4 cups)
- 1 cup of finely chopped nuts
- 1 cup of finely chopped candied cherries
- 1½ teaspoons of ground cinnamon
- ½ teaspoon of ground cloves
- 1/3 cup of light corn syrup
- 1/3 cup of brandy
- Confectioners sugar

1. Combine first five ingredients; stir-in corn syrup and brandy.
2. Shape into one-inch balls.
3. Store in air-tight container (flavor improves with storage).
4. Roll in sugar before serving.

Makes about 54 cookies.

—Mrs. Shirley Loiacano
New Sarpy (St. Charles Parish)

BUTTER FINGERS

–1 cup of butter
–5 tablespoons of powdered sugar
–2 cups of flour
–1 teaspoon of vanilla
–2 cups of nuts, broken
–Confectioners sugar

1. Work butter, sugar and flour together in a bowl.
2. Add vanilla and nuts; mix well.
3. Form into finger-shapes and bake in slow oven at 300 degrees until set, 10 to 15 minutes.
4. While warm, roll in confectioners sugar.

—Hazel Delahoussaye
New Iberia (Iberia Parish)

PECAN FUDGE

–1 can of evaporated milk
–4½ cups of sugar
–½ pound of oleo
–4 cups of pecans, chopped
–2 12-ounce bags of semi-sweet chocolate chips
–1 pint of marshmallow cream
–2 teaspoons of vanilla

1. Mix evaporated milk and sugar together in a saucepan and bring to a boil; boil gently for about 10 minutes or until it reaches the soft-ball stage.
2. Pour sugar mixture over all other ingredients, that have been mixed together in a large bowl; mix until chocolate chips and marshmallow cream are melted and well-blended.
3. Pour onto well-greased cookie sheets or large pans; let harden.
Makes five pounds.

—Cynthia Benoit
Lafayette (Lafayette Parish)

WHITE CHOCOLATE FUDGE

–3 cups of sugar
–1 cup of evaporated milk
–6 teaspoons of butter
–1 pint of marshmallow cream
–12 ounces of white chocolate, cut in small pieces
–1 cup of chopped pecans
–4 ounces of candied red cherries
–4 ounces of candied green cherries

1. Bring sugar, milk and butter to a boil over low heat, stirring constantly.
2. Cook to 237 degrees on a candy thermometer; remove from heat.
3. Add marshmallow cream, white chocolate, nuts and cherries; stir until marshmallow cream and chocolate are melted.
4. Pour into 13x9-inch buttered pan.
5. Cool before cutting.
Makes about two dozen pieces.

—Rita M. Badon
Cameron (Cameron Parish)

BROWN SUGAR CHEWS

–1 egg
–1 cup of packed brown sugar
–1 teaspoon of vanilla
–½ cup of sifted flour
–1/4 teaspoon of salt
–1/4 teaspoon of baking soda
–1 cup of coarsely chopped pecans

1. Mix egg, sugar and vanilla; add flour, salt, baking soda and nuts.
2. Bake for 18 to 20 minutes in well-greased, eight-inch pan at 350 degrees.
3. Let cool in pan; cut in squares to make 12.

—Mrs. E. K. Richards
Breaux Bridge (St. Martin Parish)

GRANDMERE'S PECAN PRALINES

- –4 cups of sugar
- –1 teaspoon of salt
- –2 cups of cream (or one large can of evaporated milk)
- –3 cups of pecans

1. Make a syrup with three cups of sugar, salt and cream. Let cook for about eight minutes.
2. In another heavy pot or heavy skillet, melt the other one cup of sugar slowly over very low heat, constantly stirring until caramelized.
3. Pour caramelized sugar into the boiling syrup at one time, stirring constantly and rapidly.
4. Boil this mixture (without stirring) to a temperature of 238 degrees, or to a soft-ball stage (about two minutes).
5. Pour into a flat pan or crock. Beat until it begins to be creamy; add the nuts.
6. Drop by the spoonful onto waxed paper to form flat, round cakes.

—Blanche Arceneaux Swann
Marksville (Avoyelles Parish)

PRALINES I

- –2 cups of sugar
- –1 teaspoon of baking soda
- –1 cup of buttermilk
- –Pinch of salt
- –2 tablespoons of butter
- –2 1/3 cups of pecan halves

1. In a large pot, combine sugar, baking soda, buttermilk and salt. Cook briskly, stirring frequently and scraping bottom and sides for five minutes or until candy thermometer reaches 210 degrees.
2. Stir well; add butter and pecan halves. Cook five minutes more. Remove from heat and cool slightly for one to two minutes.
3. Beat until thick and creamy. Drop quickly by the teaspoonful on wax paper.

—Betty Fleming
Franklin (St. Mary Parish)

PRALINES II

- –1 cup of granulated sugar
- –1 cup of light brown sugar
- –1 pinch of salt
- –½ cup of evaporated milk
- –2 tablespoons of corn syrup
- –2 tablespoons of butter
- –1 teaspoon of vanilla
- –2 cups of pecans

1. Combine sugar, brown sugar, salt, milk and corn syrup; mix and cook over medium heat to soft-ball stage.
2. Remove from heat and add butter, vanilla and pecans; beat until mixture begins to thicken.
3. Drop by the spoonful onto marble or wax paper; let harden and cool.

—Mary A. Robinson
New Roads (Pointe Coupee Parish)

PEANUT BRITTLE

–2 cups of sugar
–2 cups of raw peanuts
–½ cup of water
–½ cup of corn syrup
–1 teaspoon of baking soda

1. Mix sugar, peanuts, water and corn syrup in a saucepan; cook on high heat and stir.
2. When peanuts start popping and syrup turns brown, add baking soda.
3. When it rises, quickly spread it in a buttered pan. While it is still warm mark it with a knife so that when it cools it will break in squares.

—Ethel Roussel
Convent (St. James Parish)

CINNAMON NUTS

–1 cup of sugar
–1/3 cup of water
–1/8 teaspoon of cream of tartar
–1 teaspoon of cinnamon
–3 cups of walnuts or other nuts, chopped

1. Boil sugar, water and cream of tartar to soft-ball stage; remove from heat.
2. Sprinkle cinnamon over syrup; stir-in nuts until all are covered.
3. Pour out on wax paper; separate as soon as cool enough.

—Betty Deshotel
Elton (Jefferson Davis Parish)

CANDIED STRAWBERRIES

–24 large strawberries (about 1 pint)
–3 cups of sugar
–½ cup of light corn syrup
–½ cup of water

1. Pick over strawberries, choosing only perfect ones. (If bruised or cut, their juices will flow and dissolve the candy coating). Wash, but do not hull; dry on paper toweling. Pull back hulls and insert a wooden pick into each.
2. Mix sugar, corn syrup and water in small heavy saucepan; heat, stirring constantly, until sugar dissolves, then cook rapidly, without stirring, to 285 degrees on candy thermometer. (A teaspoon of syrup dropped into cold water will separate into strands that are hard but not brittle). Remove from heat at once.
3. Working with one berry at a time, hold by wooden pick and dip into hot syrup, turning to coat berry completely. (Work quickly; job is easier if you tip pan slightly so syrup flows to one side). Lift berry from syrup; let excess drip back into pan. Turn berry, pointed end up and hold for 10 seconds or until syrup hardens.
4. Place on a foil-covered wire rack to cool. Keep berries at room temperature and serve within two hours, because syrup cooks them just enough to make juices flow, which will dissolve coating as berries stand.

—Jackie Ipson
Lafayette Parish

Desserts & Beverages

CONTENTS

FRESH STRAWBERRY PIE

—2 cups of fresh strawberries, washed, drained and cut in half
—1 baked pie shell
—1½ cups of water
—¾ cup of sugar
—2 tablespoons of cornstarch
—1 3-ounce package of strawberry gelatin
—Whipped cream

1. Place strawberries in cooked pie shell.
2. Mix water with sugar and cornstarch; cook two to five minutes on low heat or until clear or thick.
3. Take off stove and add strawberry gelatin; stir until dissolved.
4. Pour over strawberries in crust; chill and top with whipped cream.

—Mrs. Hubert Stagg Sr.
Eunice (St. Landry Parish)

LEMON CLOUD PIE

—¾ cup of sugar
—3 tablespoons of cornstarch
—1 cup of water
—1 teaspoon of grated lemon peel
—1/4 to 1/3 cup of lemon juice
—2 egg yolks, slightly beaten
—3 ounces of creamcheese
—2 egg whites
—1/4 cup of sugar
—1 baked pie shell

1. In saucepan, combine first six ingredients; beat with rotary blender until well-blended.
2. Cook over medium heat, stirring constantly, until thick; remove from heat and add creamcheese, stirring until well-blended; cool.
3. In a small mixing bowl, beat egg whites until foamy.
4. Add one-quarter cup of sugar, gradually, continuing to beat until it stands in stiff, glossy peaks.
5. Fold into lemon mixture.
6. Pour into baked pie shell and chill at least two hours before serving.

—Mrs. Elizabeth Horecky
Church Point (Acadia Parish)

SPICY CRUST APPLE PIE

—2 pie crusts for 9-inch pie pan
—2 tablespoons of sugar
—½ teaspoon of cinnamon
—¼ teaspoon of nutmeg
—¾ to 1 cup of sugar
—1 to 2 tablespoons of flour (if apples are juicy)
—1/8 teaspoon of salt
—6 to 7 cups of peeled, sliced tart apples
—2 tablespoons of butter

1. Fit one pie crust in pie pan. Combine two tablespoons of sugar with cinnamon and nutmeg. Brush pastry with milk or water. Sprinkle with half of sugar-spice mixture.
2. Combine three-fourths to one cup of sugar with flour and salt; mix lightly through apples.
3. Heap up in pastry-lined pan. Dot with butter. Cover with top crust; cut slits for steam to escape. Brush with milk or water. Sprinkle evenly with remaining sugar-spice mixture.
4. Bake at 425 degrees 50 to 60 minutes or until pastry is lightly browned and apples are thoroughly cooked. Cover edges of pie with foil if edges start getting too brown.

—Mrs. Druci Melancon
St. Amant (Ascension Parish)

TARTE A LA BOUILLIE
(Cream Custard Pie)

–½ cup of sugar
–3 tablespoons of flour
–2 eggs
–2½ cups of milk
–2 teaspoons of vanilla
–Sweet Dough Pie Shell (Recipe follows)

1. Mix sugar and flour together; add beaten eggs.
2. Bring milk to a boil; add a small amount of hot milk to egg mixture, stirring well. Add this to remaining hot milk and cook until thick.
3. Add vanilla and cool slightly.
4. Pour into prepared Sweet Dough Pie Shell and cover top of custard with little strips of the dough.
5. Bake at 400 degrees for 30 to 35 minutes.

SWEET DOUGH PIE SHELL
–½ cup of sugar (less, if desired)
–¼ pound of butter or oil
–1 egg, beaten
–2 teaspoons of vanilla
–3 cups of flour
–2 teaspoons of baking powder
–½ cup of milk
–½ teaspoon of salt

1. Cream sugar and butter; add egg and vanilla, mixing well.
2. Alternately add flour, baking powder and milk with salt.
3. Roll out dough and place in pie plate, saving a small amount of dough for strips over the pie.

—Mrs. Lillian Schifani
Thibodaux (Lafourche Parish)

CHOCOLATE CREAM PIE

–7/8 cup of sugar (cup less two tablespoons)
–1/3 cup of flour
–1/3 cup of cocoa
–2 eggs
–1 cup of evaporated milk
–1 cup of water
–2 tablespoons of butter
–1 teaspoon of vanilla
–1 baked pie shell
–1 cup of heavy cream, whipped

1. Put sugar, flour and cocoa into saucepan; add eggs, milk and water.
2. Cook over very low heat until mixture thickens, stirring constantly.
3. Add butter and vanilla, beat until smooth and pour into baked pie shell.
4. Cool, top with whipped cream and refrigerate.

—Ida Hammatt
Ascension Parish

SWEET POTATO PIE

–1 cup of mashed cooked sweet potatoes
–¼ pound of butter, melted
–1½ cups of sugar
–3 tablespoons of flour
–2 eggs
–1 small can of evaporated milk
–1 teaspoon of lemon extract
–1 teaspoon of vanilla
–1 unbaked pie crust

1. Mix all ingredients together.
2. Pour in unbaked nine-inch pie shell; bake one hour at 350 degrees. Serve warm.

—Mrs. Hadley Fontenot
Jennings (Jefferson Davis Parish)

LEMON MERINGUE PIE

- 5 to 6 tablespoons of cornstarch
- 1 cup of water
- 1 cup of sugar
- 1 cup of milk (made by using ½ cup of evaporated milk and ½ cup of water)
- ¼ teaspoon of salt
- 3 eggs, separated
- 2 tablespoons of oleo
- 5 tablespoons of lemon juice
- Grated rind of 1 lemon
- 1 prebaked pie shell
- 6 tablespoons of sugar

1. In top of a double boiler mix cornstarch and one-half cup of cold water; blend-in one cup of sugar, remainder of water, milk and salt.
2. Cook over low heat, stirring constantly until mixture boils; cover and cook over boiling water 10 minutes.
3. Gradually pour about a cup of the hot mixture over beaten egg yolks, stirring constantly; return to double boiler and cook two minutes longer.
4. Remove from heat; add oleo, lemon juice and rind.
5. Mix well, cool and pour into prebaked pie shell.
6. Beat egg whites until stiff; gradually beat-in the six tablespoons of sugar.
7. When stiff peaks form, pile on top of pie, being sure to seal well around edges of pie; bake at 325 degrees for 15 minutes.

—Mrs. Peggy Brown
Lake Charles (Calcasieu Parish)

COCONUT PIES

- 7 cups of all-purpose flour
- 7 teaspoons of baking powder
- 4 eggs
- 1½ cups of sugar
- 1 stick of oleo
- 1 teaspoon of vanilla
- ½ cup (or more) of milk

1. Put flour and baking powder in pan; add eggs, sugar, oleo and vanilla. Mix ingredients and start adding milk. (Add more milk if needed to get pastry stiff to be rolled out).
2. Roll pastry out and cut for nine-inch pie shells.
3. Add Coconut Filling to uncooked pie shell. Decorate with extra dough.
4. Cook for 25 to 30 minutes at 250 degrees.

Makes seven pies.

COCONUT FILLING

- 4 fresh coconuts
- 1 cup of water
- 3 cups of sugar

Grate coconuts finely; add water and sugar to coconut in saucepan. Cook for an hour and a half or more until coconut is done.

—Mrs. Joseph A. Martin
Houma (Terrebonne Parish)

PECAN PIE

—1 cup of brown sugar
—½ cup of white sugar
—1 tablespoon of flour
—2 eggs
—2 tablespoons of milk
—1 teaspoon of vanilla
—¼ pound of butter, melted
—1 cup of chopped pecans
—Unbaked pie shell

1. Combine all ingredients; pour in unbaked pie shell.
2. Bake at 375 degrees for 40 minutes.

—Mrs. Goldie B. Lowe
Port Allen (West Baton Rouge Parish)

DIFFERENT PECAN PIE

—2 eggs, separated
—1½ cups of sugar
—2 tablespoons of melted butter
—3 tablespoons of milk
—2 cups of ground pecans
—1 teaspoon of vanilla
—2 pie shells, partially baked

1. Beat egg whites well and set aside.
2. Beat egg yolks until thick and add sugar gradually.
3. Add butter and milk; stir-in pecans and fold-in egg whites and vanilla.
4. Pour into pie shells and bake at 350 degrees for 30 minutes or until filling is brown on top.
Makes two medium pies or one large pie.

Note: You may wish to put pecan halves or pieces on the top of pie before baking. This recipe is different because of the absence of a jelly-like filling common to pecan pie recipes. The method of putting this pie together yields a filling that remains completely mixed throughout due to the ground pecans and beaten egg whites.

—Cathy Delaune
Houma (Terrebonne Parish)

COCONUT TURNOVERS

—½ cup of water
—1 cup of sugar
— 1 coconut, grated
—Pastry Dough (Recipe follows)

1. Boil water and sugar until it spins a thread; add coconut and cook slowly to absorb the sugar.
2. Put about one tablespoon of coconut on each circle of Pastry Dough and fold over; crimp edges to seal.
3. Bake at 350 degrees until brown.

PASTRY DOUGH
—2 cups of sifted flour
—1 teaspoon of salt
—¾ cup of shortening
—¼ cup of water

1. Combine flour and salt in mixing bowl; cut-in shortening with pastry blender until mixture is uniform.
2. Sprinkle with water a tablespoonful at a time, tossing lightly with fork.
3. When all water has been added, work dough into a firm ball; roll out one-eighth-inch thick into circles of about four inches.

—Bea Pollet
Gramercy (St. James Parish)

CHEESECAKE SUPREME

–12 ounces of creamcheese, softened
–2 tablespoons of milk
–6 tablespoons of sugar
–½ teaspoon of vanilla
–3 eggs
–½ pint of sour cream
–2 to 4 tablespoons of sugar
–Graham Cracker Crust (Recipe follows)

1. Mix creamcheese with milk until smooth.
2. Add sugar, vanilla and eggs (one at a time), beating well after each addition.
3. Pour into spring form pan that has been lined with Graham Cracker Crust; bake at 350 degrees for 30 minutes.
4. Whip sour cream with two to four tablespoons of sugar; add to top of cheesecake.
5. Return to oven for 10 minutes; chill at least two hours before serving.

GRAHAM CRACKER CRUST

–½ cup of graham cracker crumbs
–½ teaspoon of cinnamon
–1 tablespoon of sugar
–2 tablespoons of oleo or butter, melted

1. Combine graham cracker crumbs, cinnamon and sugar.
2. Add oleo and mix well.
3. Pour into spring form pan, spreading evenly on the bottom.

Serves eight.

—Peggy Lynn Vidrine
Ville Platte (Evangeline Parish)

BLACKBERRY DUMPLINGS

–4 tablespoons of butter
–1 cup of milk
–2 eggs
–3½ cups of sugar
–2 teaspoons of vanilla
–3½ cups of flour
–3 teaspoons of baking powder
–4 cups of water
–1½ quarts of blackberries

1. Melt butter and allow to cool; mix with the milk, eggs, one cup of the sugar and vanilla; add dry ingredients. Do not overmix.
2. Combine water, two and a half cups of sugar and blackberries; cook over medium heat until mixture thickens.
3. Drop dough by the spoonful or in little balls into blackberry mixture and cook until dough rises.
4. Test with fork; when it comes out clean, remove dumpling and continue adding dumplings until all dough is used.

Serve warm with blackberry mixture.
Makes three to four dozen.

—Mrs. Gayle Boudreaux
Terrebonne Parish

PEACH OR APPLE COBBLER

–1 cup of flour
–1 cup of sugar
–3 teaspoons of baking powder
–2 teaspoons of apple pie spices
–1 cup of milk
–1 can of sliced peaches or apples

1. Sift dry ingredients; add milk and beat.
2. Place fruit in bottom of buttered casserole pan and pour dough over the fruit.
3. Bake at 350 degrees for 30 minutes or until crust is firm.

—Mrs. P. B. Kelone
Marksville (Avoyelles Parish)

TARTE TATIN

–Butter
–Sugar
–8 cooking apples, peeled, cored and cut into thin wedges
–1 teaspoon of grated lemon rind
–1 pie pastry crust, unbaked
–1 egg white, slightly beaten

1. Butter a three-inch-deep pan heavily and sprinkle with sugar so that bottom is generously covered with sugar.
2. Layer apple wedges over entire bottom, overlapping them in a circular pattern; sprinkle with one-third cup of sugar and grated lemon rind and dot generously with butter.
3. Cover apples with pastry, tucking edges inside of pan; brush top of crust with egg white and prick with fork.
4. Bake at 400 degrees 30 to 45 minutes.
5. Loosen edge all around with knife and allow to set about five minutes; invert onto serving plate so that apples are on top.

Serve warm with plain or whipped cream.

—Keith E. Courrege
New Iberia (Iberia Parish)

PECAN TARTS

–1 cup of light brown sugar
–½ cup of granulated sugar
–1 tablespoon of flour
–2 eggs
–2 tablespoons of milk
–1 teaspoon of vanilla
–½ cup of butter, melted
–1 cup of pecans, chopped
–Creamcheese Pastry Tarts (Recipe follows)

1. Mix sugars and flour; beat-in eggs, milk, vanilla and butter.
2. Fold-in nuts.
3. Drop by the teaspoonful into individual unbaked Pastry Tart shells. (Can be used in single pie shell). Bake for 30 minutes at 350 degrees.

CREAMCHEESE PASTRY TARTS
–1 3-ounce package of creamcheese
–¼ pound of oleo
–1 cup (or more) of flour

1. Have creamcheese and oleo at room temperature; mix all ingredients together until smooth, using fingers, and form into balls.
2. Use fingers to press into tart pans.

—Mrs. Milton Patin
Jarreau (Pointe Coupee Parish)

PINEAPPLE TARTS

–6 cups of flour, sifted
–1 tablespoon of sugar
–½ teaspoon of salt
–2 cups of shortening
–1 packet of yeast
–3 eggs, well-beaten
–1 cup of milk
–Sugar
–Pineapple Filling (Recipe follows)

1. Sift flour with sugar and salt. Cut-in shortening.
2. Add yeast dissolved in a little warm water.
3. Add well-beaten eggs and milk, which have been mixed together. Mix well.
4. Store in refrigerator overnight.
5. Sprinkle board with sugar and roll out pastry on the sugar. Roll about a third of the pastry at a time. Roll out very thin and cut into two-inch squares.
6. Spread a teaspoon of Pineapple Filling on half of each square and fold over to form a triangle. Press edges together with a fork.
7. Place on ungreased sheet and bake at 425 degrees about 15 minutes.
Make six dozen.

PINEAPPLE FILLING
–2 tablespoons of flour
–1 can of crushed pineapple
–1 cup of sugar

Combine all ingredients. Cook until thick.

—Ann Polomsky
St. Mary Parish

BREAD PUDDING WITH RUM SAUCE

–6 eggs
–1 cup of sugar
–1½ teaspoons of vanilla
–1 teaspoon of butter flavoring
–2 quarts of milk
–1 large loaf of stale french bread, broken into bite-size pieces
–1 16-ounce can of fruit cocktail
–Raisins (optional)
–Rum Sauce (Recipe follows)

1. Mix eggs, sugar, vanilla, butter flavoring and milk in saucepan; heat until sugar dissolves.
2. Pour over bread in oblong baking dish; add fruit cocktail, juice and all; add raisins.
3. Bake uncovered at 350 degrees 45 minutes or until all juice is absorbed. Serve warm with Rum Sauce.

RUM SAUCE
–1 cup of sugar
–½ cup of cream
–½ cup of butter
–1 teaspoon of rum extract (or 2 tablespoons of dark rum)

1. Cook sugar, cream and butter in double boiler 10 minutes.
2. Just before serving stir-in rum extract or dark rum. Spoon over pudding.

—Mrs. Mary Ann Simon
Destrehan (St. Charles Parish)

OLD-FASHIONED BREAD PUDDING

–4 cups of milk
–8 slices of stale bread
–4 eggs, separated
–1½ cups of sugar
–1 small can of evaporated milk
–1 teaspoon of vanilla
–1 cup of coconut (optional)
–4 tablespoons of sugar

1. Heat milk, pour over bread and mash.
2. Cream egg yolks and sugar; add to bread mixture. Add evaporated milk, vanilla and coconut; mix well.
3. Bake uncovered in buttered pan at 375 degrees for one hour.
4. Bake egg whites with four tablespoons of sugar until stiff and sugar is dissolved. Pour over pudding; return to oven and brown at 350 degrees.

—Mrs. Ralph Gonsoulin
New Iberia (Iberia Parish)

CREAM PUFFS WITH VANILLA FILLING

–1 cup of water
–½ cup of butter or oleo
–¼ teaspoon of salt
–1 cup of flour
–4 eggs
–Vanilla Filling (Recipe follows)

1. Heat water, butter and salt to a boil; stir-in flour all at once.
2. Reduce heat and stir until mixture leaves sides of pan and forms a ball; remove from heat and cool slightly.
3. Beat-in eggs, one at a time; drop by the spoonful onto baking pan, two inches apart.
4. Bake 35 to 40 minutes at 425 degrees and cool; split on side and fill with Vanilla Filling.

VANILLA FILLING
–1/3 cup of sugar
–¼ cup of cornstarch
–½ teaspoon of salt
–2 1/3 cups of milk
–3 egg yolks, beaten
–2 tablespoons of butter or oleo
–1 teaspoon of vanilla

1. Mix sugar, cornstarch and salt in saucepan and gradually stir-in milk; cook over moderate heat, stirring constantly, until thick, and simmer one minute longer.
2. Stir a little of the hot mixture into egg yolks and then stir yolks into the hot mixture; cook one minute longer, stirring constantly.
3. Remove from heat and stir-in oleo and vanilla.

—Chuck Thibodeaux
New Iberia (Iberia Parish)

RICE PUDDING

–2 eggs
–2 cups of milk
–1¼ cups of cold, cooked rice
–1 cup of seedless raisins
–½ cup of sugar
–¼ teaspoon of salt
–1 teaspoon of vanilla extract
–Dash of ground cinnamon and nutmeg

1. Beat eggs until light and thick; add milk.
2. Lightly mix-in the other ingredients; place in a buttered one and one-half quart casserole.
3. Bake covered in a shallow pan of water at 350 degrees for one hour, or until mixture is firm.
Makes six servings.

—Mrs. Mildredge Broussard
Grand Chenier (Cameron Parish)

"TURTLES"

- —1 cup of granulated sugar
- —½ cup of light brown sugar, packed
- —½ cup of light corn syrup
- —½ cup of heavy cream
- —1 cup of milk
- —¼ cup of butter or oleo
- —1 teaspoon of vanilla extract
- —6 ounces of pecan halves
- —2 4-ounce bars of German sweet chocolate

1. Line an 8x8x2-inch baking pan with foil. Lightly butter the foil.
2. In a heavy two and one-half-quart saucepan, combine all ingredients except vanilla, nuts and chocolate. Cook, stirring with wooden spoon, over low heat until sugar is dissolved. Over medium heat, cook, stirring occasionally, to 244 degrees on candy thermometer, or until a little in cold water forms a firm ball. Remove from heat; stir-in vanilla.
3. Turn into prepared pan; let cool 30 minutes. With sharp knife, cut into 26 pieces.
4. Roll each piece into a ball; place on buttered cookie sheet about one-half inch apart.
5. To make feet and head, press five pecans into each, equidistant around edge, lengthwise, with half of each pecan overhanging the edge.
6. Melt chocolate in double boiler top over hot, not boiling water. Spoon one teaspoon of melted chocolate over each caramel, covering surface, but leaving part of the pecans showing. Refrigerate to allow the chocolate to harden slightly.

Makes 26 pieces.

—Mrs. Ulric Prather
Eunice (St. Landry Parish)

LES OREILLES DE COCHON (Pig's Ears)

- —1¾ cups of all-purpose flour
- —2 teaspoons of baking powder
- —½ teaspoon of salt
- —2 eggs
- —6 tablespoons of butter or oleo, melted and cooled
- —Oil for deep-fat frying
- —¾ cup of cane syrup
- —½ cup of chopped pecans

1. Stir together flour, baking powder and salt; set aside.
2. In mixer bowl, beat eggs until frothy; gradually add cooled butter, beating constantly. Beat-in two-thirds of the dry ingredients, a little at a time. By hand, stir-in remaining dry ingredients.
3. Divide dough into 24 portions; shape each piece of dough into ball. On lightly floured surface, roll out each ball to a thin circle, about five inches in diameter.
4. Fry dough rounds one or two at a time in deep hot fat (375 degrees). As rounds rise to surface of oil, insert one tine of long-tined fork through the center, twisting slightly to fold and curl edges (forming pig's ears). Fry until golden brown, about two minutes, turning once. Drain fried pastry on paper towels.
5. In small saucepan, combine syrup and pecans; heat just to simmering. Drizzle warm syrup-pecan mixture over pastries.

Makes 24 pastries.

Note: If cane syrup is not available, heat together one-half cup of dark corn syrup and one-fourth cup of dark molasses to drizzle over pastries.

—Mrs. Sam Broussard
New Iberia (Iberia Parish)

RIZ AU LAIT
(Rice with Milk)

–1 quart of milk
–3 eggs
–2/3 cup of sugar
–1½ cups of cooked rice
–1 teaspoon of vanilla

1. Scald milk; add beaten eggs and sugar and bring to a boil
2. When mixture boils add rice and cook slowly until it becomes thick.
3. Remove from heat and add vanilla.

—Mrs. Harvey Blanchard
Brusly (West Baton Rouge Parish)

COFFEE LIQUEUR

–4 cups of sugar
–½ cup of instant coffee
–3 cups of water
–¼ teaspoon of salt
–2½ cups of vodka
–3 tablespoons of vanilla

1. Mix sugar, coffee, water and salt in a three-quart saucepan; stir over high heat until sugar dissolves and mixture begins to boil.
2. Reduce heat to low; simmer slowly for one hour. (If mixture boils too fast, syrup will become too thick.)
3. Remove from heat and cool; stir-in vodka and vanilla.
4. Pour into bottles and close tightly. Makes one and one-half quarts.

—Sue C. McDonough
New Iberia (Iberia Parish)

CAFE BRULOT

–2 ounces of brandy or cognac
–2 sugar cubes
–2 cinnamon sticks
–2 allspice seeds
–2 whole cloves
–1 small piece of lemon peel
–1 small piece of orange peel
–2 cups of freshly made dark roast drip coffee

1. Combine all ingredients, except the coffee, in a silver bowl.
2. Ignite and ladle until the sugar has dissolved; add the coffee.
3. Serve in demitasse or special cafe brulot cups.
Serves six.

—Mrs. Roy F. Hebert
Cameron (Cameron Parish)

EGGNOG

–6 eggs, separated
–¾ cup of sugar
–1 ounce of rum
–1 quart of half-and-half cream
–1 pint of bourbon
–Grated nutmeg

1. Beat egg whites very stiff, adding one-fourth cup of sugar.
2. Beat egg yolks with one-half cup of the sugar.
3. Fold egg whites into egg yolks with rum; stir-in half-and-half cream and bourbon.
4. Serve very cold with grated nutmeg.

—Hazel Delahoussaye
New Iberia (Iberia Parish)

Unique Acadiana Cooking Traditions

The Crawfish Boil

A south Louisiana social

It is a warm and humid day in south Louisiana and guests are starting to arrive for the crawfish boil. The youngsters pile out of the car and make a mad dash for the crawfish in the big washtub, anticipating the fun they'll have poking at them with little sticks. The old folks have already arrived and are sitting in lawn chairs in the shade of the house, enjoying a beer and talking about things that old people talk about.

At a crawfish boil, everyone seems to get along well. The kids are frolicking about in the back yard and meeting new kids when they aren't poking at the crawfish. The old people are enjoying themselves, watching the kids and speaking to the twentyish and thirtyish group light-heartedly about good times they've had or seriously about some great principle involving the family or the nation. And the people whose ages are somewhere between the real old and the real young are talking about business, politics, clothing or sports. Whether related or not, everyone seems to get along well, and there is a kinship that is formed before the evening has passed.

Vegetables and fruits, salt and pepper and crab boil are brought from the house by some of the women and are placed on a table near where the crawfish will be boiled. They sit and begin to halve the lemons while discussing the question of whether onions should be halved or boiled whole.

The back yard is filling up with guests now, 15, 18, 20 of 'em. There is the steady hum of many people talking at once, punctuated by the distinct sound of a beer can being popped open or the outburst of laughter from the direction of a group of guys gathered in one corner of the yard.

The sound of gas rushing through the jet of the butane burner can be heard, as the water in the big pot begins to heat. A couple of the guys add salt and red pepper and crab boil as the water approaches boiling, and everyone in the yard notices that progress is being made toward getting those beautiful crawfish onto the table. More evidence of progress is observed by the by-standers as the host and an assistant finish pouring water out of the washtub containing the live crawfish, then the host turns to the man in charge of the pot and says, "Let's boil 'em."

The crawfish are poured into the rolling, boiling water, and everyone in attendance watches, knowing that it won't be long now. Somehow, when this happens, everyone seems to shift positions, wrap up their conversations and begin maneuvering toward the table. The beer and the bull sessions are fine, but no one wants to wait any longer than necessary before starting the meal. There is a subtle deliberateness and clearness of purpose here, in this polite though definite jockeying toward the table, for people who like crawfish love crawfish, and hungry people who love crawfish and who are about to eat them will let virtually nothing stand in their way. There are even documented cases of grown men, otherwise gentle and well-mannered, who, heading for the table and being carried away with the thought of eating crawfish, have knocked over little children and not even known it.

Once the crawfish have been boiled and are poured onto the newspaper on the table, it's amazing how the steady chatter ceases and how it becomes a near-impossibility to engage anyone in a conversation. For the first 10 or 15 minutes, no one talks. They just eat, their hands and fingers moving faster than those of guitar-players and seemingly as fast as those of good typists. Hardly anyone drinks, either, as all seem to be in deep concentration over the task they are about.

After this initial period of prolonged silence, which is broken only by a few compliments to the chef, the people do relax and start to talk as the second batch of steaming crawfish are poured onto the table. As this batch is eaten into substantially, the big eaters start to slow down and the little eaters start drifting from the table, going indoors to wash their hands and mouths.

Soon, the big eaters are finished, too, but only because there are no crawfish left. They lean back in their chairs and invariably say, "Boy, was that good!" and often, "I can't believe we ate all of 'em," and sometimes, "Ask me if I'm going to sleep well tonight."

By now it's dark, and the sounds of the butane jets and the lively chatter of people partying are gone, replaced by those of crickets and tree frogs and little kids whining to their mammas that they're tired and want to go home.

—TRENT ANGERS

BOILED CRAWFISH (For 20)

- –80 pounds of live crawfish
- –16 ounces of ground cayenne (red) pepper
- –6 pounds of salt
- –2 8-ounce bottles of liquid crab boil
- –water, as needed to fill 1/3 of a 60-quart pot

Optional vegetables, fruits and seasoning:

- –7 pounds of small red potatoes (egg-size)
- –1½ pounds of onions (preferably small whole onions, but large onions cut in half may also be used)
- –12 medium pods of garlic
- –6 lemons, halved
- –2 3-ounce bags of crab boil (don't tear the bags)

1. Pour crawfish from sack into No. 3 washtub and wash them by filling the tub with water two or three times with garden hose. (To clean them further you may want to purge them by pouring salt into the tub filled with crawfish and water, allowing crawfish to be in salted water 20 to 30 minutes.) Remove and discard any dead crawfish or debris.
2. Fill pot one-third full of water, using garden hose.
3. Add half of seasonings (for first of two 40-pound boils).
4. Bring seasoned water to a boil.
5. Add vegetables; cook until potato slides easily off a knife when stabbed in the center (about seven minutes) at medium boil.
6. Remove vegetables; set aside.
7. Add half of crawfish (about 40 pounds); stir; cover pot; return water to a boil then cook three to five minutes. Remove crawfish promptly. (Don't over-cook or crawfish will be hard to peel.)
8. Serve steaming crawfish with vegetables, pouring them directly onto table covered with newspaper.

Note: To make crawfish easier to peel, add one stick (one-fourth pound) of oleo to each batch of crawfish as they are boiling.

—Bob Guilbeau
and Lloyd Smith
Lafayette (Lafayette Parish)

Tips on putting on a successful crawfish boil

CRAWFISH COCKTAIL SAUCE
(For one or two)

–1/3 cup of ketchup
–Hot sauce, to taste (3 to 10 dashes)
–Salt, to taste
–Black pepper, to taste
–Lemon juice, squeezed from 1/8 of lemon

Mix and stir together all ingredients, then serve.

DRINKS
*1 or 2 cases of beer
*2 or 3 6-packs of soda pop

SUGGESTED EQUIPMENT AND UTENSILS
*60-quart pot (preferably aluminum)
*5-gallon butane bottle and burner
*1 large stirring apparatus of wood or metal (large spoon or small paddle)
*1 bin for receiving boiled crawfish from pot
*Beer trays (A beer tray stacked with crawfish makes an ideal serving for one adult)
*1 8- to 12-inch, handled colander or strainer

PREPARING THE TABLE: A picnic-style table is preferable. Cover it with newspaper, five or six sheets thick.

KEEPING THE CRAWFISH ALIVE: After buying your crawfish, take care to keep them alive until boiling. They should be kept moist and cool but should never be submerged in water and allowed to remain there or they will die quickly. The sack should be tied firmly at the top so the crawfish can't move around or they will pinch and kill each other. Handle the sack of crawfish gently so as not to mash and kill crawfish.

If you plan to boil on Sunday, make arrangements ahead of time to get your crawfish, since many markets are closed on Sunday and most fishermen don't fish on Sunday. If you pick up your crawfish on Saturday for a Sunday boil, refrigerate them or ice them down, especially if it is warm weather. If refrigeration isn't practical, place the sack of crawfish in an ice chest, leaving the sack bound snugly and placing some ice on it. Leave the drain on the ice chest open so the bottom of the sack isn't allowed to remain submerged.

If handled properly, crawfish will remain alive in the sack for as much as three days.

BOILING YOUR VEGETABLES AND FRUITS BEFORE BOILING YOUR CRAWFISH: It is difficult to boil vegetables and fruits properly while boiling crawfish at the same time, so don't try it unless you're a seasoned cook. The less-experienced should stick closely to the recipe on page 192.

To assure that vegetables are hot when it's time to eat, place them in the center of the table and pour the steaming crawfish over them once the crawfish are cooked.

(Continued on page 194)

(Continued from page 193)

HOW TO EAT BOILED CRAWFISH

The Tail

1. Break off tail from "head" of crawfish.
2. Peel off the first two segments of the tail shell.
3. Grasp the meat with thumb and forefinger of one hand and pinch the lower part of the tail shell with thumb and forefinger of the other hand, then pull. Meat should slide out easily.
4. If "black line" remains on top of tail meat, remove it.

The "Fat"

1. Using thumb and forefinger, remove large covering shell from the rest of the "head" to expose gill section.
2. All "fat" remaining on gills is edible. It can either be removed with index finger and then eaten or sucked directly from the crawfish.

Note: Yellowish and orange-colored "fats" are the most tasty.

CLEANING UP: Roll up the shells and other scraps in the newspaper already on the table, place paper into large plastic bags, and discard. The smell of crawfish scraps is potent, so seal plastic bags tightly and don't put them out for the garbage man to pick up until a few hours before he comes, or else dogs, cats or coons may tear open the bags, since they like crawfish, too.

LEFTOVERS: Save the leftovers for future delicious crawfish dishes: 1) Refrigerate whole, unpeeled crawfish–either in plastic bags or in vegetable drawer–and eat them within two days. 2) Peel crawfish, place meat in cellophane bags or plastic containers, refrigerate and use the next day to make crawfish stew, *etouffee* or salad. 3) Same as option No. 2, except freeze the crawfish meat for later use.

The Cochon de Lait:
An Acadiana tradition

Cochon de lait cooking today is a term broadly used to describe the art of cooking a pig before an open hardwood fire. Although its origins in Louisiana are obscure, it is known that the custom began at least a century ago and that the *cochon de lait* is most popular in northern Acadiana, particularly in the parishes of Avoyelles, Evangeline and St. Landry.

Legend has it that the traditional preparation of *cochon de lait,* French for suckling pig, came to Acadiana in the mid-19th century with veterans of Napoleon's army who settled in the northern part of the region.

Local historians say the legend may well be correct, or that the practice could just as easily have predated the arrival of the Napoleonic exiles, since feasting on roasted suckling pig is a tradition with ancient roots in Europe.

Years back, church fairs in the area specialized in what was called *cochon a la broche*, or spit-roasted pig, prepared generally the same way. The *cochon de lait* was usually a smaller pig, up to 30 pounds in weight, and was cooked for family gatherings, especially during the holiday season. Hung before the fireplace of the home, it was cooked most of the night for the noon meal the next day.

Since then, the practice has undergone some changes, but it remains basically the same. Much larger pigs are being cooked today to feed larger groups of people, with pigs up to 90 pounds regarded as excellent for open fire cooking.

In 1960 the Avoyelles Parish town of Mansura—which was first settled by Napoleon's former soldiers and was so named because the area reminded them of Mansura, Egypt—held a big *cochon de lait* for its centennial celebration. So many people enjoyed it that the pig roast became a popular annual event, and Mansura became the home of the *Cochon de Lait* Festival. But crowds at the festival became so large and sometimes unmanageable that the town eventually discontinued the celebration. Smaller versions of the festival have since been reinaugurated. Mansura remains today, by designation of the Louisiana Legislature, *"La Capital de Cochon de Lait."*

Glenn LaFleur of Ville Platte, a city also first settled by a Napoleonic veteran, is one practitioner of the art of *cochon de lait* preparation, doing it this way:

Some 48 hours before it is to be cooked, he takes a pig, up to 50 pounds in weight, and slits the inside of the carcass with a knife, liberally inserting red pepper and black pepper, garlic and salt into the slits. After this is done, the outside of the pig is given the same seasoning treatment, remembering that much of the seasoning will drip away during cooking.

After the seasoning is applied, the pig is chilled for 48 hours to allow the ingredients to penetrate the meat.

He then wraps the pig in wire mesh and mounts it (most people mount it head down) on an electric-turned spit extending from a tripod about seven feet tall, attaching rods or stakes to the front and hind legs of the pig to keep them separated.

The pig is then rotated slowly in front of the hardwood fire built three to five feet in front of it, keeping the fire constant for even cooking. The fire should be enclosed on three sides by tin sheeting.

The pig should be cooked at least one hour for every five pounds of weight, although not every pig will cook at the same rate. After three-fourths of the cooking time, the pig can be swapped, that is, placed head up.

Homemade Babyfoods

Getting your baby off
to a good start in life

Preface

There is a pure and powerful instinct that thrives in parents who are about to have a child, a burning determination to protect and provide for that child's every need, to give him the best that life has to offer, regardless of financial cost or personal sacrifice.

But, unhappily, too many parents—through lack of knowledge, not lack of caring—deprive their baby of that all-important gift that will, in many ways, have a profound effect on his wellbeing for his entire life. That gift is proper nutrition.

This special section on the preparation of homemade babyfoods is presented as a means of helping parents and parents-to-be to begin the practice of feeding their children correctly. The recipes presented here are an inexpensive and healthful alternative to the less healthy and more expensive processed jarred babyfoods and canned formulas.

What follows is not intended to be a complete collection of babyfood recipes, but rather a sampling to show you just how easy it is to feed your child properly. These recipes don't require your going out and buying all sorts of fancy or exotic foods from some specialty store, but simply opening your refrigerator or cupboard and taking out the foods which you normally buy for the rest of the family and adapting them to the baby's needs.

These foods can be fed as they are to the baby (depending on his age) or they can be used as the basis for a variety of nutritious dishes. Often times, by simply eliminating certain ingredients, such as salt, sugar or pepper, you can serve the same dishes to the baby as you are serving to the rest of the family.

Not only will this practice provide nutritious meals for the baby, but it will influence other members of your family into better eating habits. And once the habit is formed, you will be able to create many, many ways to cook healthful foods for your baby as well as the rest of your family.

The very first step to proper infant and child feeding—even before hauling out the blenders and food processors to make your own babyfoods—is breast-feeding. With very few exceptions, infants should be breast-fed at least for the first ten to twelve months of their lives. There is no substitute for it nutritionally, psychologically, or in terms of prevention of some infant diseases.

Breast milk contains antibodies that protect infants from many of the diseases the mother is immune to; it also contains elements that play a vital role in the development of the child's brain, elements that cannot be duplicated artificially. And breast-fed babies generally have fewer allergies than do bottle-fed babies.

After the first ten to twelve months, it is time to begin introducing the baby to other foods in addition to breast milk, such as some of the foods in the following pages. But steer clear of jarred babyfoods, canned formulas and any and all foods that contain refined sugar.

In your effort to formulate good eating habits for your child, it is important that you develop an ability to turn a deaf ear to those misguided souls who would have you believe that fat babies are healthy babies. Fat isn't healthy at any age. Fat kids tend to become fat adults, and they develop predispositions for diabetes and coronary heart disease, according to Doctors William F. And Laura Kremer, authors of "The Doctor's Metabolic Diet."

It is also true that kids who are bottle-fed and who eat jarred babyfood tend to be fatter than those who are breast-fed and who eat homemade babyfoods in their natural forms.

The image of a healthy kid being a chubby kid has been fostered subliminally if not blatantly by companies that produce jarred babyfoods and canned formulas. Since their products tend to fatten up the children more than pure foods and mother's milk, there is little wonder that they would promote the chubby kid as being the healthy one!

The notion that a fat child is a healthy one is also fostered by veteran mothers with blind tendencies to promote their own way of doing things. Often their opinions are expressed in an I-should-know-because-I've-been-there tone of voice. These are the ladies who—though not intending any harm—will start in on the first-time mother who is feeding her child properly with the innocent comment, "Isn't he a little thin?" then intensify the campaign with, "The poor thing is starving!" and finally come in for the kill with, "Look, he wants his grandma to feed him!" This progression of comments is a not-so-indirect attempt to establish in the first-time mother's mind that she just isn't feeding her baby enough; and if the young woman falls for this little ploy, she has thus been set up to be manipulated into letting her mother or aunt or grandmother "help with the feeding." While this sort of aid is usually promoted as a contribution to the child's well-being, it is, in fact, usually only a contribution to the relative's sense of being useful.

These relatives who would stuff the kid with all sorts of extra foods are the same ones who would take it one step further and would get a thrill out of seeing the child squeal with delight when they offer him candy. Refined sugar is not good for children of any age, or adults either. Doctors and dentists warn against it.

"In addition to the immediate problem of behavioral disturbance, one must be mindful of the long-term detrimental effects of sugar. For example, predisposition to obesity, diabetes, dental caries and perhaps even heart disease with hypertension," says Ben Feingold, M.D. and author of "The Feingold Cookbook for Hyperactive Children." He is a pediatrician and one of the world's leading authorities on the problem of hyperkinesis and learning disabilities in children.

Children learn to eat what they're served. Some parents whose kids eat candy, cookies and other junk food are shocked to see another's children eating and enjoying apples, peaches, tomatoes or carrots just as much if not more. But there is no great mystery here—just a question of what you chose to teach your children about eating.

The choice is yours. We believe that what follows is a good first step toward having a healthy, happy child.

—Leah Angers

ACKNOWLEDGEMENTS

We are indebted for the assistance rendered by Liana S. Huey (Longmont, Colo.), a La Leche League leader and mother of three who contributed recipes and valuable insight into the importance of correct feeding of infants and children; Dr. John E. Daigre (Lafayette, La.), pediatrician who reviewed the writings for technical correctness; Carolyn Hoffman (Baton Rouge, La.) Vicki Smith (Arnaudville, La.), Ann Broussard (St. Martinville, La.), and Dianne Lee and Lou Ann Gipson (both of New Iberia, La.), all of whom contributed recipes; and Christine Blonski (Carencro, La.) and Vicki Smith, whose children were used as models for toddlers in the illustration which begins this section.

—L.A.

ASHLEY MONTAGU, internationally renowned anthropologist and social biologist, has spent a lifetime examining and exposing some of the most widly held myths concerning Mankind, or Humankind, as he prefers to call it. Born June 28, 1905 in London, he came to the United States in 1927 to begin graduate studies at Columbia University in New York. He taught anatomy and anthropology at New York University in the 1930s, was awarded a Ph.D. in anthropology in 1937 at Columbia, and was professor of anthropology and chairman of the Department of Anthropology at Rutgers University from 1949 to 1955.

In a prolific book-writing career that has spanned four decades, Montagu has ventured into the controversial areas of race, child-rearing and relations between the sexes. Against a solid background of scientific evidence, he has shown the theory of racial superiority to be fallacious, has dismantled the notion that man is naturally superior to woman, and has been emphatic about the tremendous importance of proper child-rearing—sociologically, biologically and psychologically.

"The Natural Superiority of Women" (1953), "Man's Most Dangerous Myth: The Fallacy of Race" (1942), and "The Human Connection" (1979) are among his best-known books. Others include "On Being Human" (1950), "Life Before Birth" (1964), "Immortality, Religion and Morals" (1971), "Touching" (1971), "The Nature of Human Aggression" (1976), and "The American Way of Life" (1967).

Current Biography points out: "During the 1950s Montagu was perhaps the best-known anthropologist and one of the most popular university professors in the United States."

Introduction

By ASHLEY MONTAGU

Good nutrition is essential for healthy physical and mental growth.[1] This holds true from the moment of conception to the end of our days. It is especially true of the formative periods of our lives, while still in our mother's womb and during the extragestational period, which we spend as babies outside the womb, when the baby looks forward, as it were, to a continuation of the happy life he has spent in the womb, when he looks forward to what is best for him. And what is best for him? Quite simply, the satisfaction of his nutritional and emotional needs. And how is this best accomplished? Again, quite simply, by love and by breast-feeding.

Mothers know what love is without necessarily being able to define it. There is an old Hebrew saying that has it that since God could not be everywhere He created mothers. That saying will always remain true. Love is the ability to confer survival and creatively enlarging benefits upon another. The loving mother is the perfect realization of that definition. However, we live in a world which has grown quite complex and often confusing. Those with something to sell have sometimes led many women to believe that bottle-feeding, with a formula based on cow's milk, is better than breast-feeding or at least as good. Many doctors fell in line with the advertising of the formula manufacturers, and they advised mothers accordingly. Today, happily, they are revising their ideas on the subject, and the American Academy of Pediatrics has clearly stated that there is no substitute for breastmilk. The fact is that breastmilk is by far the best all-round food ever devised for the infant. Indeed, it is possible to say with complete certainty that no substitute or anything remotely equaling breastmilk will ever be found or invented. There exists no other food that even approaches the benefits which breastmilk confers upon the baby who ingests it.

The colostrum, the lemony yellowish fluid which the baby takes in from the breast during the first four or more days, contains natural antibodies which will confer immunities upon him against measles, mumps, polio and many other viral diseases; it also protects against bacterial diseases, such as those that cause diarrhea and infantile meningitis; and it affords the baby protection against respiratory infections, such as flu and pneumonia. Dr. Robbins Kimball, a distinguished pediatrician, has reported that during the first ten years of life the breast-fed youngster is more resistant to infection than the bottle-fed child. The bottle-fed child has "4 times the respiratory infections, 20 times the diarrhea, 22 times the miscellaneous infections, 8 times the eczema, 21 times the asthma, 27 times the hayfever," 11 times more tonsillectomies, 4 times more ear infections, 11 times more hospital admissions and 8 times more house calls.[2]

The colostrum serves to clean out the intestines of the newborn as nothing else can, and such a baby will seldom be colicy. In fact, the only known cure for colic in a baby is breast-feeding. In this connection it is interesting to note that adults who as babies were breast-fed rarely suffer from ulcerative colitis.

Bottle-feeding should be banned, and so should all cow's milk formulas. Cow's milk is excellent stuff for little cows, for whom it was intended, but it should never be given to babies in any form because it contains the wrong kinds and quantities of proteins, carbohydrates and other substances. The baby is unable to deal with these adequately because he has not yet developed the enzymes which help to metabolize such materials. The result may be more or less severe damage to the liver and kidneys which may not show up until years later. Allergic reactions may be immediate or delayed. For these same reasons breast-feeding mothers should not drink cow's milk because its noxious contents will get through to the baby.

After the fifth day or so the transitional milk comes into the mother's breast, and this lasts some ten days, to be followed by the permanent milk. The milk changes in its fat, carbohydrate and protein content from hour to hour, in adjustment to the baby's needs.

There is good evidence that breast-fed babies have better-developed facial bones, jaws and occlusion of the teeth than those who have not been breast-fed or who have been breast-fed for less than three months.[3] There is also good evidence that speech development, tonal quality of voice, clarity of articulation and self-confidence are superior in breast-fed children.[4] Children at seven years of age who have been breast-fed have a higher IQ than the non-breast-fed.[5]

Throughout the history of humankind humans lived as food-gatherers and hunters. The food-gathering/hunting peoples of today—such as the Australian Aborigines, the Bushmen of the Kalahari Desert and the Pygmies of the Ituri Forest—all breast-feed their children on demand, usually for not less than four years.

It should be remembered that we are mammals, the class of animals who feed their young by the breast. Mammals have been doing this for 65 million years. Humans are the only creatures who, especially in technologically advanced societies, treat their young in an unmammalian manner. The very word "mammal" is derived from the Latin meaning "breast." It is the word also from which we derive the word for mother, "mama." We should not lightly undervalue 65 million years of mammalian breast-feeding, and five or six million years of the same for human beings. Indeed, a most important part of the making of a human being consists of the experience at the maternal breast.

How long should infants be breast-fed? For as long as the nursing couple mutually enjoy the experience. Weaning will come about naturally; until it does, go on breast-feeding. Remember, breastmilk is the perfect food, and the child really needs no other to grow and develop as a healthy human being.

Quite as important as the physical benefits that breast-feeding confers upon the child are the emotional and intellectual benefits which accrue to such children. It is the emotional and social interactions which transpire between mother and child at the breast that lay the foundations of his education in becoming a healthy, warm, loving human being. Health, especially mental health, is the ability to love, to work, to play and to use one's mind soundly. More than 400 years ago the English writer William Painter described the breast as "That most sacred fountaine of the body, the educatour of mankind."

The evidence indicates that babies should be breast-fed at the very least for a year, and that solid foods should not be given the baby until after that period. It should be noted that the milk teeth do not complete their eruption until the end of the second year. This in itself should tell us something.

When the child is ready for solid foods commercial baby foods should be avoided. I say this because many of these baby foods have been very damaging to babies; furthermore, at the present time their manufacture is not properly regulated by the Food and Drug Administration. Home-prepared foods are by far the best. It is, therefore, a great boon for mothers to have a special section such as this, created by Leah and Trent Angers, which provides mothers with the recipes for a variety of delicious and fully nutritious natural foods for their infants.

It is important to understand several things about such foods: 1. They are free of artificial additives, coloring materials and acids, as well as unnecessary amounts of sugars, starches and salts, all of which are known to be damaging. 2. Such foods are very pleasant, and babies early establish a familiarity and taste for them, which will continue into the later years. 3. They are completely nourishing. 4. The ingestion of food one enjoys is an emotionally satisfying experience, and this is why most of us enjoy eating so much! Such enjoyable experiences reinforce the child's taste for natural foods, so that as he grows older he finds it easy to avoid junk foods.

Always remember that feeding and eating are social occasions and should always be pleasant ones for everyone concerned. Infants should never be forced to eat. If they enjoy eating—and usually infants do—they will nurse and eat when they feel like it. Babies should be nursed on demand. Later, when they are old enough, and solid foods are provided for them, they should also be fed on demand. Regular scheduling is not a good idea because the growing child's needs are very different from the time-clocking habits of adults. Loving mothers will know when their child needs to eat, and the little one will usually make his need quite clear.

The important point is for both of you to enjoy each other and to be happy and well-fed.

REFERENCES

1. David A. Levitsky (editor), *Malnutrition, Environment and Behavior,* Ithaca, N. Y., Cornell University Press, 1979; Nevin S. Scrimshaw and John E. Gordon (editors), *Malnutrition, Learning and Behavior,* Cambridge, Mass., MIT Press, 1968. Two collections of articles by leading authorities, highly readable and informative.
2. Robins E. Kimball, "How I Get Mothers to Breastfeed," *Physicians Management,* June 1968; see also R. L. Jackson *et al.,* "Growth of 'Well-born' American Infants Fed Human and Cow's Milk," *Pediatrics,* Vol. 33, p. 642, 1964. These two articles show why breastfed babies are healthier than artificially fed babies.

   –La Leche League International. *Womanly Art of Breastfeeding,* Franklin Park, Illinois, La Leche League International, 1977. The best practical guide to the art of breastfeeding.

   –An excellent book on breastfeeding for the mother *and* father is the paperback by Marvin S. Eiger and Sally Wendos Olds, *The Complete Book of Breastfeeding,* New York, Bantam Books, 1973.

   –The most authoritative book on breastfeeding and human milk is by Derrick B. Jelliffe and E. F. Patrice Jelliffe, *Human Milk in the Modern World,* New York, Oxford University Press, 1978.

   –BOOKS ON NUTRITION:

   Lewis Coffin, *Grandmother Conspiracy Exposed,* New York, Bantam Books, 1976. Nutritional myths exposed, with common-sense suggestions for well-fed kids using natural foods.

   Adelle Davis, *Let's Have Healthy Children,* New York, New American Library, 1972. Complete nutritional guide for expectant mothers, babies and growing children.
3. F. M. Pottenger Jr. and B. Krohn, "Influence of Breast-Feeding on Facial Development," *Archives of Pediatrics,* Vol. 67, pp. 451-461, 1950; F. M. Pottenger, "The Responsibility of the Pediatrician in the Orthodontic Problem," *California Medicine,* Vol. 65, pp. 169-170, 1946; F. M. Bertrand, "The Relationship of Prolonged Breast-Feeding to Facial Features," *Central African Journal of Medicine,* Vol. 14, pp. 226-227, 1968.

   –For the report of the studies relating to the superior jaw, teeth and occlusal development, as well as speech development and higher IQ, see Ashley Montagu, *Touching,* second edition, New York, Harper & Row, 1978.
4. Frances Broad, "The Effects of Infant Feeding on Speech Quality," *New Zealand Medical Journal,* Vol. 76, pp. 28-31, 1972; Frances Broad, "Further Studies on the Effects of Infant Feeding on Speech Quality," *New Zealand Medical Journal,* Vol. 82, pp. 373-376, 1975; Frances Broad, "Suckling and Speech," *Parents Centres Bulletin* 53, pp. 4-6, Nov. 1972.
5. C. Hoefer and M. C. Hardy, "Later Development of Breast Fed and Artificially Fed Infants," *Journal of the American Medical Association,* Vol. 96, pp. 615-619, 1929; Marcelle Geber, "The Psychomotor Development of African Children in the First Year and the Influence of Maternal Behavior," *Journal of Social Psychology,* Vol. 47, pp. 185-195, 1958; M. D. S. Ainsworth, *Infancy in Uganda,* Baltimore, The Johns Hopkins Press, 1967.

Starting your baby on solid foods...

For generations mothers have wrestled with the question of when to begin feeding their babies solid foods. Some begin the process at six months of age and some at 12 to 18 months, but most pediatricians are now advising parents to wait until the latter part of the first year of life. They recommend starting breast-fed babies on solids at 11 or 12 months and bottle-fed babies two or three months sooner.

But the best guide to starting the baby on solids is the baby himself. He is usually ready to begin eating solid foods toward the end of the first year, when he develops the ability to pick up food with his thumb and forefinger and to place it in his mouth (rather than all over his face). This is also the time when he has developed a sufficient tooth structure to bite and chew the food–which is nature's way of saying that the baby's digestive system is ready for solid foods.

But don't be misled into thinking the baby is ready for solid foods at five or six months of age just because he starts putting toys and food into his mouth. This is normally an act of exploration or of imitation of his parents or an attempt to scratch or soothe his gums, which are aching and itching because he is cutting his first teeth.

The process of starting babies on solid foods can take six to twelve months, depending on the age at which you introduce the first solid food. But it should be a gradual process which allows you to determine if the baby is allergic to any of the foods you are feeding him. To find out, introduce only one new food per week and look for any signs of an allergic reaction, such as rashes, itching or bumps. If a reaction should occur, discontinue feeding that food and try another food a week later. If there is no reaction, introduce another food the following week and alternate feeding it with the food introduced the first week. Continue this process, introducing one new food per week. (The older a baby is before starting him on solid foods, the less likely he is to develop food allergies. If there is a family history of a particular food allergy, then that food should not be given at all or should be delayed until the child is at least 18 months old. It is also useful to know that breast-fed babies generally have fewer allergies than those who are bottle-fed.)

Introducing babies to solid foods should be a methodical and orderly process, geared to the little one's ability to digest different foods as he grows older. Solid foods should be introduced in the following order:

–yellow fruits (peaches, apricots, bananas, etc.)
–other fruits (apples, pears, strawberries, etc.)
–yellow vegetables (squash, pumpkin, corn, carrots, etc.)
–other vegetables (zucchini, spinach, peas, etc.)
–meats (including liver, heart, kidneys, etc.)
–whole grains (rice, wheat, flour, rye, wheatgerm, etc.)
–dairy products (eggs, yogurt, milk, cheese, etc.) Dairy products should not be introduced any sooner than one year of age.

Babies often go through stages of eating one food freely and then refusing to eat it at all; they may also switch completely from eating mostly yellow fruits and vegetables to eating only green vegetables and meats; and sometimes the quantity of food they eat will vary widely. Don't be alarmed by this, because babies generally eat what they have real nutritional needs for; their cravings and preferences are good indicators of their real nutritional needs.

These seemingly eratic eating habits often raise the question in parents' minds: Is my baby being properly nourished? The baby will usually give you the answer himself! He is being properly nourished if there is a gleam in his eye and a smile on his face, if he is content, if there is a sheen to his hair and if his skin is moist and elastic.

Your baby's first experience with eating solid foods should be made as pleasant and satisfying as possible. The best time of day to introduce him to his first solid foods is when he is rested and in good spirits. Serving him after naptime gives you a chance to prepare the food while he's sleeping, so that when he awakes you can give him your undivided attention. It is preferable that you and the baby be seated at the same eye level so he can see what you are doing and what you're about to feed him. Feed him yourself the first few times, then let him try his hand at it. You'll be pleased and surprised at how willing he is to attempt this big step. Give your baby the time he needs to eat his food in his own way; it will be an enjoyable experience for both of you.

Teething Foods

Teething foods are given to babies cutting their first teeth, not so much as a source of nourishment, but as a means of easing the pain of those aching and itching gums.

One of the advantages of giving your baby teething foods—rather than plastic or rubber teething rings—is that in gnawing on them he tastes their juices and begins to cultivate a taste for these healthful and nourishing foods. (Parents should avoid store-bought teething foods containing salt, sugar and preservatives; it is usually better for the baby and easier on the pocketbook to use homemade zwieback toast or raw vegetables from the refrigerator, such as carrots or celery.)

Foods you can give your baby to teeth on include the following:

–Celery (Wash well and refrigerate. Works well until the baby learns to bite off a piece, in which case it should be discontinued until his molars have grown out.)

–Carrots (Wash well and cut off the pointed tip. This also works well for a time but will have to be cooked once the child is able to bite into it.)

–Whole wheat bread (Toast or air-dry for crispness)

–Zwieback toast (See recipe in this section)

Following are recipes for other teething foods:

BANANA POPS

–1 or 2 bananas
–2 cups of plain yogurt
–2 tablespoons of corn syrup
–1 tablespoon of honey

1. Blend one to two bananas to make one cup.
2. Add yogurt, corn syrup and honey to blender and blend well.
3. Pour into popsicle molds and freeze.

Note: Teething toddlers love this!

FRUIT POPS

–2 cups of unsweetened fruit juice
–¼ cup of pureed fruit

Mix ingredients together and fill Tupperware popsicle molds. Freeze until firm.

TEETHING BISCUITS

–1 egg yolk, beaten
–4 tablespoons of molasses
–2 tablespoons of cooking oil
–1 teaspoon of vanilla flavoring
–3/4 cup of whole wheat flour
–1 tablespoon of soy flour
–2 tablespoons of wheatgerm

1. Mix liquid ingredients; add dry ingredients to mixture and mix well.
2. Roll dough out to about one-fourth inch thick; cut into strips about one-half inch by two inches.
3. Bake on ungreased cookie sheet at 325 degrees about 15 minutes.
4. When cooked, remove from baking sheets to cool completely.
5. Store in airtight container.

HOMEMADE ZWIEBACK

Cut store-bought or homemade whole grain bread into thirds or fourths. Bake at 250 degrees for about an hour, until dried out and hard.

Breakfast Foods

OAT PORRIDGE

–¾ cup of oatmeal
–¼ cup of rye flakes
–1 tablespoon of cornmeal
–1 tablespoon of raw wheatgerm
–1 tablespoon of bran
–2¾ cups of water

1. Mix all ingredients and cook on low for 15 to 20 minutes.
2. Sweeten with honey and add butter, to taste.

Makes five one-half-cup servings.

Note: This is appropriate for older infants or toddlers who have previously eaten the five different main ingredients. It can be blended or put through a food processor before adding the water, to make a finer mixture.

HOMEMADE RAISIN BRAN

–½ cup of honey
–2 tablespoons of molasses
–1 teaspoon of vanilla
–2 cups of raw wheatgerm
–2 cups of bran

1. Warm honey and add molasses and vanilla; stir.
2. Add this to wheatgerm and bran in a large bowl.
3. Spread on cookie sheet and bake 15 minutes at 300 degrees.
4. Store in a closed container; serve with raisins and milk.

WHOLE WHEAT PANCAKES

–1 cup of whole wheat flour
–2½ teaspoons of baking powder
–½ teaspoon of salt (optional)
–¼ cup of toasted wheatgerm
–½ teaspoon of vegetable oil
–1 cup of milk
–¼ cup of molasses
–1 egg
–2 tablespoons of vegetable oil

1. Mix flour, baking powder, salt and wheatgerm in bowl.
2. Heat griddle with one-half teaspoon of oil spread over it.
3. Mix milk, molasses, egg and two tablespoons of oil; add to dry mixture and mix until smooth.
4. Pour in small amounts on griddle and cook on both sides.
Makes about four servings.

FRENCH TOAST

–3 eggs
–½ cup of milk
–¼ teaspoon of cinnamon
–¼ teaspoon of nutmeg
–1 teaspoon of vanilla
–Sliced whole wheat bread

1. Beat all ingredients except bread until smooth.
2. Dip bread in mixture, coating both sides evenly.
3. Cook in lightly buttered frying pan on medium low heat, turning and browning on both sides.
4. Serve with butter and/or pure maple or pure cane syrup.

GRITS AND CHEESE

–Long-cooking grits
–1 tablespoon of cheese of your choice, grated
–½ tablespoon of butter

1. For one serving, cook grits according to directions on package.
2. Let cheese and butter melt into grits; stir to mix.

Great for chilly afternoon lunch!

ORANGE FRENCH TOAST

–2 eggs, beaten
–½ cup of orange juice
–1 to 2 tablespoons of honey
–Whole wheat bread

1. Mix eggs, orange juice and honey.
2. Dip slices of bread into the mixture.
3. Cook in buttered skillet three minutes on each side.

PEACHES AND CREAM

–½ peach, pureed and refrigerated from the preceeding day
–¼ cup of whole milk
–1 egg yolk
–1 teaspoon of wheatgerm

Blend all ingredients at high speed for 30 seconds or until foamy. Serve chilled in baby cup.

WHOLE GRAIN BREAD

- 1½ cups of whole wheat flour
- 1½ cups of unbleached flour
- ½ cup of instant nonfat dry milk
- 1 tablespoon of salt
- 2 packages of active dry yeast
- 3 cups of water
- ½ cup of honey
- 2 tablespoons of vegetable oil
- 1 cup of whole wheat flour
- ½ cup of soyflour
- ¾ cup of wheatgerm
- 1 to 1¼ cups of whole wheat flour
- 1¾ to 2 cups of unbleached flour

1. Grease two 9x5- or 8x4-inch loaf pans with butter.
2. In a large bowl, mix together the first five ingredients.
3. Warm in a saucepan over low heat three cups of water, honey and vegetable oil.
4. Pour warm liquid over flour mixture; blend one minute with mixer at low speed and two minutes at medium speed.
5. By hand stir-in one cup of whole wheat flour, then soyflour, wheatgerm, one and one-fourth cups of whole wheat flour and one and three-fourths to two cups of unbleached flour.
6. Knead five minutes. Put in a greased bowl; turn over. Cover and let rise 45 to 60 minutes (til doubled in bulk). Punch down, let rise again. Punch down a third time. Shape, place in pans, cover and let rise 30 to 45 minutes, until light and doubled. Bake at 350 degrees for 40 to 45 minutes.

CARROT BREAD

- 2½ cups of whole wheat flour
- 1 teaspoon of baking powder
- 1 teaspoon of baking soda
- 1 teaspoon of ground cinnamon
- ½ teaspoon of salt (optional)
- 2/3 cup of honey
- 1 tablespoon of molasses
- 3 eggs
- ½ cup of oil
- ½ cup of whole milk
- 2 cups of shredded carrots
- ½ cup of chopped pecans

1. Grease 9x5-inch loaf pan and dust with flour.
2. Combine dry ingredients and sift together; add honey and molasses.
3. Beat eggs, oil and milk; combine with dry ingredients.
4. Stir-in carrots and nuts.
5. Bake at 325 degrees for one hour and 20 to 30 minutes.
6. Cool on wire rack for ten minutes; remove from pan and completely cool on rack.
7. Wrap in plastic or aluminum foil.

This bread tastes better the following day. It may be frozen for later use.

CARROT CAKE MUFFINS

- –2 cups of whole wheat pastry flour
- –2 teaspoons of cinnamon
- –½ teaspoon of sea salt (optional)
- –1 teaspoon of baking powder
- –2 teaspoons of soda
- –1½ cups of oil
- –4 eggs
- –1 teaspoon of vanilla
- –3 cups of grated carrots
- –3/4 cup of raw honey

1. Mix dry ingredients well.
2. Add oil, eggs, vanilla, carrots and honey, and blend together.
3. Bake in muffin cups at 350 degrees for 25 minutes.

QUICK OATMEAL-RAISIN BREAD

- –1 1/3 cups of whole wheat flour
- –½ cup of honey
- –1 tablespoon of molasses
- –1 tablespoon of baking powder
- –1 teaspoon of salt (optional)
- –½ teaspoon of nutmeg
- –1 cup of raisins
- –1½ cups of rolled oats
- –1 1/3 cups of whole milk
- –1 egg
- –¼ cup of melted butter

1. Mix flour, honey, molasses, baking powder, salt and nutmeg in a large bowl; add rest of ingredients and stir just enough to mix.
2. Pour batter into three greased, well-cleaned, empty cans (about two cups each) or one loaf pan.
3. Bake at 325 degrees (moderate oven) 50 to 60 minutes or until loaf shrinks from sides of pan; remove from cans or loaf pan at once and cool thoroughly. Wrap and freeze for later use.

HOMEMADE BUTTER

- –1 quart of unsweetened whipping cream, at room temperature
- –Pinch of salt (optional)

1. Using a mixer, blender or food processor, whip cream until it coagulates, usually after about five minutes.
2. After butter globules form, put them in bowl and press out milk.
3. Refrigerate.

Soups

BEAN SOUP

- –1 16-ounce can of whole tomatoes
- –1 6-ounce can of tomato paste
- –1 onion, chopped
- –2 garlic cloves, minced
- –1 ham hock
- –1 pound of dried white beans
- –2 to 4 quarts of water, depending on consistency desired

1. Put all ingredients in a large heavy-bottomed soup pot; bring to a boil and reduce to simmering.
2. Simmer for five or six hours, or until beans have broken apart.
3. Remove hock; any leftover ham may be used in the soup.

SPLIT PEA SOUP

–1 16-ounce package of split peas
–5 bacon slices
–½ pound of ham, cut in small pieces
–2 medium onions, chopped
–3 ribs of celery, chopped
–2 quarts of water (approximately)
–1 bay leaf
–2 carrots, diced or shredded

1. Rinse and sort peas. Soak in cold water over night.
2. Fry bacon in skillet over medium heat; remove bacon and set aside; remove all but three tablespoons of bacon drippings.
3. Saute ham, onions and celery until seasonings are wilted.
4. Add split peas, water, bay leaf, three slices of crumbled bacon and carrots.
5. Bring soup to a boil; then simmer for one hour, stirring occasionally. Garnish with two slices of crumbled bacon.

CREAM OF VEGETABLE SOUP

–1 tablespoon of butter
–1 cup of whole milk
–1 tablespoon of whole wheat flour
–1 cup of pureed vegetables

1. Make a white sauce by heating butter and milk in a saucepan and stirring-in flour.
2. Add vegetables and stir while heating.

CORN CHOWDER

–4 ears of corn (or 1 pint of frozen cream-style corn)
–2 small onions, chopped
–2 small bellpeppers, chopped
–4 tablespoons of butter
–Whole wheat flour
–1 quart of whole milk
–4 fresh tomatoes, peeled and chopped (or 1 can of tomatoes, drained)
–1 cup of cream
–2 tablespoons of butter

1. Scrape corn from cob; saute with onion and bellpepper in oleo for five minutes, stirring constantly.
2. Sprinkle with a small amount of flour; mix until smooth. Add milk, tomatoes and seasonings; simmer 30 minutes, stirring often.
3. If mixture has a tendency to curdle, add a pinch of soda and stir.
4. When ready to serve, add cream and butter.

Serves six or seven adults and two toddlers.

RICE AND CARROTS

–1 teaspoon of butter
–¼ cup of whole milk
–½ teaspoon of whole wheat flour
–¼ cup of pureed cooked carrots
–¼ cup of cooked rice
–¼ cup of Ricotta cheese

1. Make a white sauce by heating butter and milk in a saucepan and stirring-in flour.
2. Stir-in remaining ingredients, and heat.

HONEY CARROTS

–¼ cup of honey
–1 tablespoon of butter
–1 pound of fresh carrots, cut into 3-inch pieces
–Dash of cinnamon

Heat honey and butter; add carrots and cook until they are warm.

BAKED CARROTS

–Carrots
–Butter
–Honey

1. Skin carrots and slice lengthwise.
2. Lay in a flat casserole and dot lightly with butter.
3. Sprinkle lightly with honey.
4. Cover and bake at 350 degrees for one hour.

GREEN BEANS WITH CREAMCHEESE

–1 can of green beans
–3 ounces of creamcheese
–1 tablespoon of butter

1. Drain beans, then puree in blender.
2. Melt butter and creamcheese in saucepan; add beans and stir until warm.
3. Season with a few drops of lemon juice, if desired.

Note: As baby gets older, leave beans whole. They're a little messy, but they make great finger food or beginning fork food. And the baby will eat more because he'll be pleased with feeding himself.

VEGETABLE KEBABS WITH BUTTER

–1 cup of cherry tomatoes
–2 medium-sized zucchini squash, cut into one-inch pieces
–6 mushroom caps
–½ cup of butter, melted

1. Arrange cherry tomatoes, zucchini and mushrooms on skewers.
2. Brush butter over vegetables.
3. Place over hot coals and grill about 10 minutes or until done, turning and brushing with butter occasionally.

SWEET POTATO CRUNCH

–2 large sweet potatoes, peeled
–2 tablespoons of honey
–1 tablespoon of orange juice
–1 teaspoon of cinnamon
–½ cup of raw wheatgerm
–¼ cup of finely chopped pecans
–¼ cup of slivered almonds
–¼ cup of coconut

1. Cut potatoes into small pieces and place in saucepan with enough water to cover; cover and cook over medium heat for 30 minutes or until soft.
2. Mash potatoes, using as much of the cooking liquid as needed for a soft consistency.
3. Add honey, orange juice and cinnamon; blend well.
4. Add remaining ingredients and mix well. Serve with pat of butter on top.

TUNA-NOODLE CASSEROLE

–½ cup of thin noodles, cooked
–2 teaspoons of butter
–½ cup of pureed tuna
–½ cup of pureed green peas

Mix ingredients together; heat in casserole dish in 300 degree oven for 15 to 20 minutes; serve.

LIVER-EGG DISH

–2 chicken livers
–½ cup of water
–1 hard-cooked egg

1. Simmer chicken livers in water until tender, about 30 minutes.
2. Puree chicken liver in blender or food processor, adding as much of the cooking liquid as needed to obtain smooth consistency.
3. Add finely chopped egg to liver, then serve.
Enough for two to three servings.

POACHED MEAT

–½ pound of raw chicken, lean beef, liver or fish
–1½ cups of water

1. Simmer meat in water for 45 minutes to one hour, depending on type of meat used.
2. Puree meat in blender or food processor, adding cooking liquid to obtain smooth consistency.
3. Place meat mixture in plastic ice cube trays and freeze.
4. Pop cubes out as needed, thaw and heat.

MEAT AND GRAVY DINNERS

Take a small piece of meat (any kind) and chop finely; place in blender with some gravy and blend. If potatoes were cooked for the meal, add a small amount of potatoes to the meat and gravy and blend together. If you feel your gravy is too spicy, add a little whole milk or yogurt to the mixture.

BAKED LIVER AND ONIONS

–1 cup of whole wheat flour
–1½ pounds of sliced calf liver, skinned and membrane removed
–Salad oil
–6 medium onions, thinly sliced
–4 slices of bacon, fried and crumbled
–½ cup of hot water

1. Dredge liver in flour.
2. Lightly brown liver in hot oil; drain and place in a shallow two-quart casserole.
3. Top with onion slices and sprinkle with bacon; add water.
4. Cover and bake at 350 degrees for 30 minutes; uncover and bake an additional 10 minutes.

RED BEANS AND RICE

Take some beans, add some of the bean juice and mash or blend to desired consistency. Rice can be stirred-in, blended-in or mashed-in.

PIMENTO CHEESE

–½ pound of cheddar cheese, grated (about 2½ cups)
–½ cup of chopped, drained canned pimentos
–1 teaspoon of grated onion
–½ cup of mayonnaise

Mash ingredients in a bowl. Cover and refrigerate. (Will keep for a few days.)

To make a toasted sandwich, cut bread into thirds, toast slightly in hot oven (400 degrees), spread with cheese mixture and return to oven until cheese melts.

Note: Makes good finger food for toddlers; spread in celery or on bread or crackers.

ARTICHOKE CASSEROLE

–2 14-ounce cans of artichoke hearts, drained and chopped
–½ cup of butter
–2 cups of Italian-style breadcrumbs
–1 cup of Romano cheese, grated

1. Saute artichokes in butter; add breadcrumbs and mix well.
2. Place in a casserole and sprinkle with cheese.
3. Bake at 350 degrees until cheese is melted.

BANANA-PECAN YAMS

–6 medium yams, cooked and mashed (canned or fresh)
–¼ cup of mashed bananas
–2/3 cup of honey
–1 teaspoon of cinnamon
–1 cup of chopped pecans
–¼ cup of butter, softened
–1 teaspoon of lemon juice

1. Combine all ingredients and mix well until blended.
2. Place in a one-quart casserole and bake uncovered at 325 degrees for 30 to 40 minutes or until lightly browned.

SQUASH AU GRATIN

–2 pounds of yellow squash, sliced
–1 medium onion, chopped
–½ teaspoon of salt (optional)
–1 tablespoon of butter
–1 cup of cracker crumbs
–1 cup of grated cheddar cheese
–½ cup of whole milk
–1 egg

1. Cook squash and onion until tender; remove from heat.
2. Add salt, butter, cracker crumbs, half the grated cheese, milk and egg; stir until well-blended.
3. Pour into casserole; sprinkle remaining grated cheese over top.
4. Cover casserole and bake at 350 degrees for 20 minutes. Garnish with parsley.

Makes seven adult servings and two toddler servings.

VEGETABLE CASSEROLE

–½ cup of butter, melted
–½ cup of whole wheat flour
–1 quart of whole milk
–2 cups of grated cheese
–1 8-ounce can of peas, drained
–1 8-ounce can of sliced carrots
–1 8-ounce can of cut up asparagus, drained

1. Combine butter and flour in large skillet.
2. Add milk slowly to keep sauce smooth; add one cup of grated cheese.
3. Cook until thick; pour half of white sauce in casserole dish.
4. Arrange vegetables in order given over white sauce in casserole; pour remaining white sauce over vegetables; top with remaining grated cheese.
5. Bake uncovered at 350 degrees for 30 minutes. Casserole may be frozen. Allow to thaw before heating.

YAM-STUFFED APPLES

- –1½ cups of mashed yams
- –1 cup of honey
- –1 tablespoon of molasses
- –1 egg, well-beaten
- –¼ teaspoon of cinnamon
- –¼ teaspoon of salt (optional)
- –1 teaspoon of vanilla
- –2 tablespoons of melted butter
- –6 large apples
- –Syrup (Recipe follows)
- –6 tablespoons of chopped nuts

1. Mash yams and set aside.
2. Mix honey, molasses, egg, cinnamon, salt, vanilla and butter.
3. Wash apples, core and scoop out, leaving shells about one-eighth inch thick.
4. Preheat oven to 325 degrees.
5. Blend apple meat in electric blender, then combine with mashed yams and honey-egg mixture.
6. Fill apple shells with this mixture.
7. Pour some of the Syrup into individual buttered custard cups; place one apple in each cup.
8. Cook for 40 to 45 minutes.
9. Cool for ten minutes, sprinkle with additional Syrup, then sprinkle nuts over all.

SYRUP

- –2/3 cup of honey
- –1 cup of water
- –2 tablespoons of butter
- –½ teaspoon of ground cinnamon
- –½ teaspoon of ground nutmeg

Combine ingredients and bring to hard boil.

ZUCCHINI CASSEROLE

- –1 cup of chopped onion
- –½ cup of chopped bellpepper
- –½ cup of chopped celery
- –Olive oil
- –1 large zucchini, sliced
- –1 large fresh tomato, blanched and peeled
- –1 cup of whole wheat breadcrumbs
- –½ cup of grated cheddar cheese

1. Pre-heat oven to 375 degrees.
2. In a large skillet, saute onion, bellpepper and celery, using a small amount of olive oil.
3. Add zucchini and tomato and cover; simmer over low heat 30 minutes. Stir-in one-half cup of breadcrumbs.
4. Pour mixture into 9x9 casserole dish and top with grated cheddar cheese and remainder of breadcrumbs.
5. Bake uncovered for 20 minutes or until brown and bubbly.

BAKED ZUCCHINI PROVOLONE

- –3 cups of green zucchini squash, sliced or diced
- –1 onion, chopped
- –2 cups of canned Italian tomatoes, pureed
- –1 cup of water
- –2 tablespoons of breadcrumbs
- –2 ounces of sharp provolone cheese, chopped
- –Oregano

1. Layer ingredients in greased baking dish.
2. Bake at 350 degrees for 25 to 30 minutes.

BANANA SHAKE

–2 cups of whole milk
–½ cup of plain yogurt
–1 egg
–2 teaspoons of vanilla
–2 teaspoons of nutmeg
–1 cup of instant nonfat dry milk
–1 medium banana, cut in chunks
–Juice of two fresh oranges

Blend until well-mixed.
Makes four servings of one cup each.

BANANA FRUIT SHAKE

–2 bananas
–3 cups of any type of fruit juice

Mix in blender.

EGGNOG

–2 eggs
–1 cup of whole milk
–1 tablespoon of honey
–¼ teaspoon of cinnamon
–¼ teaspoon of nutmeg
–1 tablespoon of wheatgerm

1. Heat all ingredients for five minutes in a small saucepan over low heat, stirring constantly.
2. Pour into blender and blend at high speed for three minutes.
3. Serve hot or chilled.

FRUIT SHAKES

–1 cup of fruit (fresh and unsweetened)
–1½ cups of whole milk
–1 teaspoon of vanilla
–1 tablespoon of wheatgerm
–2 eggs
–1 teaspoon of honey
–Dash of cinnamon

Place all ingredients in blender and blend at high speed until foamy.

Great as an afternoon snack for the older kids, too!

FRUIT SLUSH

–1 cup of fresh fruit (strawberries, bananas, peaches, pineapple, etc.)
–½ cup of orange juice or grape juice

1. Wash fruit and put in plastic bag or container and freeze overnight or about 12 hours.
2. Add one-fourth cup of frozen fruit and all of the juice to blender. Cover and blend at medium speed, adding the rest of the fruit slowly until blended smoothly. Serve right away.

Note: Two or more fruits can be used together with a variety of juices.

PEACH FUZZIES

–2 to 3 fresh peaches
–Juice of one fresh lemon, plus water to make 10 ounces of liquid
–2 tablespoons of honey
–1 cup of ice cubes

1. Remove pit of peaches, leaving peelings on; slice peaches.
2. Place all ingredients in blender and blend to the consistency of a snowball.

PEANUT BUTTER DRINK

–1 cup of whole milk
–1 tablespoon of honey
–1 tablespoon of peanut butter

Mix in blender.

STRAWBERRY JUICE

–1 pint of fresh sliced strawberries
–1 quart of water (or 1 pint of water and one pint of ice cubes)

Blend at medium to high speed until smooth. Chill and serve. May be strained to remove seeds, if desired.

VANILLA MILK

–1 8-ounce cup of ice cold whole milk
–¼ teaspoon of vanilla
–½ teaspoon of honey

Mix all ingredients and serve.

This is a good afternoon treat, and it may make the non-milk-drinkers surprise you.

Snacks

FRUIT DELIGHT

–1 11-ounce can of pears, peaches or apricots
–2 tablespoons of vanilla yogurt
–1 tablespoon of honey

1. Drain fruit; blend with yogurt and honey.
2. Chill to baby's liking and serve.

Note: This can be partially frozen and made into a slush for the older children.

CREAMY PEACH PUDDING

–1 cup of chopped fresh peaches
–½ cup of creamed cottage cheese
–½ cup of plain yogurt
–1 tablespoon of honey
–½ teaspoon of vanilla

1. Arrange peaches in bottom of flat, one-quart dish.
2. Blend remaining ingredients until smooth and creamy, and pour over peaches.
3. Stir to mix; cover and refrigerate three hours or overnight before serving.

YOGURT

–2½ cups of whole milk
–¼ cup of evaporated milk
–½ cup of non-instant powdered milk
–1 envelope of yogurt-starter, or 3 tablespoons of yogurt

1. Mix first three ingredients in saucepan, and heat until warm (test drops on wrist), beating with rotary beater.
2. Add yogurt-starter or three tablespoons of yogurt from previous batch; mix well with beater.
3. Pour into yogurt-maker, cover and incubate about three hours or until thickened. (If you don't have a yogurt-maker, you can pour the prepared mixture into a prewarmed jar, cover and put into hot water bath to be kept at 110 to 115 degrees.)
4. Place in refrigerator to chill.

Note: This is a good substitute for sour cream and can be made into salad dressings and desserts.

PEACH YOGURT

–½ cup of plain, unsweetened yogurt
–½ ripe peach

Chop peach slices into very small pieces and stir-in to yogurt. Serve chilled.

YOGURT DIP

–1 small container of plain natural yogurt
–1 envelope of Blue Cheese dressing
–1 tablespoon of cold pressed mayonnaise

Mix all ingredients together and serve with any raw vegetable your children enjoy eating. (Other dressing mixes can be used for different taste.)

A great after-school snack that won't spoil appetites for supper.

SPICY APPLE TREAT

–2 tablespoons of butter
–¼ cup of raw honey
–Dash of cloves
–¼ teaspoon of nutmeg
–4 apples, cored
–4 cinnamon sticks

1. Let butter stand at room temperature until soft and pliable.
2. Combine butter, honey, cloves and nutmeg and blend until smooth.
3. Place apples on 6 x 6-inch pieces of aluminum foil; spoon mixture into apple cores and top with cinnamon sticks.
4. Wrap apples in foil and bake at 355 degrees for 45 minutes. Serve hot or cold.

DATE AND NUT BREAD

–1 cup of dates, cut up
–1 teaspoon of baking soda
–3/4 cup of boiling water
–1 egg, beaten
–3/4 cup of pecans, chopped
–1 3/4 cups of whole wheat pastry flour
–2/3 cup of honey
–1 tablespoon of molasses
–1 tablespoon of melted butter

1. Combine dates, baking soda and water; let stand until cool.
2. Add remaining ingredients, stirring thoroughly.
3. Put into a greased loaf pan and bake at 325 degrees for 45 minutes to an hour.
4. Cool, slice and serve.

FRUIT CAKE SQUARES

–2 eggs
–2/3 cup of honey
–1 tablespoon of molasses
–½ teaspoon of vanilla
–½ cup of chopped nuts
–2 cups of chopped dried fruits
–3/4 cup of whole wheat pastry flour
–1 teaspoon of baking powder

1. Beat eggs and add honey and molasses gradually; add vanilla, nuts and fruits, and mix.
2. Combine flour and baking powder in another bowl and stir-in the fruit mixture.
3. Spread about one-half inch thick in a shallow greased pan and bake at 325 degrees for 30 to 40 minutes.
4. Cut into squares when cool.

SESAME CHEESE WAFERS

–½ cup of soft butter
–½ pound of shredded American cheese
–1 cup of sifted whole wheat flour
–Dash of paprika
–Dash of onion powder
–Sesame seeds, toasted

1. Combine butter and cheese.
2. Add the other ingredients (except the sesame seeds) and mix well.
3. Form into balls about the size of large marbles and flatten with the palm of your hand.
4. Dip into toasted sesame seeds.
5. Bake on ungreased cookie sheet at 375 degrees for 12 to 15 minutes.

SESAME CANDY

–2 cups of unhulled sesame seeds
–¼ cup of honey
–2 tablespoons of melted butter
–1 teaspoon of vanilla
–¼ teaspoon of cloves (optional)
–½ teaspoon of cinnamon (optional)

1. Roast sesame seeds until crunchy.
2. Grind sesame seeds in blender or food processor.
3. Add remaining ingredients and mix.
4. Shape as desired or press onto cookie sheet and cut into pieces.

PEANUT BUTTER CANDY

–½ cup of peanut butter (without added salt or sugar)
–½ cup of honey
–1 cup of nonfat dry milk powder

1. Combine the three ingredients and turn out onto waxed paper on cookie sheet.
2. Pat until one-half inch thick.
3. Cut into small shapes; can decorate with raisins.
4. Chill; leave on waxed paper or cookie sheet.

TOMATO SNACK

–1 large ripe fresh tomato
–¼ cup of Romano or Parmesan cheese

1. Slice tomato and place on a baking sheet that has been lightly greased with olive oil.
2. Sprinkle slices with cheese.
3. Bake at 475 degrees for 10 minutes.

NUTTY FRUIT TOPPING

–1 cup of creamed cottage cheese
–1 cup of applesauce
–½ cup of finely chopped peanuts or chunky peanut butter

Combine all ingredients in blender or food processor.

Serve over fruits.

Good Food Sources

PROTEIN: legumes, seeds, nuts, eggs, dairy products (milk, yogurt, cottage cheese, cheese), fish, poultry, organ and other meats.

VITAMINS

Vitamin D: sunshine (interacts with oils on the surface of the skin, creating vitamin D which is then absorbed. Bathing before or within several hours after being in the sun negates the effect of the sun), egg yolks, organ meats, bone meal, irradiated milk, canned salmon and tuna.

Vitamin E: dark leafy greens, eggs, liver, organ meats, wheatgerm, vegetable oils, desiccated liver.

Vitamin C: citrus fruits, dark leafy greens, sweet and hot peppers, broccoli, cabbage.

Folic Acid: liver, organ meats, leafy greens, fruit, nutritional yeast, milk, dairy products, oysters, salmon, whole grains, mushrooms.

Niacin: nutritional yeast, seafood, lean meats, milk, milk products, poultry, rice bran, peanuts, seeds, whole grains, legumes.

Riboflavin: blackstrap molasses, nutritional yeast, brown rice, organ meats, whole grains, mushrooms, dark leafy greens.

Thiamine: blackstrap molasses, nutritional yeast, brown rice, fish, meat, nuts, organ meats, whole grains.

Vitamin B_6*:* blackstrap molasses, nutritional yeast, leafy greens, meat, organ meats, whole grains, wheatgerm, prunes.

Vitamin B_{12}*:* cheese, milk, milk products, fish, organ meats, eggs (people who have been complete vegetarians for years have the only known deficiencies).

MINERALS

Calcium: milk, cheese, yogurt, organ meats, almonds, bone meal, dolomite, sesame seeds, soybeans, legumes, dark leafy greens.

Phosphorus: eggs, fish, grains, glandular meats, meat, poultry, yellow cheese, bran, seeds, legumes.

Iodine: seafood, kelp, dulse, dark leafy greens, iodized salt.

Iron: blackstrap molasses, eggs, fish, organ meats, wheatgerm, dulse, kelp, rice bran, seeds, legumes.

Magnesium: bran, honey, green vegetables, nuts, beans, seafood, spinach, bone meal, kelp.

Zinc: nutritional yeast, liver, seafood, soybeans, spinach, sunflower seeds, mushrooms.

---

*From "Life Before Birth." Reprinted with permission of the author, Ashley Montagu, and the publisher, The American Library, Inc., New York.

Index

This index applies to the main body of this book,
but not to the babyfoods section

A

B

C

D

Q

R

S

T

V

W

Y

Z

Books & Magazines

by Acadian House Publishing

(Please turn the page)

ACADIAN HOUSE PUBLISHING, based in Lafayette, Louisiana, is the nation's leading publisher of authentic Cajun recipes. It also publishes and markets a line of books about Louisiana history, heritage, culture, tourism and other topics, both historical and contemporary. Acadian House is affiliated with *Acadiana Profile*, "The Magazine of the Cajun Country," which has been featuring recipes and stories from south Louisiana since 1968.

The cream of the crop of Cajun recipes (Book 1)

Cajun Cooking, Book 1 contains about 400 of the best Cajun recipes, like Jambalaya, Crawfish Pie, Filé Gumbo, Cochon de Lait, Chicken & Okra Gumbo, Sauce Piquante. Special features include a section on homemade babyfoods and drawings of classic south Louisiana scenery. (ISBN: 0-925417-03-3. Price: $17.95)

B-1

B-2

The cream of the crop of Cajun recipes (Book 2)

Cajun Cooking, Book 2 picks up where Book 1 left off. It contains such delicious dishes as Shrimp & Crab Bisque, Fresh Vegetable Soup, Seafood-Stuffed Bellpepper, Broiled Seafood Platter, Yam-Pecan Cake. The recipes appear in the same easy-to-follow format as in Part 1, except they're in real large print for arm's-length reading. (ISBN: 0-925417-05-X. Price: $14.95)

The classics of Louisiana cooking

A 218-page hardcover book that just may be the most beautiful book on Louisiana cuisine in existence today. It features many of the real classics of Louisiana cooking, as well as nutritional data on the content of each of these recipes. It also features stories about 25 of the state's most fun-filled festivals, plus colorful illustrations which reflect the themes of these festivals. (ISBN: 0-925417-10-6. Price: $24.95)

B-9

The best gumbo cooks in the world have agreed to share their secrets...

There's no dish in the world quite like Cajun or Creole gumbo, and this cookbook shows you how to master the art.

The *Louisiana Gumbo Cookbook* reveals the secrets of the best gumbo cooks to be found anywhere - the women (and some men) who run the kitchens in the homes of south Louisiana, plus the chefs who work in some of the best restaurants in this corner of the world.

The main features of this 192-page hardcover book include these:

- ✓ Over 100 gumbo recipes.
- ✓ The complete history of gumbo: how long it's been around, who "invented" it, how it has evolved over the past few hundred years. (Spanish, French and Africans all had a hand in it.)
- ✓ The story behind filé (Created by the Choctaw Indians of Louisiana)
- ✓ How to make a good roux - with or without oil - on the stove, or in the oven, or in the microwave (7 recipes).
- ✓ How to prepare rice correctly the first time, every time, whether white, brown, yellow, etc.
- ✓ How to make stocks that will enhance the flavor of your gumboes. (ISBN: 0-925417-13-0. Price: $15.95)

B-12

B-14

From the kitchens of south Louisiana

A 48-page saddle-stitched softcover book containing 100 recipes selected by the editors of *Acadiana Profile,* "The Magazine of the Cajun Country." For example, Boudin, Couche Couche, Maque Choux, Mirliton, Crawfish Etouffee, Chicken Fricassee, Pralines - the classics of South Louisiana cuisine. (ISBN: 0-925417-20-3. Price: $6.95)

A useful little book for those just starting out in Cajun cooking

Cajun Cooking For Beginners is a 48-page saddle-stitched softcover book that teaches the basics of authentic Cajun cooking. It contains about 50 simple, easy-to-follow recipes; cooking tips and hints; a glossary of Cajun food terms, such as roux, gumbo, jambalaya and etouffee; and definitions of basic cooking terms, such as beat, blend, broil, saute' and simmer. (ISBN: 0-925417-23-8. Price: $6.95)

B-17

The Children's CORNER

B-32

Nicky The Swamp Dog: A True Story is a 40-page hardcover book about an intriguing little dog that lives in the Atchafalaya Basin in south Louisiana. She and her master ("Half Pint" Guillory) rescue lost and injured animals – such as nutria, beavers and owls – and bring them back to their houseboat. Here, they feed them, shelter them and nurse them back to health. Then, when they are well, they release them back into the wilds. Lavishly illustrated with photographs of Nicky, her furry and feathered friends, and the swamp environment in which they live.
(ISBN: 0-925417-36-X. Price: $14.95)

The Legend of Catfish and Little Bream is a 40-page hardcover book about a big fish who gets bored with life in a little pond in the South. He sets out on a great adventure to the North, and along the way learns some of life's most important lessons – that friendship is priceless, that home is where the heart is, and that the grass isn't always greener on the other side of the hill. Magnificently illustrated! (ISBN: 0-925417-26-2. Price: $19.95)

B-21

T-1

The 50-minute cassette tape includes a dramatic reading of the book and a beautiful musical rendition of the story. (ISBN: 0-925417-31-9. Price $9.95)

Book on Tape

For a steady dose of Cajun recipes, Cajun humor, and Cajun history and culture...

Subscribe to

S-1

If you like the recipes in the book you're holding now, you're going to love the magazine that published many of them first.

Since 1968, this bimonthly magazine has been profiling the people, places and events that make the Cajun Country the warm, rich, unique land that it is.

There's something in each issue for every member of your family. From recipes and genealogy columns to business news and people features to beautiful nature photography. There are stories on hunting and fishing, travel and tourism, health and medicine, and even a bit of philosophy and humor.

Do something nice for yourself or your friends and relatives – subscribe today!

The magazine is published six times a year. Rates: 6 issues for $17; 12 issues for $33; 18 issues for $49; 24 issues for $65. To subscribe, use the Order Form on the last page of this book, or call (800) 850-8851.

Other Louisiana regional books by Acadian House Publishing

The Truth About the Cajuns is a 120-page book that describes the French-Acadian, or Cajun, people with the accuracy and dignity to which they are entitled – contrary to the shallow, stereotyping manner in which they have been depicted by many of the news media. Illustrated. (ISBN: 0-925417-04-1. Price: $11.95) **B-3**

Louisiana's French Heritage is a 192-page hardcover book about the French contribution to the colonization of the New World. It describes the settlement of the Acadian Peninsula, the discovery and exploration of the Mississippi River, the development of the first Louisiana colony and the exile of the French-Acadians from Canada. Illustrated. (ISBN: 0-925417-02-5. Price: $15.95) **B-5**

Dudley LeBlanc: A Biography. A 104-page softcover book about Dudley LeBlanc, the most famous Cajun of all time. The political leader of the Cajun people in the 1930s thru the 1960s, "Coozan Dud" also invented and promoted HADACOL into the best-selling patent medicine in America in its time. (ISBN: 0-925417-12-2. Price: $9.95) **B-11**

Live Oak Gardens: A Place of Peace & Beauty is a 48-page softcover book, 6x9 size, filled with striking color photographs of Live Oak Gardens and the historic Joseph Jefferson House. (ISBN: 0-925417-08-4. Price: $7) **B-6**

Tour Guide: Louisiana's Beautiful Scenic Byways is a 124-page guide to six of south Louisiana's Scenic Byways, with simplified location maps, write-ups on some 280 tourist attractions, and brilliant color photography. (ISBN: 0-925417-28-9. Price: $7) **B-20**

Cajun Humor is a softcover book filled with dozens of jokes and humorous stories by several of south Louisiana's funniest people. (ISBN: 0-925417-22-X. Price: $7.95) **B-16**

The New Orleans Saints: 25 Years of Heroic Effort (Book 1) is a 112-page hardcover book that describes the colorful history of the New Orleans Saints from 1967 thru 1987. Highlights include Tom Dempsey's record-breaking 63-yard field goal, Archie Manning's brilliant quarterbacking, the amusing "baghead" era, etc. Illustrated with photos. (ISBN: 0-925417-09-2. Price: $11.95) **B-7**

The New Orleans Saints: 25 Years of Heroic Effort (Book 2) is a 184-page hardcover book that details the history of the Saints from 1988 thru the 1991 season, picking up where Book 1 left off. This book is about victory, about the winning years. It features players including Bobby Hebert, Dalton Hilliard, Morten Andersen and "The Dome Patrol." Illustrated with photos. (ISBN: 0-925417-11-4. Price: $14.95) **B-8**

ORDER FORM

To order, simply fill in this Order Form (or a photocopy of it) and mail it along with your check or credit card authorization to: Acadian House Publishing, P.O. Box 52247, Lafayette, LA 70505.

Quantity	Item Number	Title / Item Description	Price Per Item	Total Price

If more room is needed for listing your order, please do so on a separate piece of paper or on a photocopy of this form.

☐ Enclosed is my check or money order for $____________

☐ I'd rather charge it. Please charge $______ to my ☐ VISA ☐ MC

Acct. # ☐☐☐☐☐☐☐☐☐☐☐☐☐☐☐☐

Expiration Signature

Sub-Total	
Sales Tax: 7.5% for LA residents	
Shipping & Handling: $2.50 first book $1.00 each book thereafter	
TOTAL	

* When placing orders for shipment out of the U.S., add 50% to shipping & handling rates.

Ordered by:

Name

Address

City, State, Zip

Ship to

Name

Address

City, State, Zip

Questions? Call (800) 850-8851
(337) 235-8851

www.acadianhouse.com • info@acadianhouse.com

Acadian House
PUBLISHING
Lafayette, Louisiana